GARY WIGGLESWORTH

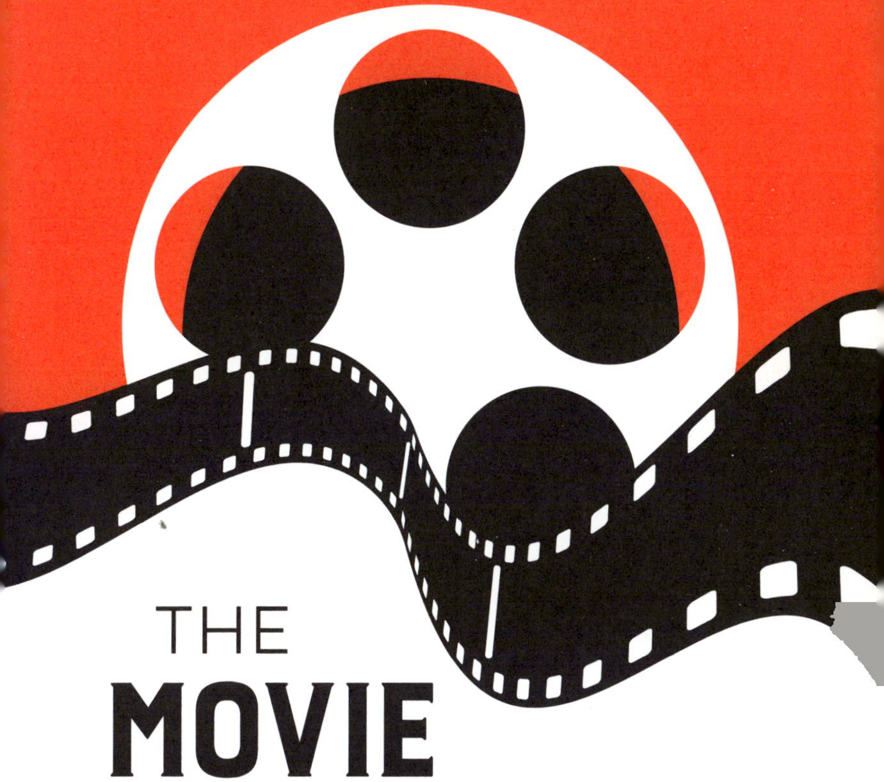

THE MOVIE LOVER'S QUIZ BOOK

OVER 900 QUESTIONS ON YOUR FAVOURITE FILMS, MOVIE STARS AND DIRECTORS

summersdale

THE MOVIE LOVER'S QUIZ BOOK

The Last Picture Show illustrations by Gary Wigglesworth; film projector © thenatchdl/ Shutterstock.com

An Hachette UK Company
www.hachette.co.uk

Summersdale Publishers
Part of Octopus Publishing Group Limited
Carmelite House
50 Victoria Embankment
LONDON
EC4Y 0DZ
UK

www.summersdale.com

This FSC® label means that materials and other controlled sources used for the product have been responsibly sourced

MIX
Paper | Supporting responsible forestry
FSC® C016973

The authorized representative in the EEA is Hachette Ireland, 8 Castlecourt Centre, Dublin 15, D15 XTP3, Ireland (email: info@hbgi.ie)

Printed and bound in China

ISBN: 978-1-83799-607-0
eISBN: 978-1-83799-608-7

For Caroline and my brother Neil

CONTENTS

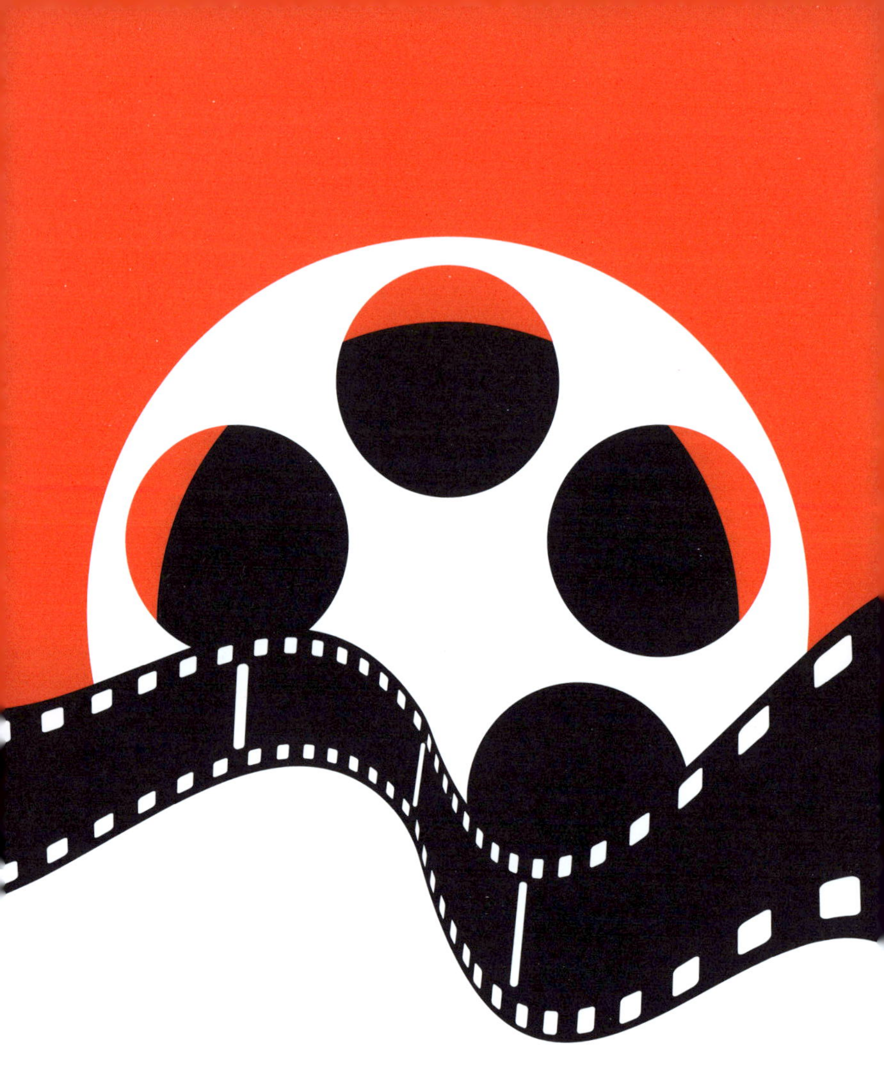

INTRODUCTION

Hello, and welcome to *The Movie Lover's Quiz Book*! Inside you'll find 20 quizzes all about movies, directors, actors, soundtracks... all the things that make seeing a movie so memorable.

I love movies! (And, yes, I also love quizzes.) And I love *all* kinds of movies; the ones that make you laugh, make you cry, make you sit on the edge of your seat or make you jump out of it! So, I've included movies of all genres and styles of film-making. My only criterion for including a movie is that I've heard of it, but it was a real pleasure to include some of my favourites.

Each quiz is divided into five rounds. The first round features ten questions with a lot of multiple-choice options, red herrings and clues to aid guessing. The rounds after that are a mixture (though some feature in every quiz) to keep it fresh. I have named each of these rounds after a movie, which was fun – trying to think of the most apposite title. Then the final round in each quiz is a picture round (The Last Picture Show – choosing that name was easy), where I have drawn six picture clues to six famous movies. You will also find some interesting extras on the answer pages, little titbits I just had to pass on to you. Oh, and Quiz 20 is all about Christmas movies – so save that one for the festive period.

That's all from me, I won't keep you, you have quizzes to do.

Happy quizzing!

Gary

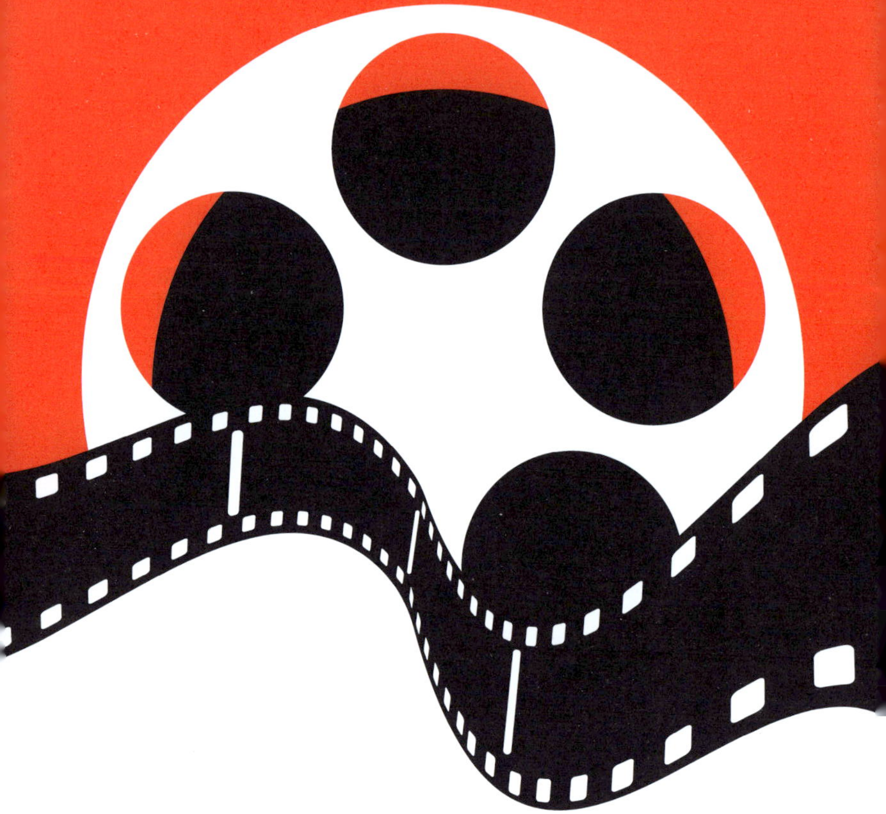

QUIZ 1

ROUND 1

STARTER FOR 10

Ten questions to begin!

1. THE FIRST QUESTION

Which of these "Last" films was released first?

a) *The Last of the Mohicans*

b) *Last Tango in Paris*

c) *Last Exit to Brooklyn*

2. THE ANAGRAM

Unscramble the actor's name: IT SCOWLED A TON

3. FILM QUOTE

What film is the following quote from?

"I feel the need... the need for speed!"

a) *Le Mans* (1971)

b) *Top Gun* (1986)

c) *Speed* (1994)

d) *Quadrophenia* (1979)

4. THUMBS DOWN

What film is this the one-star review of?

"At one point she is advised that she needs to do less – but by this point I was yelling at the screen, 'How is this possible???' The pace is so slow that it is practically backwards..."

a) *Sex and the City* (2008)

b) *Eat Pray Love* (2010)

c) *Joy* (2024)

5. ODD ONE OUT

Which of these films was not directed by Spike Lee? Bonus point if you know who it was directed by.

a) *He Got Game* (1998)

b) *She's Gotta Have It* (1986)

c) *They Live* (1988)

6. RHYMING FILMS

I'll give you the initials of two films whose titles rhyme with each other. I'll also give you one of the stars and the years they were released, just name the films for a point each.

TD, Denzel Washington (2001) and CW, Al Pacino (1993).

7. CELLULOID OR CELLULIED?

Which of the following is true about Steve McQueen?

a) In one of McQueen's first films, monster movie *The Blob* (1958), McQueen's father, a shopkeeper, provided the jam the Blob is made of.

b) McQueen refused to be filmed next to Paul Newman in *The Towering Inferno* (1974) because Newman was taller than him.

c) In *The Great Escape* (1963), McQueen wasn't allowed to perform the jumping-the-fence stunt, so he donned a German uniform and "chased himself".

8. WHAT MIGHT HAVE BEEN

Which of these roles did Sean Connery turn down?

a) Jimmy "Popeye" Doyle (*The French Connection* – 1971)

b) Gandalf (*The Lord of the Rings* trilogy – 2001–2003)

c) Willy Wonka (*Willy Wonka and the Chocolate Factory* – 1971)

9. WHAT YEAR?

In what year did the following things happen?

Films released this year include: *The Bourne Identity*, *Ice Age*, *Minority Report*, *Gangs of New York*, *Die Another Day* and *Catch Me if You Can*. *A Beautiful Mind* wins the Best Picture Oscar at the Academy Awards. *Spider-Man*, directed by Sam Raimi, becomes the first film to earn $100 million in one weekend. Jenna Ortega and Finn Wolfhard are born. Dudley Moore, Rosemary Clooney, Rod Steiger, Richard Harris and James

Coburn pass away. *Amélie* starring Audrey Tautou becomes the highest-grossing French-language film in the USA ever. But what was the year?

10. GIVE ME FIVE

A chance for five points! Name me five films directed by Alfred Hitchcock with one-word titles. There are 18 possible answers.

ROUND 2

1. THE HIDDEN

The titles of these classic comedy films can be found in capital letters within the descriptions. Unscramble them to name the film for a point.

a) Neal and Del, while attempting to get home for Christmas, find IMPONDERABLE ASSAULTS, NOT IN A deliberate attempt to stop them – they are just really unlucky! (1987)

b) When Cameron accidently causes the destruction of his father's prized possession (a 1961 Ferrari 250 GT California Spyder) he finds it ABSURDLY OFFERS RELIEF. (1986)

c) Billy Ray Valentine breaks a vase and is concerned, but once PLACATED, GRINS and asks, "You want me to break something else?" (1983)

d) As bounty hunter Jack Walsh spends more time with Jonathan "The Duke" Mardukas he comes to realize he wouldn't MIND HURTING him. (1988)

e) When Warner Huntington III breaks up with his girlfriend because she isn't serious enough, will ELLE GO BLANDLY? No, she has a plan... (2001)

2. ONE OF OUR ______ IS MISSING!

Just fill in the missing word – there's always a theme, and this time it's... weather.

a) *Little Miss* ________ (2006)
b) ________ *and Lightfoot* (1974)
c) *A Mighty* ________ (2003)
d) *Black* ________ (1989)
e) ________, *Caesar!* (2016)

ROUND 3

1. NEXT

A round about sequels. I'll give you a film, you tell me the name of the sequel.

a) *The Mask* (1994)
   i) *Somebody Stop Him*
   ii) *The Mask Rides Again*
   iii) *Son of the Mask*

b) *Gregory's Girl* (1981)
   i) *Gregory's Two Girls*
   ii) *Gregory Strikes Out*
   iii) *Grow Up Gregory!*

c) *Donnie Darko* (2001)
   i) *Donnie Darker*
   ii) *S. Darko*
   iii) *Donnie in Wonderland*

d) *The NeverEnding Story* (1984)
   i) *The NeverEnding Story II: The Next Chapter*
   ii) *The NeverEnding Story Never Ends*
   iii) *The NeverEnding Story: The Bux Stops Here*

e) *Gremlins* (1984)
   i) *Gremlins 2: Gremlins Take Manhattan*
   ii) *Gremlins 2: The New Batch*
   iii) *Gremlins 2: Search for Gizmo*

2. THE ODD COUPLE

I'll describe an actor and a film character that share the same initials. A point for each you can name.

a) **Actor:** American actor born in 1926. Née Norma Jeane Mortenson, she became one of the icons of the twentieth century, starring in films including *Niagara* (1953), *Gentlemen Prefer Blondes* (1953), *The Seven Year Itch* (1955) and *Some Like It Hot* (1959). **Character:** First appeared in *Halloween* (1978) by John Carpenter. In his trademark mask and boiler suit, he stalks and attempts to murder Jamie Lee Curtis. He was still chasing her in the 2022 film *Halloween Ends*.

b) **Actor:** American actor born in 1983. Combines low-budget dramas such as *Frances Ha* (2012), *Paterson* (2016) and *Marriage Story* (2019) with blockbusters such as *Star Wars: Episode VII – The Force Awakens* (2015), in which he plays Kylo Ren, *Ferrari* (2023) and *Megalopolis* (2024). **Character:** The central character from *Gone Girl* (2014) portrayed by Rosamund Pike. At the beginning of the film, Pike's character is missing and suspicion falls on her husband, Nick, portrayed by Ben Affleck.

c) **Actor:** American, born in 1982. As a child she first appeared on screens aged six in *Purple People Eater* (1988). She is probably best known for two roles, Enid Coleslaw in *Ghost World* (2001) and Jane Burnham in *American Beauty* (1999). **Character:** A man who is unaware that his entire life is, and has always been, filmed for a TV show and that all his friends, family and neighbours are actors. Portrayed by Jim Carrey in a film released in 1998, directed by Peter Weir.

d) **Actor:** French actor born in 1966. First found fame in *La Haine* (1995), while other French-language successes include *Mesrine* (2008) and *The Specials* (2019). He has also appeared in English-speaking films, including *Ocean's*

Twelve (2004) and *Ocean's Thirteen* (2007), *Eastern Promises* (2007) and *Black Swan* (2010). **Character:** The head of the family in Francis Ford Coppola's *The Godfather* (1972) portrayed in that film by Marlon Brando, with Robert De Niro playing a younger version in *The Godfather Part II* (1974). Both actors won Academy Awards, though Brando sent Sacheen Littlefeather to decline his as a statement against Hollywood's portrayal of Native Americans.

e) **Actor:** Swedish actor born in 1905. One of the great icons of the silent and golden eras of Hollywood. The silent film *Flesh and the Devil* (1926) made her a star in the USA. Some of her talkies included *Mata Hari* (1931), *Grand Hotel* (1932) and *Anna Karenina* (1935). She retired from acting in 1941, rejecting the role of Norma Desmond in *Sunset Boulevard* (1950). **Character:** Appears in *Wall Street* (1987) and *Wall Street: Money Never Sleeps* (2010), portrayed both times by Michael Douglas. This "corporate raider" is best remembered for his "greed, for lack of a better word, is good" line. Douglas won the Best Actor Oscar for the first film.

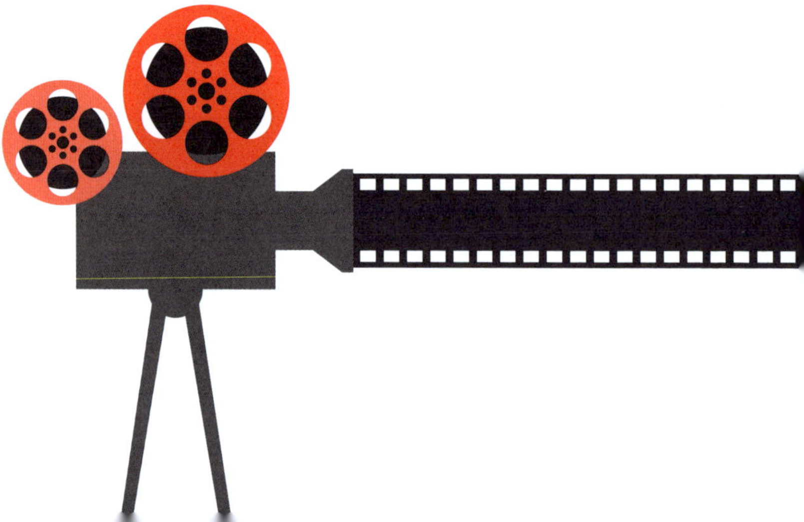

ROUND 4

1. BRAINSTORM

Complete the lists and spot the links – a point for each correct answer.

a) What connects Peter Finch in *Network* (1976) with Heath Ledger in *The Dark Knight* (2008)?

b) Which singer and actor appeared in *The Rocky Horror Picture Show* (1975), *Fight Club* (1999) and *Spice World* (1997)?

c) John "Stumpy" Pepys – bizarre gardening accident. Eric "Stumpy Joe" Childs – choked on vomit, origin unknown. Peter "James" Bond – spontaneously combusted on stage. Mick Shrimpton – exploded. What connects these characters and their untimely demises?

d) What comes next in this list? *Legacy* (2012), *Ultimatum* (2007), *Supremacy* (2004)...?

e) Which historical figure was played by Gérard Depardieu, Georges Corraface and Jim Dale in the same year?

2. IT FOLLOWS

The first letter of each answer follows the first letter of the last. So, if the answer to c) is "Apple", the answer to d) will begin with "B". If you get to Z, go to A. Each question is worth one point.

a) *El laberinto del fauno* is the Spanish title for which 2006 Guillermo del Toro film?

b) Name the Captain of the *Orca* in Steven Spielberg's *Jaws* (1975) played by Robert Shaw.

c) In Powell and Pressburger's 1948 classic, what colour are the titular shoes?

d) Which notorious sci-fi flop from 1980 starred Kirk Douglas, Farrah Fawcett and Harvey Keitel and had a script by Martin Amis?

e) In which 1982 film is Dustin Hoffman credited twice, once as Michael Dorsey and once as Dorothy Michaels?

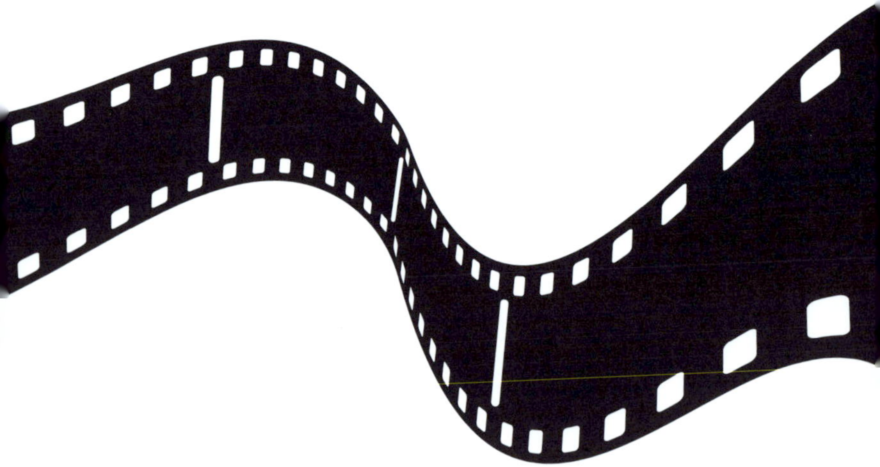

ROUND 5

THE LAST PICTURE SHOW

Say what you see! Can you identify the films from these picture clues? Each picture is worth a point.

1

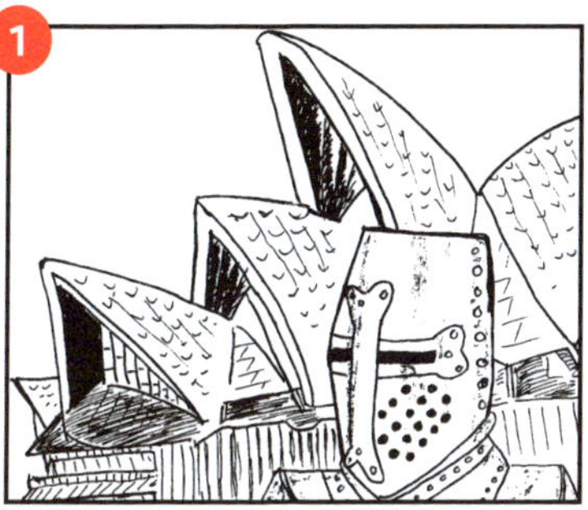

2

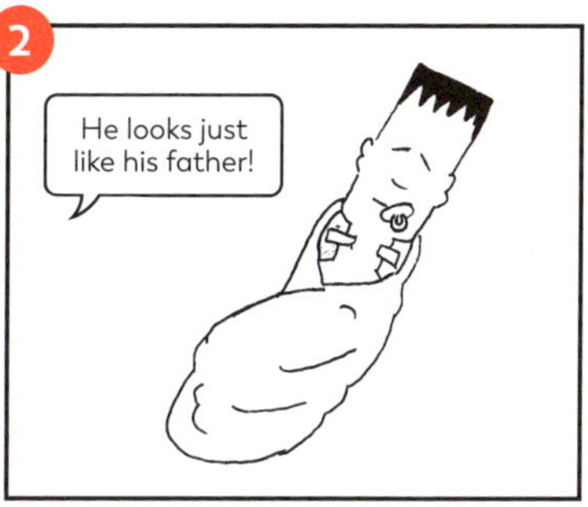

3

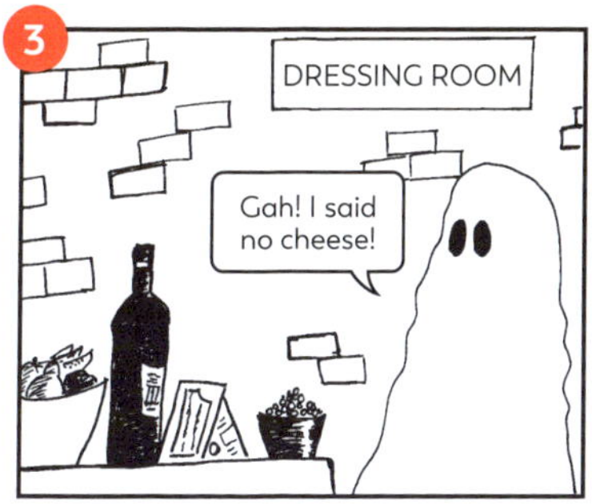

4

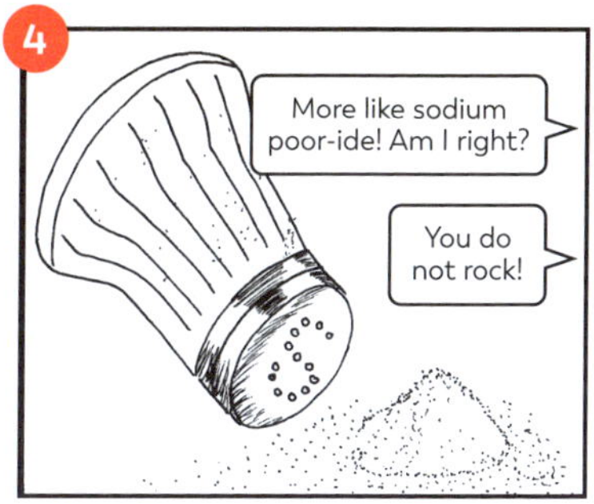

5

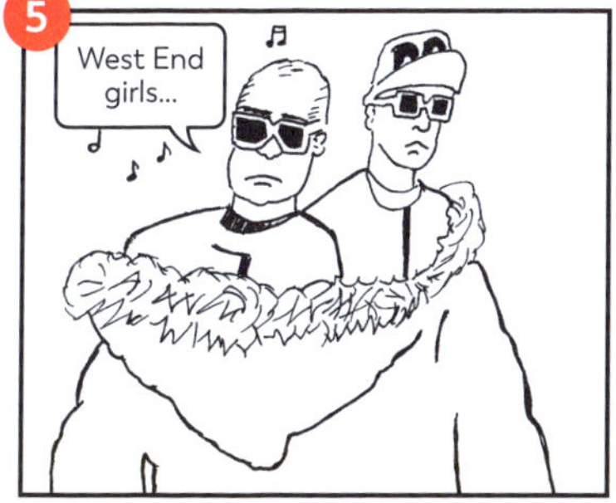

6

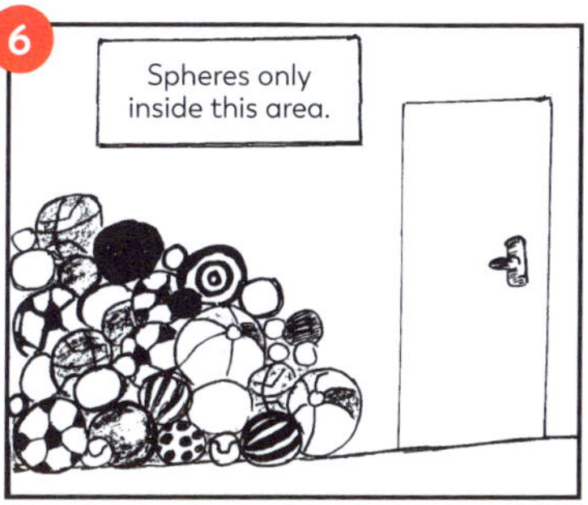

ANSWERS

ROUND 1

1. b) *Last Tango in Paris* (1972). *Last Exit to Brooklyn* was 1989, *The Last of the Mohicans* was 1992.

2. Clint Eastwood

3. b) *Top Gun*

4. b) *Eat Pray Love*

5. c) *They Live* by John Carpenter.

6. *Training Day* and *Carlito's Way*.

7. c) In *The Great Escape*, McQueen wasn't allowed to perform the jumping-the-fence stunt, so he donned a German uniform and "chased himself".

While filming *The Towering Inferno*, he reportedly insisted that he and Newman had the same number of lines (cutting some of his to accommodate this) so that it was a level playing field that would allow his superior talent to show through.

8. b) Gandalf (*The Lord of the Rings* trilogy)

9. 2002

10. *Downhill* (1927), *Champagne* (1928), *Blackmail* (1929), *Murder!* (1930), *Mary* (1931), *Sabotage* (1936), *Rebecca* (1940), *Suspicion* (1941), *Saboteur* (1942), *Lifeboat* (1944), *Spellbound* (1945), *Notorious* (1946), *Rope* (1948), *Vertigo* (1958), *Psycho* (1960), *Marnie* (1964), *Topaz* (1969) and *Frenzy* (1972).

ROUND 2

1. a) *Planes, Trains and Automobiles*

1. b) *Ferris Bueller's Day Off*

1. c) *Trading Places*

1. d) *Midnight Run*

1. e) *Legally Blonde*

2. a) *Sunshine*

2. b) *Thunderbolt*

2. c) *Wind*

2. d) *Rain*

2. e) *Hail*

ROUND 3

1. a) iii) *Son of the Mask* (2005)

1. b) i) *Gregory's Two Girls* (1999)

1. c) ii) *S. Darko* (2009)

1. d) i) *The NeverEnding Story II: The Next Chapter* (1990)

1. e) ii) *Gremlins 2: The New Batch* (1990)

> Surprisingly (to me) *Gremlins* 2 was a failure at the box office, taking only $41,483,050 from an estimated budget of $50,000,000.

2. a) Marilyn Monroe and Michael Myers.

Famously, Myers's mask was a William Shatner/Captain Kirk one. The production manager actually bought two masks – the other being a clown mask – but John Carpenter chose the Shatner.

2. b) Adam Driver and Amy Dunne.

2. c) Thora Birch and Truman Burbank.

2. d) Vincent Cassel and Vito Corleone.

2. e) Greta Garbo and Gordon Gekko.

ROUND 4

1. a) Both actors won the Best Actor Oscar award posthumously. Coincidentally, they were also both Australian.

1. b) Meat Loaf

1. c) They are the (ex) drummers from the fictional band Spinal Tap – from the 1984 film *This Is Spinal Tap*.

1. d) *Identity* – these are the titles of the (Jason) *Bourne* films in reverse order from fourth to first. (There is also a fifth film simply entitled *Jason Bourne*.)

1. e) Christopher Columbus. Depardieu in *1492: Conquest of Paradise* (1992), Corraface in *Christopher Columbus: The Discovery* (1992) and Dale in *Carry on Columbus*, also (1992).

None of the three films were hits but *Carry on Columbus* lost the least money as its budget was a mere £2.5 million.

2. a) *Pan's Labyrinth*

2. b) Quint

2. c) Red

2. d) *Saturn 3*

2. e) *Tootsie*

ROUND 5

1. *A Night at the Opera* (1935)
2. *Young Frankenstein* (1974)
3. *Ghost Rider* (2007)
4. *Saltburn* (2023)
5. *Boyz n the Hood* (1991)
6. *Strictly Ballroom* (1992)

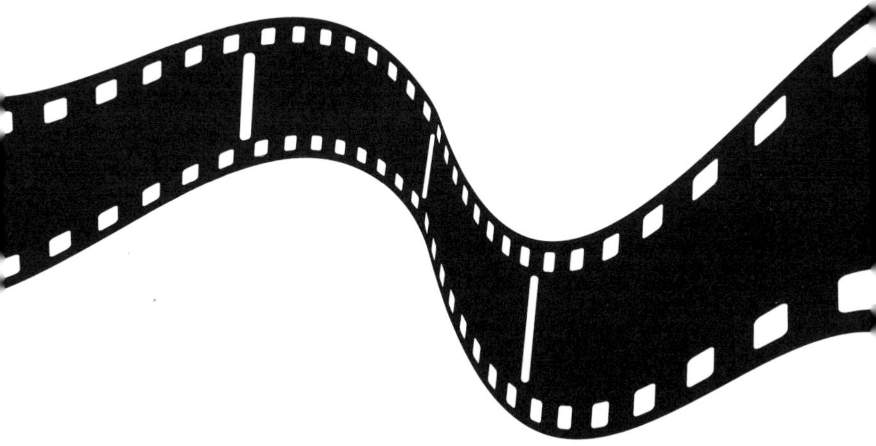

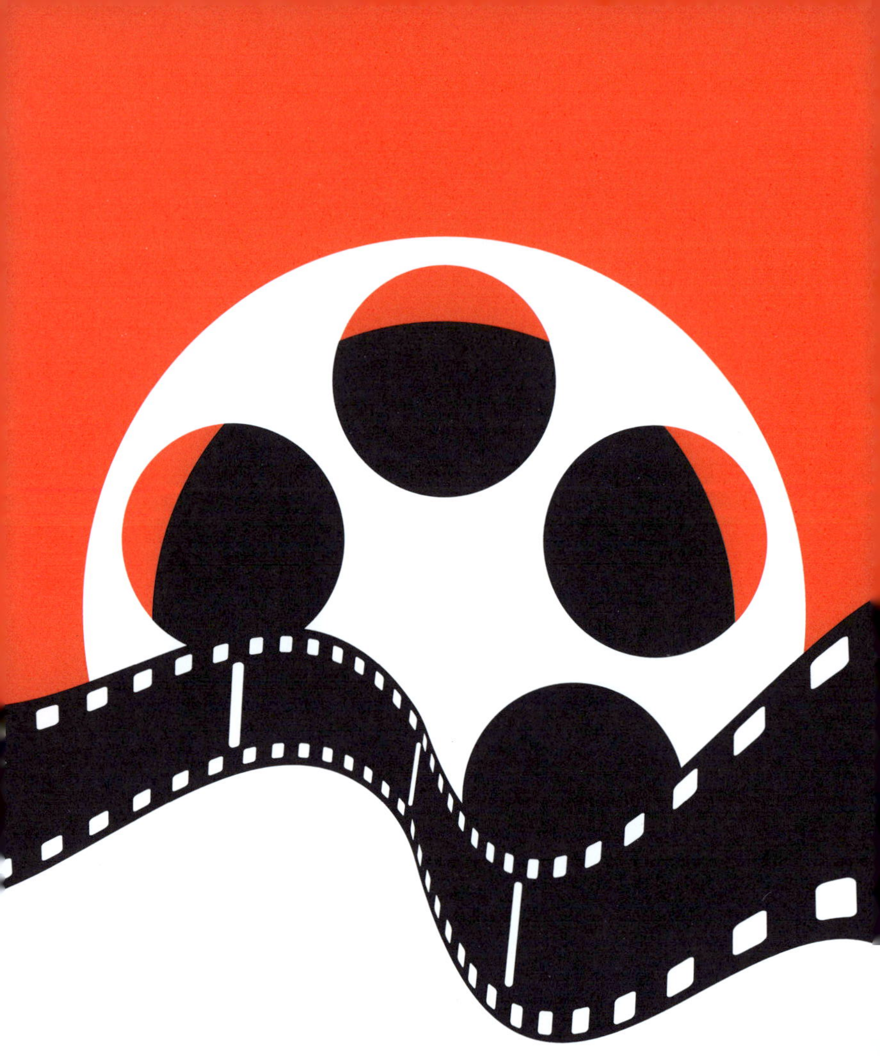

QUIZ 2

ROUND 1

STARTER FOR 10

Ten questions to begin!

1. THE FIRST QUESTION

Which of these child stars was born first?

a) Haley Joel Osment

b) Daniel Radcliffe

c) Macaulay Culkin

2. THE ANAGRAM

Unscramble the actor's name: A NOMINAL PET RAT

3. FILM QUOTE

What film is the following quote from?

"You're a big man, but you're in bad shape. With me it's a full-time job. Now behave yourself."

a) *Get Carter* (1971)

b) *High Noon* (1952)

c) *Taken* (2008)

d) *King Kong* (1933)

4. THUMBS DOWN

What film is this the one-star review of?

"... essentially, it's a truck being chased for a few days in a given direction across a desert then it turns round and goes back again. Genius!"

a) *Mad Max: Fury Road* (2015)

b) *Duel* (1971)

c) *The Vanishing* (1988)

5. ODD ONE OUT

Which of these films was not directed by David Cronenberg? Bonus point if you know who it was directed by.

a) *Scanners* (1981)

b) *Suspiria* (1977)

c) *Videodrome* (1983)

6. RHYMING FILMS

I'll give you the initials of two films whose titles rhyme with each other. I'll also give you one of the stars and the years they were released, just name the films for a point each.

DLN, Donald Sutherland (1973) and OBWAT, George Clooney (2000).

7. CELLULOID OR CELLULIED?

Which of the following is true about Mark Wahlberg?

a) Mark Wahlberg's 1992 autobiography is dedicated to Madonna.

b) Mark Wahlberg's 1992 autobiography is dedicated to his personal trainer.

c) Mark Wahlberg's 1992 autobiography is dedicated to his penis.

8. WHAT MIGHT HAVE BEEN

Which of these roles did Daniel Day-Lewis turn down?

a) Withnail (*Withnail and I* – 1987)

b) Francis "Franco" Begbie (*Trainspotting* – 1996)

c) Edward Scissorhands (1990)

9. WHAT YEAR?

In what year did the following things happen?

Films released this year include: *Seven*, *Bad Boys*, *Toy Story*, *GoldenEye* and *12 Monkeys*. *Forrest Gump* wins the Best Picture Oscar and *Color of Night* wins the Worst Picture award at the Razzies. Lana Turner, Dean Martin, Peter Cook, Michael Hordern and Doug McClure all pass away, and Timothée Chalamet is born. The Dogme movement is begun by Lars von Trier and Thomas Vinterberg and *Die Hard with a Vengeance* is the year's top-grossing film worldwide. But what was the year?

10. GIVE ME FIVE

A chance for five points! You have a choice here: Name me five of the seven actors who made up the original *Magnificent Seven* (1960) or who made up the seven in the remake from 2016.

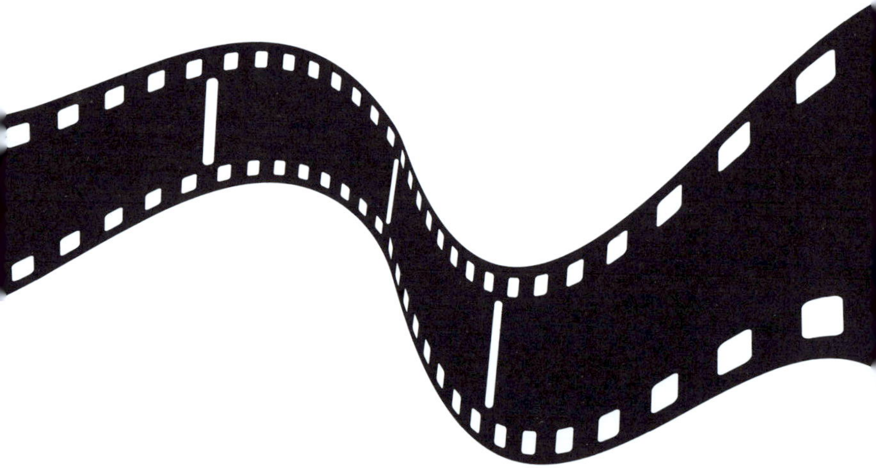

ROUND 2

1. DEATH WATCH

In each question, I'm going to describe three death scenes. I will only use actor names, not characters. One actor links all three. Name the actor for one point, name each film for bonus points. Four points available per question. SPOILER ALERT!

a) ______

i) Blown up by Jean Reno, who he has just shot in the back. (1994)

ii) Bludgeoned with a hammer by his lover Alfred Molina. (1987)

iii) Beheaded by Winona Ryder, having had his throat slit by Keanu Reeves. (1992)

b) ______

i) Dies in the electric chair (off camera) having just broken down and begged for mercy (1938).

ii) Shot, he collapses onto the snowy steps of a church, where he is cradled by Gladys George (1939).

iii) Shouts "Made it, Ma! Top of the world!" atop a large gas storage tank, then blown up by said tank exploding (1949).

c) ______

i) Has her heart torn out by Robert De Niro (and is later brought back to life, in a way, by Kenneth Branagh) (1994).

ii) Shoved into a large oven by Johnny Depp (2007).

iii) Explodes after being hit by a spell from Julie Walters' wand (2011).

d) _______

- **i)** Killed by a small creature bursting from his chest (1979).
- **ii)** Slapped by Uma Thurman's giant thumbs (1993).
- **iii)** Suffocates due to his deformities when he decides to sleep lying down (1980).

e) _______

- **i)** Falls to his death from the Golden Gate Bridge after a fight with Roger Moore (1985).
- **ii)** Shot by Victor Argo on the subway, he makes it to a taxi but dies in the back seat (1990).
- **iii)** Shoots himself in the head playing Russian Roulette (1978).

2. ONE OF OUR _______ IS MISSING!

Just fill in the missing word – there's always a theme, and this time it's… bands with one-word names.

a) *The African* _______ (1951)

b) *Punch-Drunk* _______ (2002)

c) *The Trial of the* _______ *7* (2020)

d) _______ *of the Spider Woman* (1985)

e) _______ *Guy* (2021)

ROUND 3

1. LINK

I will give you a word that ends one film title and begins another, plus the star and the year – name both for two points.

a) The link is "Liar". Film one – Tom Courtenay (1963). Film two – Jim Carrey (1997).

b) The link is "Everything". Film one – Eddie Redmayne (2014). Film two – Michelle Yeoh (2022).

c) The link is "Hunter". Film one – Robert De Niro (1978). Film two – Gerard Butler (2018).

d) The link is "Wild". Film one – Meryl Streep (1994). Film two – Nicolas Cage (1990).

e) The link is "Velvet". Film one – Elizabeth Taylor (1944). Film two – Ewan McGregor (1998).

2. THE ODD COUPLE

I'll describe an actor and a film character that share the same initials. A point for each you can name.

a) **Actor:** American actor born in 1962. Initially best known for comedic roles such as Brick Tamland in *Anchorman: The Legend of Ron Burgundy* (2004), Andy in *The 40-Year-Old-Virgin* (2005) and Evan Baxter in *Evan Almighty* (2007), he later secured serious roles in *Foxcatcher* (2014), *Little Miss Sunshine* (2006) and *The Big Short* (2015). He is also the voice of Gru in the *Despicable Me* series (2010–2024). **Character:** The mother of John, she attempts to protect her son from seemingly unstoppable killing machines in

The Terminator series of films (1984–2019). Played in the first two films and *Terminator: Dark Fate* (2019) by Linda Hamilton, the character has also been played by Emilia Clarke.

b) **Actor:** Also a director, writer and singer born in France in 1969. Early acting roles included Zoe in *Killing Zoe* (1993) and Dominque in Krzysztof Kieślowski's *Three Colours* trilogy (1993–1994). Perhaps best known for her starring role in Richard Linklater's *Before* trilogy (1995–2013), in which she stars with Ethan Hawke. **Character:** First portrayed by Sylvester Stallone in 1995 and then by Karl Urban in 2012. A ruthless lawman taken from the pages of cult British sci-fi comic *2000 AD*.

c) **Actor:** American, born in 1893. One of the most influential stars of the silent film era. He performed many of his own stunts and the trick shot of him dangling from a clock face in *Safety Last!* (1923) has become iconic. **Character:** Portrayed by Orson Welles in Carol Reed's *The Third Man* (1949). Although absent from the first two-thirds of the film, Welles's character is central to the plot, and some might say grabs the best lines (the "Cuckoo Clock" speech, for example).

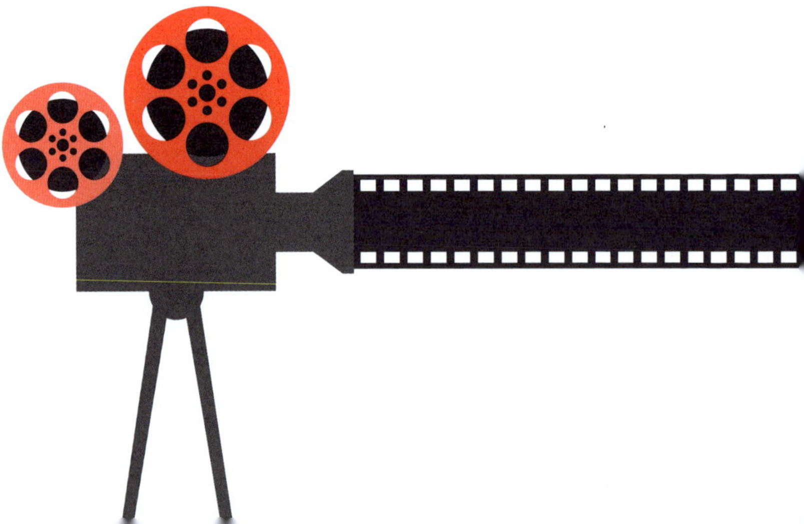

d) **Actor:** American, born in 1976. She rose to prominence in the *Scary Movie* series of films (2000–2013), going on to star in films including *The House Bunny* (2018) and the 2018 remake of *Overboard*. Her 2017 memoir *Unqualified* became a *New York Times* bestseller. **Character:** Portrayed by Gregory Peck in the 1962 film version of *To Kill a Mockingbird*. The principled attorney who is hired to defend a young black man against a charge of rape. Peck won the Oscar for this role.

e) **Actor:** Welsh, born in 1925. One of the most acclaimed actors of his generation, he starred in films such as *Look Back in Anger* (1959), *Cleopatra* (1963), *Who's Afraid of Virginia Woolf?* (1966) and *Where Eagles Dare* (1968). Nominated seven times for an Oscar, but never won. His final film was the 1984 version of *Nineteen Eighty-Four*. **Character:** Portrayed by Humphrey Bogart in the 1942 film *Casablanca*. He runs a nightclub and gambling den that is one day visited by his ex-love Ilsa Lund (Ingrid Bergman), forcing him to make a tough decision.

ROUND 4

1. BRAINSTORM

Complete the lists and spot the links – a point for each correct answer.

a) Who comes next in this list? Sebastian Koch, Timothy Olyphant, Jeremy Irons, William Sadler and ________?

b) What (specifically) links Sean Connery in *Sir Billi* (AKA *Guardian of the Highlands* in the US – 2012), Orson Welles in *The Transformers: The Movie* (1986), James Stewart in *An American Tail: Fievel Goes West* (1991) and Donald Sutherland in *Ozi: Voice of the Forest* (2023)?

c) What role connects Peter Sellers, Steve Martin and Alan Arkin?

d) What film title links Ralph Macchio in 1986, Britney Spears in 2002, and Hedy Lamarr in 1942?

e) What colour appears in the titles of films for Seth Rogen in 2011, Tom Hanks in 1999 and Dev Patel in 2021?

2. IT FOLLOWS

The first letter of each answer follows the first letter of the last. So, if the answer to c) is "Apple", the answer to d) will begin with "B". If you get to Z, go to A. Each question is worth one point.

a) A 1954 Billy Wilder film starring Audrey Hepburn and Humphrey Bogart, it was remade in 1995 by Sydney Pollack starring Harrison Ford and Julia Ormond. What are they (both) called?

b) In the 1976 sci-fi classic *Logan's Run*, at what age are the population terminated?

c) Which film was the first to be nominated for both Best Picture and Best Animated Feature at the Academy Awards?

d) Which artist has been portrayed on film by Kirk Douglas, Tim Roth and Willem Dafoe?

e) What was the surname of brothers Harry, Albert, Sam and Jack who founded a film studio in 1923?

ROUND 5

THE LAST PICTURE SHOW

Say what you see! Can you identify the films from these picture clues? Each picture is worth a point.

1

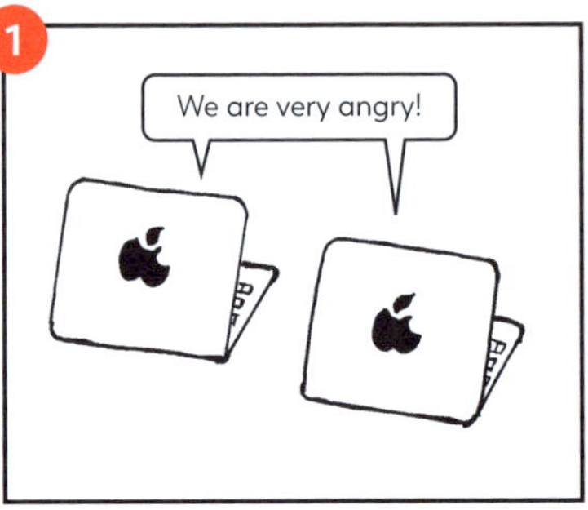

2

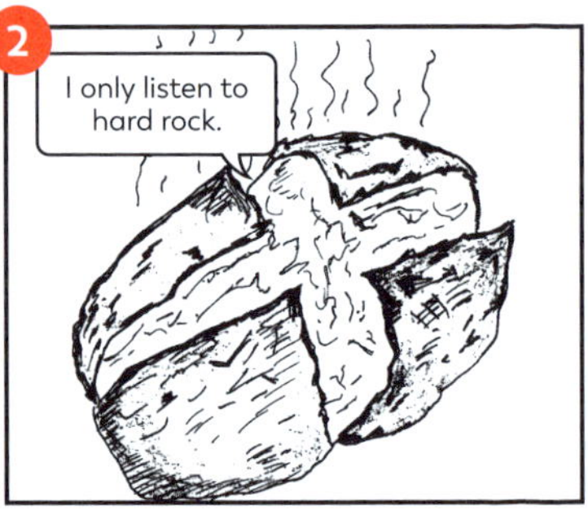

3

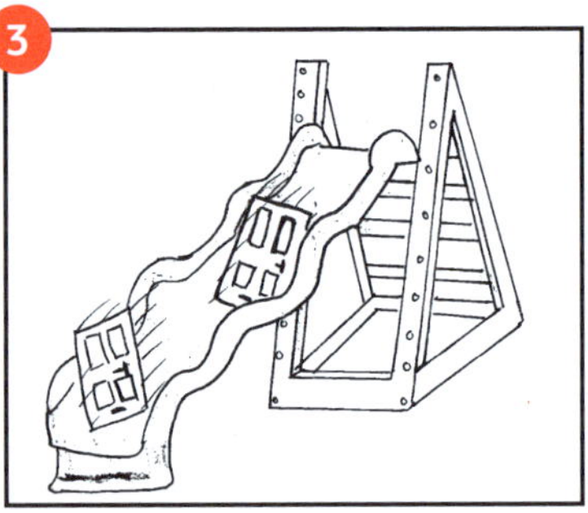

4

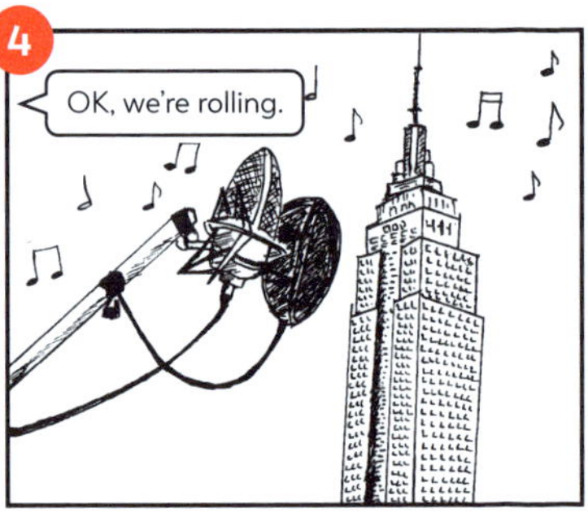

5

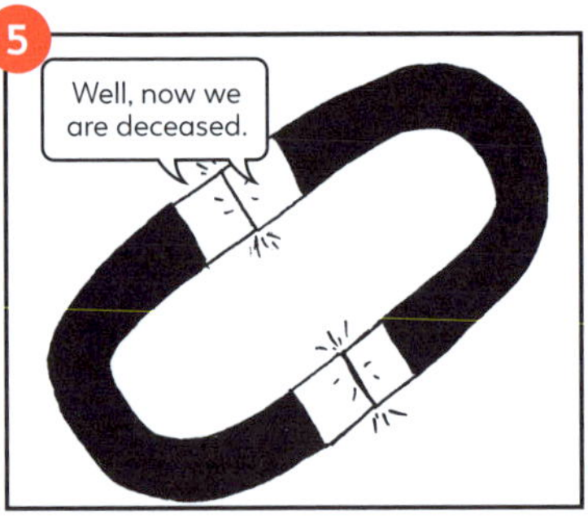

6

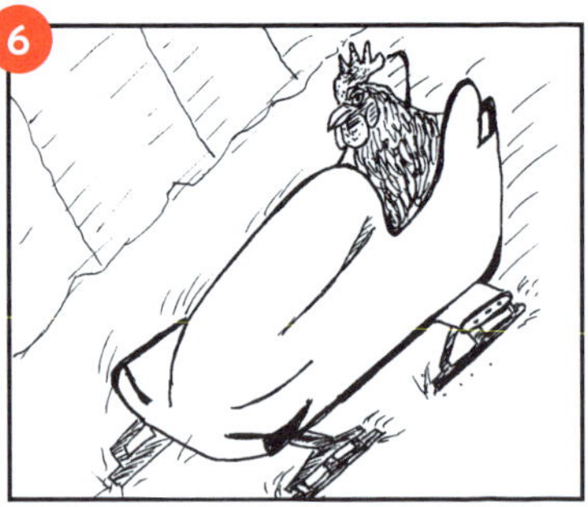

ANSWERS

ROUND 1

1. c) Macaulay Culkin, 1980 (Osment, 1988 and Radcliffe, 1989).

2. Natalie Portman

3. a) *Get Carter*

> The actor Michael Caine is talking to is Bryan Mosley (who is then thrown by Caine from the roof of a car park), also known as Alf Roberts in UK soap opera *Coronation Street*.

4. a) *Mad Max: Fury Road*

5. b) *Suspiria* by Dario Argento.

6. *Don't Look Now* and *O Brother, Where Art Thou?*

7. c) Mark Wahlberg's 1992 autobiography is dedicated to his penis.

> The book began "I wanna dedicate this book to my dick". He later regretted this decision saying, "I thought it would be funny."

8. a) Withnail

Richard E. Grant has often thanked Day-Lewis for not taking the part. He got to thank him in person while filming *The Age of Innocence* (1993) – "I said, 'Oh Daniel, I owe you my career.' And he said, 'Arise!' Then he didn't acknowledge me for the next three months because his character hated my character and he's a method actor."

9. 1995

10. 1960: Yul Brynner, Steve McQueen, Horst Buchholz, James Coburn, Charles Bronson, Robert Vaughn, Brad Dexter.

2016: Denzel Washington, Chris Pratt, Ethan Hawke, Vincent D'Onofrio, Lee Byung-hun, Manuel Garcia-Rulfo, Martin Sensmeier.

ROUND 2

1. a) Gary Oldman

1. a) i) *Léon: The Professional*

1. a) ii) *Prick Up Your Ears*

1. a) iii) *Bram Stoker's Dracula*

1. b) James Cagney

1. b) i) *Angels with Dirty Faces*

1. b) ii) *The Roaring Twenties*

1. b) iii) *White Heat*

Debate rages over whether Cagney's character in *Angels with Dirty Faces*, William "Rocky" Sullivan, really breaks down or is doing as his friend Father Jerry Connolly (Pat O'Brien) has asked (to stop the local kids idolizing him). Cagney has said "it is virtually impossible to say which course Rocky took – which is just the way I wanted it".

1. c) Helena Bonham Carter

1. c) i) *Frankenstein*

1. c) ii) *Sweeney Todd: The Demon Barber of Fleet Street*

1. c) iii) *Harry Potter and the Deathly Hallows: Part 2*

1. d) John Hurt

1. d) i) *Alien*

1. d) ii) *Even Cowgirls Get the Blues*

1. d) iii) *The Elephant Man*

1. e) Christopher Walken

1. e) i) *A View to a Kill*

1. e) ii) *King of New York*

1. e) iii) *The Deer Hunter*

2. a) *Queen*

2. b) *Love*

2. c) *Chicago*

2. d) *Kiss*

2. e) *Free*

ROUND 3

1. a) *Billy **Liar** Liar*

1. b) *The Theory of **Everything** Everywhere All at Once*

1. c) *The Deer **Hunter** Killer*

1. d) *The River **Wild** at Heart*

1. e) *National **Velvet** Goldmine*

2. a) Steve Carell and Sarah Connor.

2. b) Julie Delpy and Judge Dredd.

> Stallone's version is (rightly) not well thought of. Sly himself later commented, "It probably should have been much more comic, really humorous, and fun. What I learned out of that experience was that we shouldn't have tried to make it *Hamlet*; it's more Hamlet and Eggs."

2. c) Harold Lloyd and Harry Lime.

2. d) Anna Faris and Atticus Finch.

2. e) Richard Burton and Rick Blaine.

ROUND 4

1. a) Alan Rickman – these are the villains in the *Die Hard* series (1988–2013), in reverse order, from *A Good Day to Die Hard* (2013) back to the first *Die Hard* (1988).

1. b) They are all those actors' final film performance, and they are all voice only – all those films are animated.

> Sean Connery had retired but briefly returned to acting for this role. It seems his wife's grandchildren became enamoured by the sample DVD Connery had been sent and encouraged him to participate. Though not highly thought of, *Sir Billi* was also Scotland's first CGI animated movie.

1. c) Inspector Clouseau – Peter Sellers: *The Pink Panther* (1963), *A Shot in the Dark* (1964), *The Return of the Pink Panther* (1975), *The Pink Panther Strikes Again* (1976) and *Revenge of the Pink Panther*

(1978). Alan Arkin: *Inspector Clouseau* (1968). Steve Martin: *The Pink Panther* (2006) and *The Pink Panther 2* (2009).

1. d) *Crossroads*

1. e) Green – *The Green Hornet*, *The Green Mile* and *The Green Knight*.

2. a) *Sabrina*

2. b) Thirty

2. c) *Up* (2009)

> ***Up*** **was also the first Pixar film presented in 3D and Pixar's first win for Best Score (Randy Newman).**

2. d) Vincent van Gogh. Douglas in *Lust for Life* (1956), Roth in *Vincent & Theo* (1990), and Dafoe in *At Eternity's Gate* (2018).

2. e) Warner

ROUND 5

1. *Mad Max* (1979)
2. *Full Metal Jacket* (1987)
3. *Sliding Doors* (1998)
4. *Empire Records* (1995)
5. *Fatal Attraction* (1987)
6. *Chicken Run* (2000)

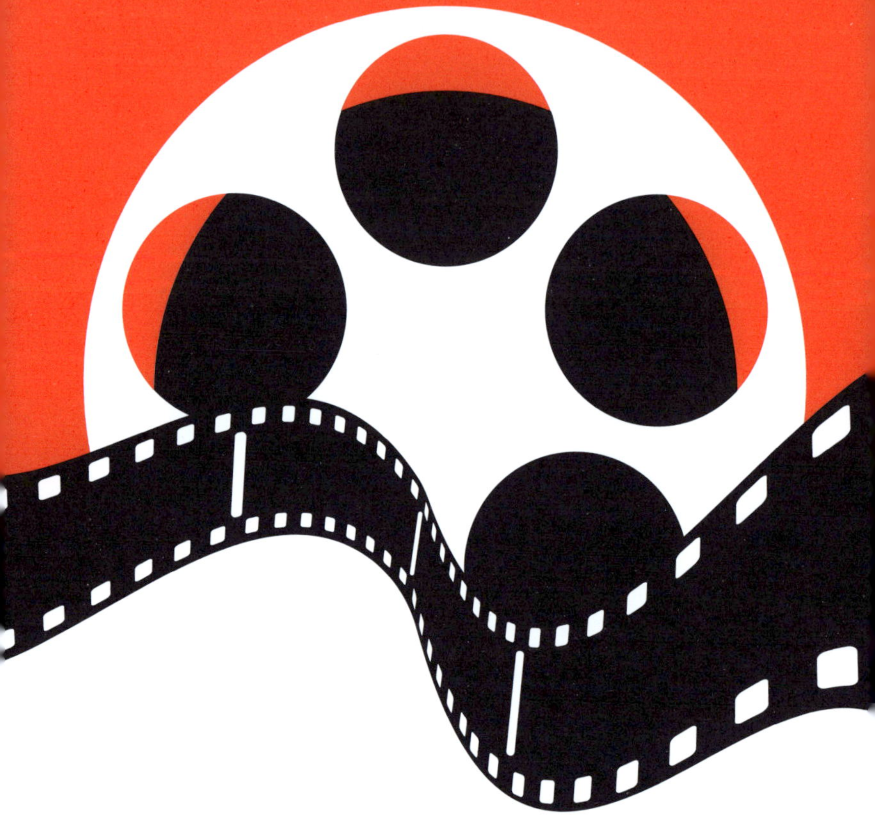

QUIZ 3

ROUND 1

STARTER FOR 10

Ten questions to begin!

1. THE FIRST QUESTION

Which of these cartoon characters appeared on cinema screens first?

a) Buzz Lightyear (*Toy Story*)

b) Remy (*Ratatouille*)

c) Shrek

2. THE ANAGRAM

Unscramble the actor's name: WALTZ NEEDS HONING

3. FILM QUOTE

What film is the following quote from?

"Get busy living, or get busy dying."

a) *As Good as It Gets* (1997)

b) *The Shawshank Redemption* (1994)

c) *The Color Purple* (1985)

d) *Dawn of the Dead* (1978)

4. THUMBS DOWN

What film is this the one-star review of?

"Abysmal soundtrack, mumbling dialogue, weird back-and-forth time jumps... Awful doom-laden intrusive music – and FAR TOO LONG!"

a) *Gladiator* (2000)

b) *The Time Traveler's Wife* (2009)

c) *Oppenheimer* (2023)

5. ODD ONE OUT

Which of these films was not directed by Alejandro González Iñárritu? Bonus point if you know who it was directed by.

a) *Babylon* (2022)

b) *Birdman* (2014)

c) *Babel* (2006)

6. RHYMING FILMS

I'll give you the initials of two films whose titles rhyme with each other. I'll also give you one of the stars and the years they were released, just name the films for a point each.

PAHR, Rachel Roberts (1975) and ATB, John Boyega (2011).

7. CELLULOID OR CELLULIED?

Which of the following is true about Jack Nicholson?

a) To prepare for an upcoming film, in the late sixties, Nicholson spent three months naked.

b) To prepare for an upcoming film, in the late seventies, Nicholson spent three months in an asylum.

c) To prepare for an upcoming film, in the late eighties, Nicholson spent three months listening only to the artist Prince.

8. WHAT MIGHT HAVE BEEN

Which of these roles did Russell Crowe turn down?

a) Judge Dredd (*Dredd* – 2012)

b) Wolverine (*X-Men* – 2000)

c) Iron Man (2008)

9. WHAT YEAR?

In what year did the following things happen?

Films released this year include: *E.T. The Extra Terrestrial, Tootsie, First Blood, Star Trek II: The Wrath of Khan, The Dark Crystal, Fanny and Alexander* and *Britannia Hospital. Tron* is the first film to feature extensive use of computer animation. *Chariots of Fire* wins the Best Picture Oscar and the Bafta. Eddie Redmayne, Kirsten Dunst and Hayley Atwell are born. John Belushi is found dead of a drug overdose at the Chateau Marmont hotel in Los Angeles. Ingrid Bergman, Henry Fonda, Jacques Tati and Marty Feldman also pass away. Eddie Murphy makes his film debut in *48 Hours*. But what was the year?

10. GIVE ME FIVE

A chance for five points! Name five actors who provided voices for the toys in *Toy Story* (1995). There are ten possible answers.

ROUND 2

1. A FEW GOOD MEN

Can you complete these film titles? They all end with "Man". I'll give you the year of release, the director and one of the stars.

a) 1973, Robin Hardy, Edward Woodward.

b) 2023, Richard Linklater, Glen Powell.

c) 1992, Brett Leonard, Pierce Brosnan.

d) 2009, Tom Ford, Colin Firth.

e) 1952, John Ford, John Wayne.

2. ONE OF OUR ______ IS MISSING!

Just fill in the missing word – there's always a theme, and this time it's... birds.

a) *Black* ________ (2010)

b) *Hudson* ________ (1991)

c) *The* ________ *Kid* (1984)

d) *Red* ________ (2018)

e) *The* ________ *Has Landed* (1976)

ROUND 3

1. ENCORE

Here are five film titles with alliterative missing words – can you fill the words in? A point for each title completed.

a) *Something's* _ _ _ _ _/_ _ _ _ (2003)

b) *How the* _ _ _ _ /_ _ _/_ _ _ (1962)

c) _ _ _ _ _ _ _ _ _/_ _ _ _ _ _ _/ *Jenkins* (2016)

d) _ _ _/_ _ _/ *Afternoon* (1975)

e) *Those* _ _ _ _ _ _ _ _ _ _ _ _ / _ _ _/ *in Their Flying Machines* (1965)

2. THE ODD COUPLE

I'll describe an actor and a film character that share the same initials. A point for each you can name.

a) **Actor:** American actor born in 1931. One of the finest actors of his generation, his roles include Boo Radley in *To Kill a Mockingbird* (1962 – his debut), Tom Hagen in *The Godfather* (1972), Lieutenant Colonel Bill Kilgore in *Apocalypse Now* (1979) and Prendergast in *Falling Down* (1993). He won the Best Actor Oscar for his portrayal of Mac Sledge in *Tender Mercies* (1983). **Character:** The main protagonist in *Blade Runner* (1982) by Ridley Scott. Portrayed by Harrison Ford, the character hunts down replicants (synthetic humans). The character also appears in a smaller role in the 2017 sequel *Blade Runner 2049*.

b) **Actor:** British actor born in 1913. He became popular in the 1940s playing mostly romantic leads, appearing in films such as *The Man in Grey* (1943) playing Rokeby, *King Solomon's Mines* (1950) playing Allan Quatermain and portraying Rudolf Rassendyl/King Rudolf V in *The Prisoner of Zenda* (1952). **Character:** The servant but also close friend and companion of Frodo Baggins throughout Peter Jackson's *The Lord of the Rings* trilogy (2001–2003). He was played by Sean Astin.

c) **Actor:** Irish actor born in 1991. The daughter of U2 singer Bono and his wife Ali. Her roles include Mary in *This Must Be the Place* (2011), Maid Marian in the 2018 version of *Robin Hood* starring Taron Egerton, and Flora in *Flora and Son* (2023). **Character:** The main protagonist of the *Mission: Impossible* film series, portrayed by Tom Cruise. A highly skilled field agent, he works for the Impossible Missions Force (the IMF).

d) **Actor:** British actor born in 1993. She made her film debut in Lars von Trier's *Nymphomaniac* (2013) where she met the father of her child, Shia LaBeouf. She is probably best known for the roles of Maxine Minx and Pearl in Ti West's *X* trilogy of horror films (*X* 2022, *Pearl* 2022 and *MaXXXine* 2024). **Character:** The Police Chief from the Coen brothers' *Fargo* (1996), played by Frances McDormand for which she won her first Oscar for Best Actress.

e) **Actor:** British actor born in 1990. Came to worldwide fame by starring in Danny Boyle's *Slumdog Millionaire* (2008) as Jamal Malik. His other roles include Saroo Brierly in *Lion* (2016) and the titular role in *The Personal History of David Copperfield* (2019). In 2024, he was included in *Time* magazine's list of the 100 most influential people in the world. **Character:** The ruthless oilman played by Daniel Day-Lewis in Paul Thomas Anderson's *There Will Be Blood* (2007). Day-Lewis won his second Best Actor Oscar for the role.

ROUND 4

1. BRAINSTORM

Complete the lists and spot the links – a point for each correct answer.

a) What word comes after *Casino* ________ (1967 and 2006), *Battle* ________ (2000) and *Bad Times at the El* _____ (2018)?

b) In which film would you find Randall, Fidgit, Strutter, Og, Wally and Vermin?

c) What connects Hayley Mills in 1961 with Jeremy Irons in 1988 and Tom Hardy in 2015?

d) In *Point Break* (1991), a gang, led by Patrick Swayze, perform robberies wearing the masks of ex-presidents of the USA, but which ex-presidents were they? A point for each!

e) Which composer connects a St Bernard dog (1992), Gary Oldman (1994) and Clifford David (1989)?

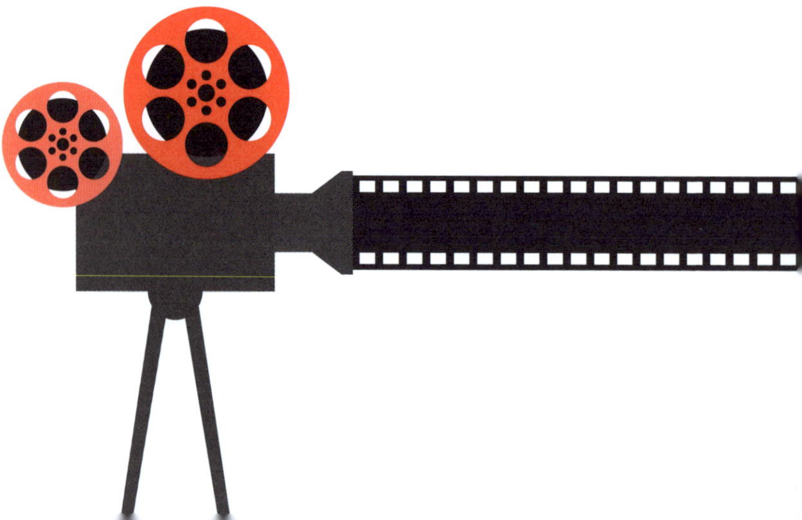

2. IT FOLLOWS

The first letter of each answer follows the first letter of the last. So, if the answer to c) is "Apple", the answer to d) will begin with "B". If you get to Z, go to A. Each question is worth one point.

a) What is the name of the West London-based production company best known for its run of comedies including *Kind Hearts and Coronets* (1949), *Passport to Pimlico* (1949), *The Lavender Hill Mob* (1951) and *The Ladykillers* (1955)?

b) What is the name of the first animated film to be given an X certificate? Released in 1972, it was based on a comic strip by Robert Crumb.

c) Which comedy actor's real first names were Julius Henry?

d) Which legendary country singer has been portrayed by George Hamilton, Henry Thomas and Tom Hiddleston?

e) What was the first film in "Phase One" of the Marvel Cinematic Universe?

ROUND 5

THE LAST PICTURE SHOW

Say what you see! Can you identify the films from these picture clues? Each picture is worth a point.

1

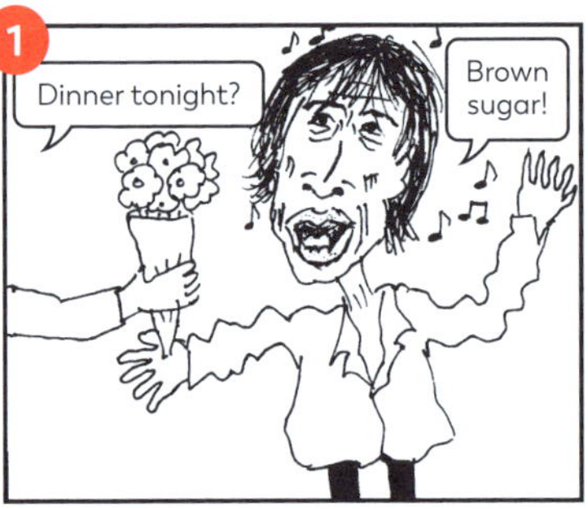

2

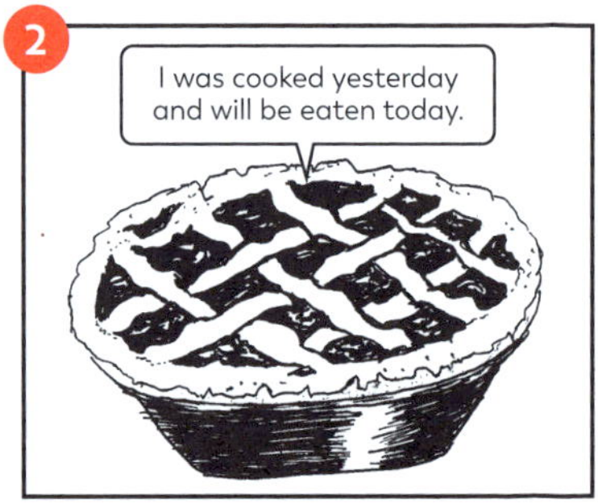

3

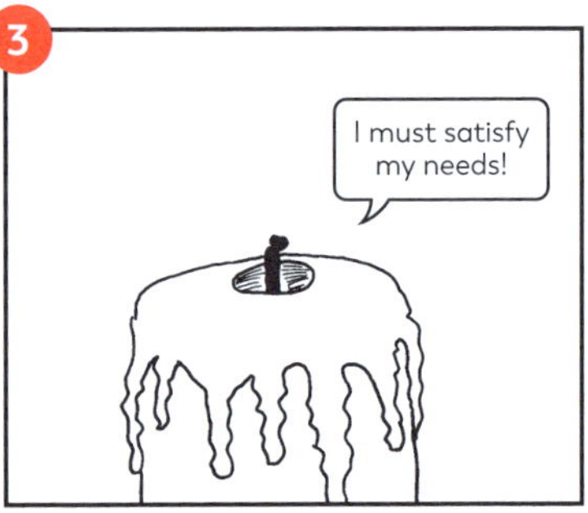

4

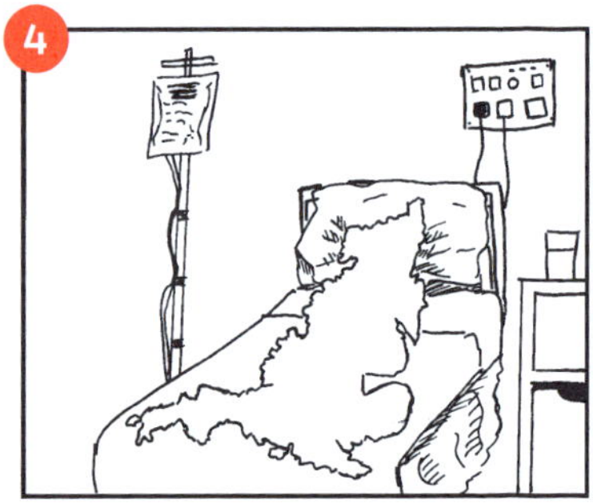

5

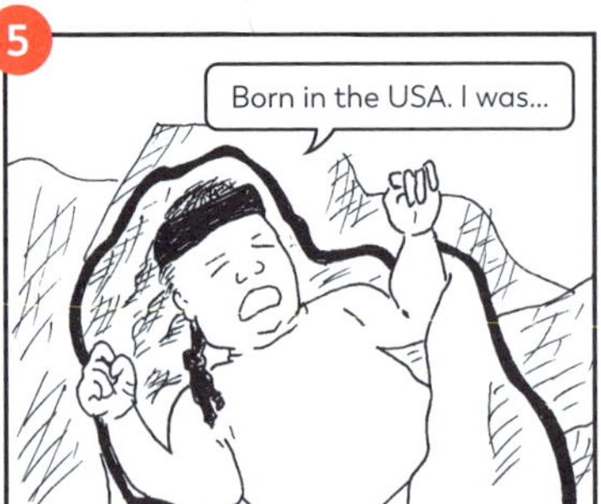

6

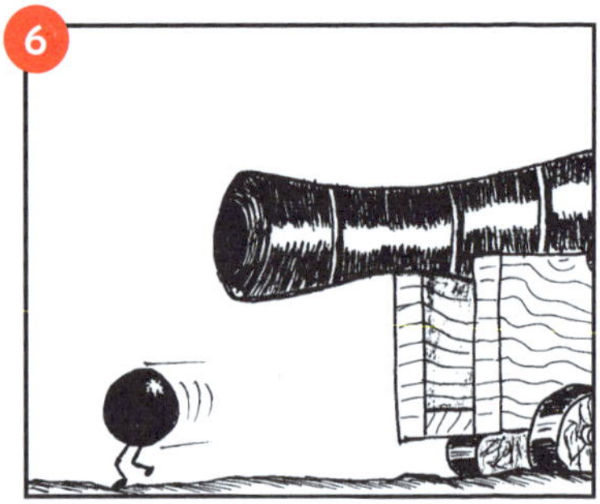

ANSWERS

ROUND 1

1. a) Buzz Lightyear in *Toy Story* (1995). *Ratatouille* was 2007 and *Shrek* was 2001.

2. Denzel Washington

3. b) *The Shawshank Redemption*

4. c) *Oppenheimer*

5. a) *Babylon* by Damien Chazelle.

6. *Picnic at Hanging Rock* and *Attack the Block*.

7. a) To prepare for an upcoming film, in the late sixties, Nicholson spent three months naked.

> He said, "I felt it was totally necessary... I'm self-conscious about body image. I don't have a great body shot. And it was an era of 'Let's get free'."

8. b) Wolverine (*X-Men*)

> In an interview, Crowe explained, "If you remember, Maximus (*Gladiator*) has a wolf at the centre of his cuirass, and he has a wolf as his companion... which I thought was going to be a bigger deal... So I said no because I didn't want to be 'Wolfy the General' then 'Wolfy the Other Bloke' and become like 'Mr Wolf Man'."

9. 1982

10. Tom Hanks (Woody), Tim Allen (Buzz Lightyear), Annie Potts (Bo Peep), Don Rickles (Mr Potato Head), Jim Varney (Slinky Dog), Wallace Shawn (Rex), John Ratzenberger (Hamm), R. Lee Ermey (Sarge), Jack Angel and Jeff Pidgeon (various).

A trading card for John Ratzenberger's *Star Wars* character, "Derlin", stated: "at the Mos Eisley Cantina, everybody knows his name". Derlin is never actually seen at the Cantina, it's a reference to the theme tune of the TV show *Cheers*, in which Ratzenberger played Cliff Clavin.

ROUND 2

1. a) *The Wicker Man*

1. b) *Hit Man*

1. c) *The Lawnmower Man*

1. d) *A Single Man*

1. e) *The Quiet Man*

I have seen this many times as it was my dad's favourite film – supplying his favourite movie plot, a man who is very good at fighting but doesn't want to anymore, but then "has" to. See also *John Wick*, *Taken*, *The Equalizer*, etc.

2. a) *Swan*

2. b) *Hawk*

2. c) *Flamingo*

2. d) *Sparrow*

2. e) *Eagle*

ROUND 3

1. a) *Something's Gotta Give*

1. b) *How the West Was Won*

1. c) *Florence Foster Jenkins*

1. d) *Dog Day Afternoon*

1. e) *Those Magnificent Men in Their Flying Machines*

2. a) Robert Duvall and Rick Deckard.

2. b) Stewart Granger and Samwise Gamgee.

Stewart Granger's real name is James Stewart. He changed it as James Stewart was already a successful American actor at this time. Granger was his Scottish grandmother's maiden name.

2. c) Eve Hewson and Ethan Hunt.

2. d) Mia Goth and Marge Gunderson.

2. e) Dev Patel and Daniel Plainview.

ROUND 4

1. a) "Royale". *Casino Royale*, *Battle Royale* and *Bad Times at the El Royale*.

1. b) *Time Bandits* (1981). These are the time bandits that Kevin befriends at the beginning of the film.

1. c) They took both roles as a pair of twins. Hayley Mills in *The Parent Trap*, Jeremy Irons in *Dead Ringers* and Tom Hardy in *Legend*.

Initially Irons used two dressing rooms (one for each twin) and went shopping on different days for their clothes. This was abandoned when Irons realized (after watching the unedited footage) it was too easy to tell the twins apart.

1. d) Ronald Reagan, Jimmy Carter, Richard Nixon and Lyndon B. Johnson.

1. e) Beethoven. A St Bernard dog was the titular character of the 1992 film *Beethoven*, Gary Oldman played the composer in the 1994 biopic *Immortal Beloved* and Clifford David played him in *Bill and Ted's Excellent Adventure* in 1989.

2. a) Ealing Studios

2. b) *Fritz the Cat*

2. c) Groucho Marx

2. d) Hank Williams. George Hamilton in *Your Cheatin' Heart* (1964), Henry Thomas in *The Last Ride* (2011) and Tom Hiddleston in *I Saw the Light* (2015).

2. e) *Iron Man* (2008)

ROUND 5

1. *Romancing the Stone* (1984)

2. *Life of Pi* (2012)

3. *Wicked* (2024)

4. *The English Patient* (1996)

5. *The Boss Baby* (2017)

6. *The Cannonball Run* (1981)

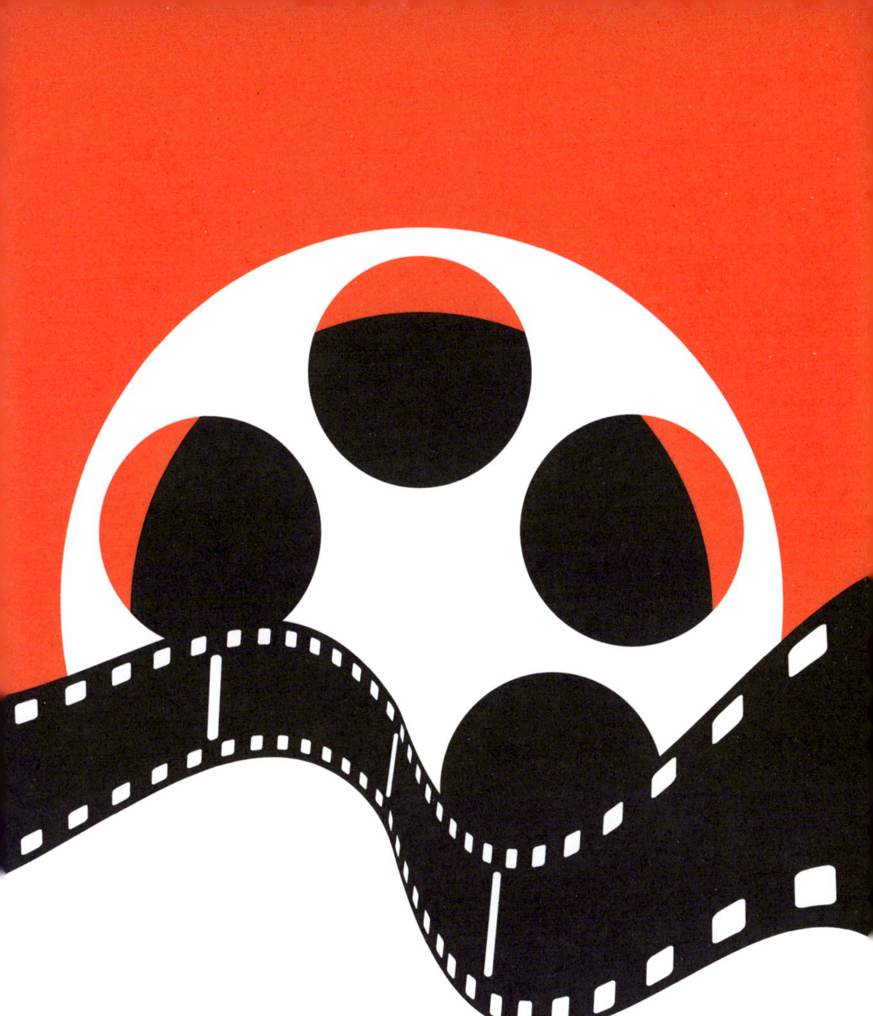

QUIZ 4

ROUND 1

STARTER FOR 10

Ten questions to begin!

1. THE FIRST QUESTION

Which of these actors was first to win an Oscar?

a) Michael Caine

b) Anthony Hopkins

c) Meryl Streep

2. THE ANAGRAM

Unscramble the actor's name: LOP THE CHERRIES

3. FILM QUOTE

What film is the following quote from?

"Are you gonna bark all day little doggie? Or are you gonna bite?"

a) *Rocky IV* (1985)

b) *Man Bites Dog* (1992)

c) *Reservoir Dogs* (1992)

d) *Lady and the Tramp* (1955)

4. THUMBS DOWN

What film is this the one-star review of?

"Dreadful, dreadful film, set in NY in Victorian times, but the singing is more like something from *The Voice*, or *Britain's Got Talent*, nobody sang like that in those times."

a) *Sweeney Todd: The Demon Barber of Fleet Street* (2007)

b) *The Greatest Showman* (2017)

c) *My Fair Lady* (1964)

5. ODD ONE OUT

Which of these films was not directed by Denis Villeneuve? Bonus point if you know who it was directed by.

a) *Dune* (2021)

b) *Arrival* (2016)

c) *Interstellar* (2014)

6. RHYMING FILMS

I'll give you the initials of two films whose titles rhyme with each other. I'll also give you one of the stars and the years they were released, just name the films for a point each.

MJB, Brad Pitt (1998) and TWWB, Steve Carell (2013).

7. CELLULOID OR CELLULIED?

Which of the following is true about Michael Keaton?

a) Michael Keaton's real name is Michael Caine.

b) Michael Keaton's real name is Michael Douglas.

c) Michael Keaton's real name is Michael Sheen.

8. WHAT MIGHT HAVE BEEN

Which of these roles did Will Smith turn down?

a) Blade (1998)

b) Jack Ryan (*Patriot Games* – 1992)

c) Neo (*The Matrix* – 1999)

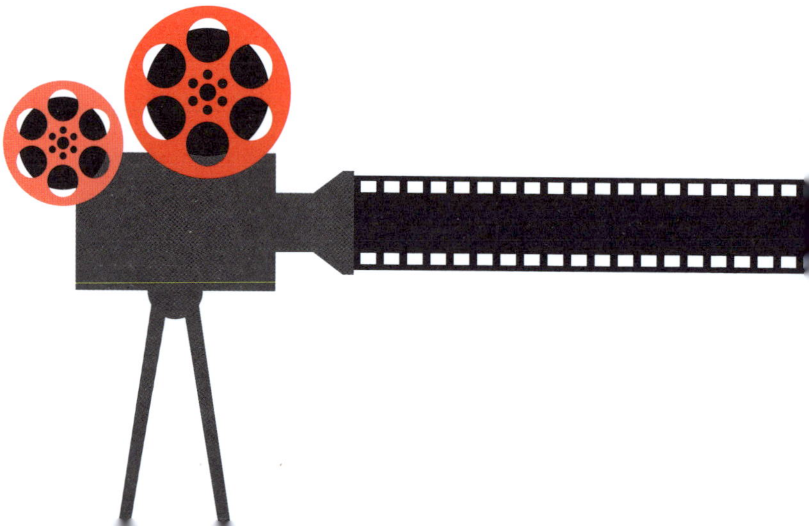

9. WHAT YEAR?

In what year did the following things happen?

Films released this year include: *Diamonds are Forever, Get Carter, Dirty Harry, The French Connection, A Clockwork Orange, The Blood on Satan's Claw* and *Bedknobs and Broomsticks*. Ewan McGregor, Sofia Coppola, Mark Wahlberg and Winona Ryder are born. The silent-film legend Harold Lloyd passes away only three months before his son, Harold Lloyd Jr, Richard Roundtree makes his film debut in (and as) *Shaft* and the highest-grossing independent film of the year is *Sweet Sweetback's Baadasssss Song* by Melvin Van Peebles. But what was the year?

10. GIVE ME FIVE

A chance for five points! Name five films with one-word titles that have won the Best Picture Academy Award (up to the 96th ceremony in 2024). There are 27 possible answers. Or, if you'd prefer something trickier, name five of the six that begin with the letter "C".

ROUND 2

1. THE LAST WORD

Here are five pairs of films where the title ends with the same word. I will give you that word, one actor from the film and the years they were released. Name both films – a point for each.

a) The word is "Dragon". Film one was released in 2000 starring Chow Yun-Fat. Film two was released in 2010 and starred Jay Baruchel (voice performance).

b) The word is "Wedding". Film one was released in 1994 starring Toni Collette. Film two was released in 2002 starring Nia Vardalos.

c) The word is "Place". Film one was released in 2018 starring Emily Blunt. Film two was released in 1950 starring Humphrey Bogart.

d) The word is "Water". Film one was released in 2017 starring Sally Hawkins. Film two was released in 2016 starring Chris Pine.

e) The word is "Woman". Film one was released in 1981 starring Meryl Streep. Film two was released in 2020 starring Carey Mulligan.

2. ONE OF OUR ______ IS MISSING!

Just fill in the missing word – there's always a theme, and this time it's... flavours of ice cream.

a) ________ *Sky* (2001)
b) *Like Water for* ________ (1992)
c) ________ *Falls* (1999)
d) *The* ________ *Blonde* (1941)
e) ________ *and Cigarettes* (2003)

ROUND 3

1. RHYME AND REASON

All these films have titles that rhyme. I'll give you the year of release, one of the stars and the initials of the titles.

a) 1993, Bette Midler, HP.

b) 1991, Rik Mayall, DDF.

c) 2007, Dustin Hoffman, MMWE.

d) 2008, Jack Black, BKR.

e) 2022, Lesley Manville, MHGTP.

2. THE ODD COUPLE

I'll describe an actor and a film character that share the same initials. A point for each you can name.

a) **Actor:** American, born in 1940. Widely considered as one of the greatest actors of his generation. Some of his key roles include Michael Corleone in *The Godfather* (1972), and its sequels, Sonny Wortzik in *Dog Day Afternoon* (1975), Frank Serpico in *Serpico* (1973) and Tony Montana in *Scarface* (1983). He won the Best Actor Oscar for *Scent of a Woman* (1992). **Character:** Created and portrayed by Mike Myers, this spoof of the *James Bond* films has appeared, so far, in three films beginning in 1997.

b) **Actor:** American, born in 1949. Character actor, probably best known for playing Sergeant Bob Barnes in *Platoon* (1986), a role for which he was Oscar nominated. His other performances include Jake Taylor in *Major League* (1989) and Sergeant Tom Beckett in *Sniper* (1993). **Character:**

Portrayed by Robert De Niro. The central character from Martin Scorsese's *Taxi Driver* (1976), a loner whose deteriorating mental state leads to extreme violence.

c) **Actor:** American character actor born in 1960, some of his roles include Tommy Fawkes in *Funny Bones* (1995), Porthos in the 1993 version of *The Three Musketeers* and Bob Zelnick in *Frost/Nixon* (2008). He is, perhaps, better known for his TV work on *Fargo* (Series 1, 2014) and the role of Uncle Jimmy in *The Bear* (2022–present day). **Character:** The supreme commander of the Autobots in the *Transformers* film series. He has been primarily voiced by Peter Cullen.

d) **Actor:** English actor born in 1942. His first film role was Harry Brown in *The Wild and the Willing* (1962) and he has worked consistently since then with a recent recurring role (Winston Scott) in the *John Wick* (2014–present day) series of films. He is also known for his TV appearances, including the title role in *Lovejoy* (1986–1994) and Al Swearengen in *Deadwood* (2004–2006). **Character:** Portrayed by Mandy Patinkin in the 1987 film *The Princess Bride*, he is a Spanish fencer searching for his father's killer. When he finally confronts him, he says the famous line, "Hello. My name is [REDACTED]. You killed my father. Prepare to die."

e) **Actor:** English actor born in 1927. Best known for being the third actor to portray James Bond on screen. His tenure began with *Live and Let Die* (1973) and ended with *A View to a Kill* (1985). **Character:** The central character, portrayed by Jack Nicholson, in Miloš Forman's *One Flew Over the Cuckoo's Nest* (1975). The character feigns mental illness to avoid hard labour but, after being placed in a mental institution, he clashes with Nurse Ratched (Louise Fletcher).

ROUND 4

1. BRAINSTORM

Complete the lists and spot the links – a point for each correct answer.

a) Which French cabaret connects films directed by Sidney Lanfield, John Huston and Baz Luhrmann?

b) Which film completes the *Eastrail 177* trilogy by M. Night Shyamalan: *Unbreakable* (2000), *Split* (2016) and ________?

c) In three films directed by Lindsay Anderson – *If....* (1968), *O Lucky Man!* (1973) and *Britannia Hospital* (1982) – there is a character called Mick Travis. Which actor played him?

d) Which character has been played by Johnny Weissmuller, Christopher Lambert and Alexander Skarsgård?

e) Which film series' subtitles include *Citizens on Patrol* (1987), *Assignment Miami Beach* (1988), *City Under Siege* (1989) and *Mission to Moscow* (1994)?

2. IT FOLLOWS

The first letter of each answer follows the first letter of the last. So, if the answer to c) is "Apple", the answer to d) will begin with "B". If you get to Z, go to A. Each question is worth one point.

a) Who became the first Native American to be nominated for an Oscar in 2024?

b) What 2020 film was the last film appearance of Chadwick Boseman? His performance earned him a posthumous Academy Award nomination.

c) Which singer songwriter acted in the films *Ghosts... of the Civil Dead* (1988), *Johnny Suede* (1991) and *The Assassination of Jesse James by the Coward Robert Ford* (2007)?

d) What is the real name of the Penguin – an antagonist in *Batman Returns* (1992) and *The Batman* (2022)?

e) Which first name connects a 1994 film directed by Stephan Elliott starring Guy Pearce, Hugo Weaving and Terence Stamp, and a 2023 film starring Cailee Spaeny and directed by Sofia Coppola?

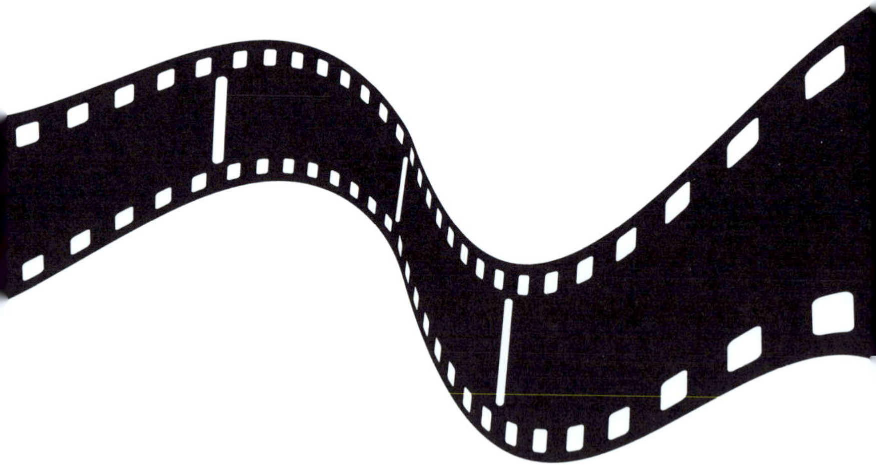

ROUND 5

THE LAST PICTURE SHOW

Say what you see! Can you identify the films from these picture clues? Each picture is worth a point.

1

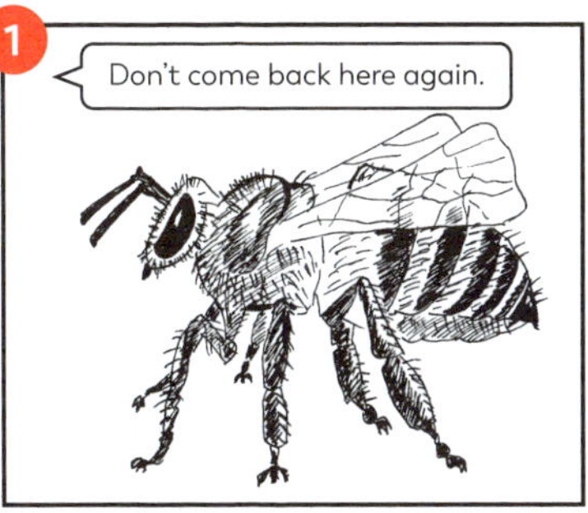

2

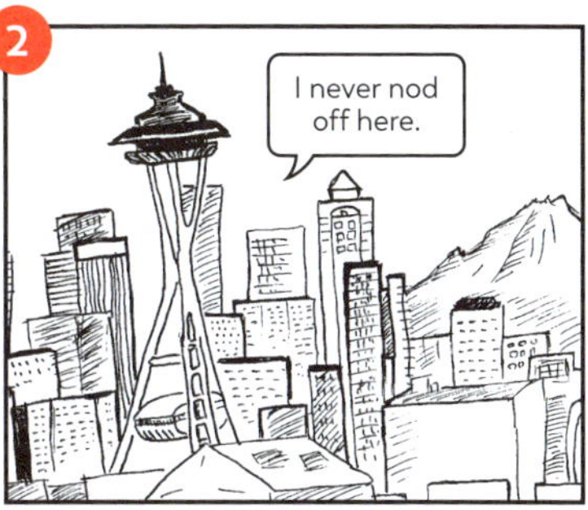

3

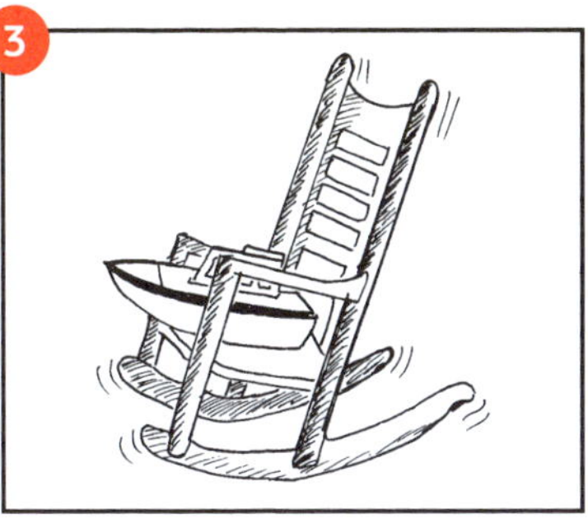

4

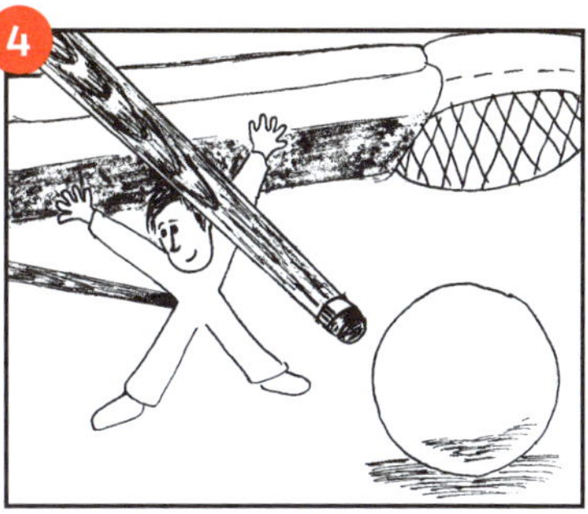

5

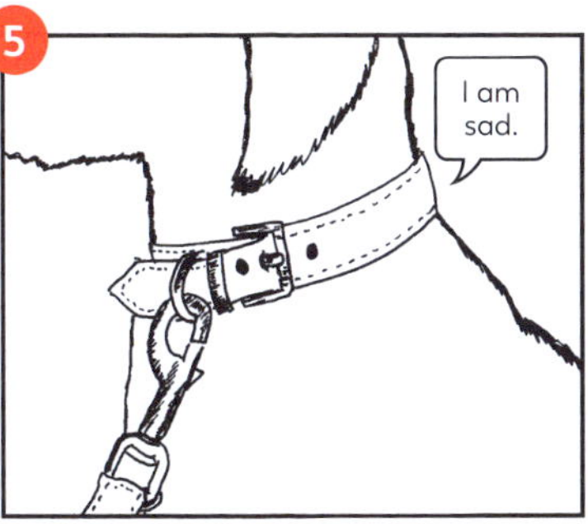

6

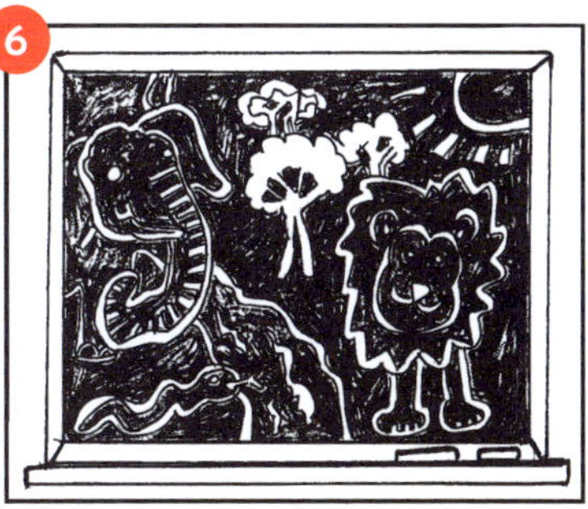

ANSWERS

ROUND 1

1. c) Meryl Streep in 1979 for *Kramer vs. Kramer* (Best Supporting Actress). Michael Caine was 1986 for *Hannah and Her Sisters* (Best Supporting Actor). Anthony Hopkins was 1991 for *The Silence of the Lambs* (Best Actor).

2. Christopher Lee

3. c) *Reservoir Dogs*

4. b) *The Greatest Showman*

5. c) *Interstellar* by Christopher Nolan.

6. *Meet Joe Black* and *The Way Way Back*.

7. b) Michael Keaton's real name is Michael Douglas.

There's a myth that Keaton chose that name as a tribute to Diane Keaton. It is not true. He merely looked at the Ks in the phone book and thought it was "inoffensive".

8. c) Neo (*The Matrix*)

Smith decided to make *Wild Wild West* (1999) instead.

9. 1971

10. *Wings* (1927), ***Cimarron*** (1931), ***Cavalcade*** (1933), *Rebecca* (1940), ***Casablanca*** (1942), *Hamlet* (1948), *Marty* (1955), *Gigi* (1958), *Oliver!* (1968), *Patton* (1970), *Rocky* (1976), *Gandhi* (1982), *Amadeus* (1984), *Platoon* (1986), *Unforgiven* (1992), *Braveheart*

(1995), *Titanic* (1997), *Gladiator* (2000), **Chicago** (2002), **Crash** (2004), *Argo* (2012), *Spotlight* (2015), *Moonlight* (2016), *Parasite* (2019), *Nomadland* (2020), **CODA** (2021), *Oppenheimer* (2023).

ROUND 2

1. a) *Crouching Tiger, Hidden Dragon* and *How to Train Your Dragon.*

1. b) *Muriel's Wedding* and *My Big Fat Greek Wedding.*

1. c) *A Quiet Place* and *In a Lonely Place.*

1. d) *The Shape of Water* and *Hell or High Water.*

1. e) *The French Lieutenant's Woman* and *Promising Young Woman.*

2. a) *Vanilla*

2. b) *Chocolate*

2. c) *Cherry*

2. d) *Strawberry*

2. e) *Coffee*

ROUND 3

1. a) *Hocus Pocus*

1. b) *Drop Dead Fred*

1. c) *Mr. Magorium's Wonder Emporium*

1. d) *Be Kind Rewind*

1. e) *Mrs. Harris Goes to Paris*

2. a) Al Pacino and Austin Powers.

2. b) Tom Berenger and Travis Bickle.

2. c) Oliver Platt and Optimus Prime.

2. d) Ian McShane and Inigo Montoya.

2. e) Roger Moore and Randle McMurphy.

ROUND 4

1. a) *Moulin Rouge. Moulin Rouge* (1934) by Sidney Lanfield, *Moulin Rouge* (1952) by John Huston and *Moulin Rouge!* (2001) by Baz Luhrmann.

In Luhrmann's film, the Green Fairy (Kylie Minogue) lets out an ear-piercing scream at the end of her song, which was actually provided by Ozzy Osbourne.

1. b) *Glass* (2019)

1. c) Malcolm McDowell

1. d) Tarzan. Weissmuller played him 12 times from 1932 to 1948, Lambert played him in *Greystoke: The Legend of Tarzan, Lord of the Apes* (1984) and Skarsgård in *The Legend of Tarzan* (2016).

Legendary screenwriter Robert Towne hated the end version of *Greystoke* so much that he gave the writing credit to his dog. That makes P. H. Vazak the only dog to ever be nominated for an Oscar for Best Screenplay.

1. e) *Police Academy* (1984–1994)

2. a) Lily Gladstone for *Killers of the Flower Moon* (2023).

2. b) *Ma Rainey's Black Bottom* (2020)

2. c) Nick Cave

2. d) Oswald Chesterfield Cobblepot

2. e) Priscilla. *The Adventures of Priscilla, Queen of the Desert* (1994) and *Priscilla* (2023).

ROUND 5

1. *Barbie* (2023)
2. *Sleepless in Seattle* (1993)
3. *The Boat that Rocked* (2009)
4. *Spider-Man* (2009)
5. *Blue Collar* (1978)
6. *Blackboard Jungle* (1955)

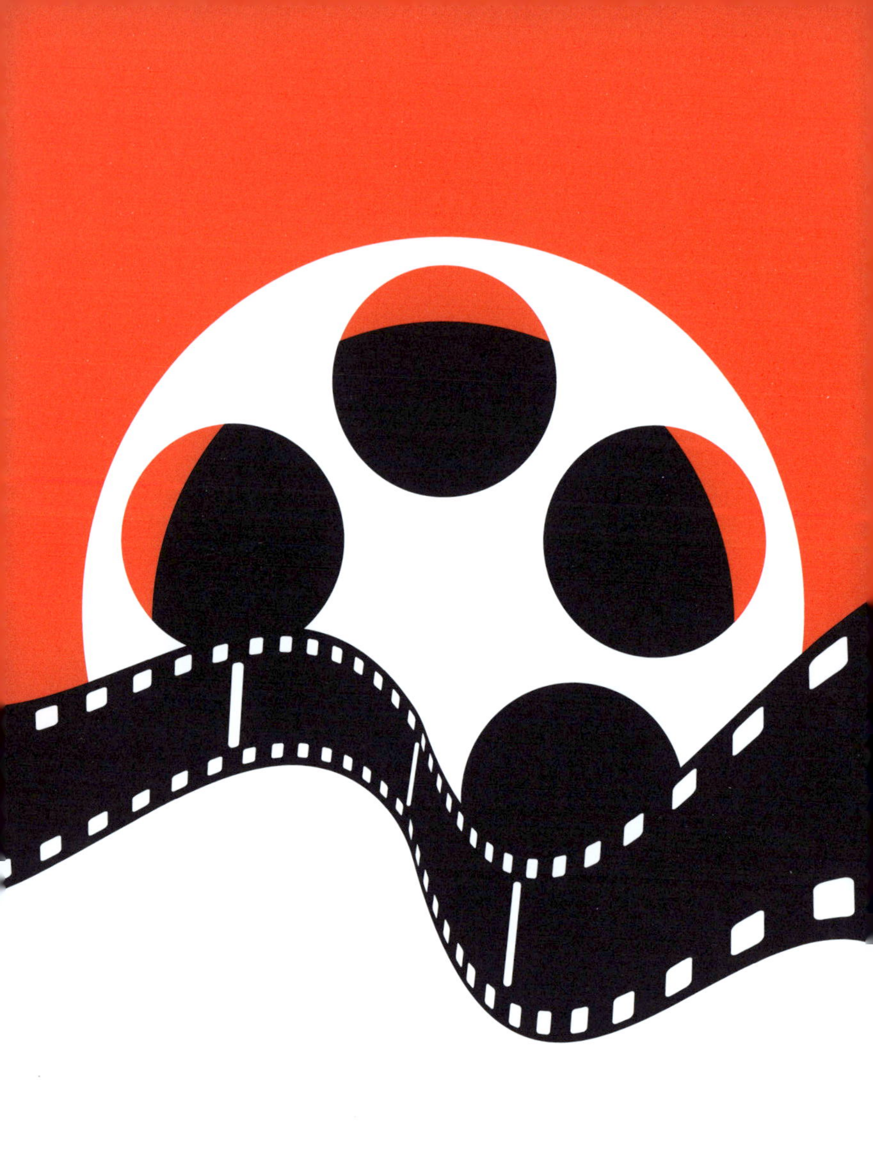

QUIZ 5

ROUND 1

STARTER FOR 10

Ten questions to begin!

1. THE FIRST QUESTION

Which of these actors named Tom was born first?

a) Tom Hardy

b) Tom Cruise

c) Tom Hanks

2. THE ANAGRAM

Unscramble the actor's name: FINDS A HORROR

3. FILM QUOTE

What film is the following quote from?

"That's the way it crumbles, cookie-wise."

a) *The Maltese Falcon* (1941)

b) *Forrest Gump* (1994)

c) *The Apartment* (1960)

d) *The Menu* (2022)

4. THUMBS DOWN

What film is this the one-star review of?

"The 'whip-smart' dialogue is the worst kind of American drivel, and there are whole scenes where the characters talk about literally nothing of interest, or even anything to drive the (slow, largely non-existent) story along."

a) *There Will Be Blood* (2007)

b) *Pulp Fiction* (1994)

c) *Annie Hall* (1977)

5. ODD ONE OUT

Which of these films was not directed by Sofia Coppola? Bonus point if you know who it was directed by.

a) *Frida* (2002)

b) *Priscilla* (2023)

c) *Marie Antoinette* (2006)

6. RHYMING FILMS

I'll give you the initials of two films whose titles rhyme with each other. I'll also give you one of the stars and the years they were released, just name the films for a point each.

EOL, Olivia Colman (2022) and ITHOTN, Sidney Poitier (1967)

7. CELLULOID OR CELLULIED?

Which of the following is true about Sean Bean?

a) While filming *The Lord of the Rings* (2001–2003), Sean Bean would spend 2 hours climbing to film the mountain scenes as he hates flying.

b) While filming *The Lord of the Rings* (2001–2003), Sean Bean requested his scenes be filmed early in the schedule to enable him to return to the UK for the start of the football season.

c) While filming *The Lord of the Rings* (2001–2003), Sean Bean helped himself find his character by only eating venison (from red deer) that he had caught himself.

8. WHAT MIGHT HAVE BEEN

Which of these roles did Doris Day turn down?

a) Mrs Robinson (*The Graduate* – 1967)

b) Marion Crane (*Psycho* – 1960)

c) Baby Jane Hudson (*What Ever Happened to Baby Jane?* – 1962)

9. WHAT YEAR?

In what year did the following things happen?

Films released this year include: *Home Alone*, *Pretty Woman*, *Ghost*, *Total Recall*, *Miller's Crossing*, *Goodfellas*, *La Femme Nikita* and *The Hunt for Red October* (the first time we see Jack Ryan on screen). Liam Hemsworth, Kristen Stewart, Jennifer Lawrence, Dev Patel and Aaron Taylor-Johnson are born. Ava Gardner, Greta Garbo,

Jim Henson and Sammy Davis Jr pass away. *Dances With Wolves*, Kevin Costner's directorial debut, is released; it later goes on to win seven Oscars, including Best Director and Best Picture. Tom Cruise and Nicole Kidman marry and release *Days of Thunder*; they then divorce 11 years later. Universal Pictures change their logo for the first time in 27 years. But what was the year?

10. GIVE ME FIVE

A chance for five points! Name me five films from the *Carry on...* (1958–1992) series where the third word begins with a "C". There are eight possible answers.

ROUND 2

1. FIVE EASY PIECES

I'll list five central characters from a film and give you the year of release. Just name the film.

a) Mikey, Brand, Chunk, Mouth and Data (1985).

b) Fenster, Keaton, Hockney, McManus and Verbal (1995).

c) Professor Marcus, Major Claude Courtney, Louis Harvey, Harry Robinson and "One-Round" Lawson (1955).

d) Soap, Bacon, Eddy, Big Chris and Plank (1998).

e) Lone Starr, Barf, Princess Vespa, Dot Matrix and Lord Dark Helmet (1987).

2. ONE OF OUR _____ IS MISSING!

Just fill in the missing word – there's always a theme, and this time it's... relatives.

a) *In the Name of the* _______ (1993)

b) *Our Idiot* _______ (2011)

c) *All About My* _______ (1999)

d) *Coal Miner's* _______ (1980)

e) _______ *Buck* (1989)

ROUND 3

1. LINK

I will give you a word that ends one film title and begins another, plus the star and the year – name both for two points.

a) The link is "Man". Film one – Arnold Schwarzenegger (1987). Film two – Denzel Washington (2004).

b) The link is "Hot". Film one – Marilyn Monroe (1959). Film two – John Cusack (2010).

c) The link is "Day". Film one – John Wayne (1962). Film two – Lori Cardille (1985).

d) The link is "Rain". Film one – Gene Kelly (1952). Film two – Dustin Hoffman (1988).

e) The link is "Do". Film one – Tom Hanks (1996). Film two – Danny Aiello (1989).

2. THE ODD COUPLE

I'll describe an actor and a film character that share the same initials. A point for each you can name.

a) **Actor:** English actor born in 1971. Appeared in films such as *A Beautiful Mind* (2001), *Master and Commander: The Far Side of the World* (2003) and *Wimbledon* (2004) before finding international fame as Vision in the Marvel Cinematic Universe. He married Jennifer Connelly in 2003. **Character:** The main protagonist of Mary Harron's *American Psycho* (2000) played by Christian Bale. He is an investment banker who seems to lead a double life as a serial killer.

b) Actor: American actor born in 1921. One of the highest paid stars of the 1940s, she starred in films such as *Dr. Jekyll and Mr. Hyde* (1941), *The Postman Always Rings Twice* (1946), *Peyton Place* (1957) and *Imitation of Life* (1959). **Character:** The titular world-renowned conductor in the 2022 film directed by Todd Field, played by Cate Blanchett – who won the BAFTA for Best Actress in a Leading Role.

c) Actor: Australian actor born in 1979. Though she has appeared in an eclectic mix of films, she is probably best known for comedic roles, including *Bridesmaids* (2011), *Spy* (2015) and *Neighbors* (2014). She also plays Moira MacTaggert in the *X-Men* series that began with *X-Men: First Class* (2011). **Character:** The leader of the renegade Nexus-6 replicants hunted by Harrison Ford's character in *Blade Runner* (1982). He's portrayed by Rutger Hauer, who helped rewrite the now famous "Tears in rain" speech.

d) Actor: French Actor born in 1985. Her breakthrough role was in *Blue Is the Warmest Colour* (2013), and she later found international fame as Madeleine Swann in the *James Bond* films *Spectre* (2015) and *No Time to Die* (2021). **Character:** Created by Stieg Larsson in his trilogy of books known as the *Millennium* series, this central character has been portrayed by three different actors: Noomi Rapace in 2009, Rooney Mara in 2011 and Claire Foy in 2018. Rapace in three films, Mara in *The Girl with the Dragon Tattoo* (2011) and Foy in *The Girl in the Spider's Web* (2018).

e) Actor: American actor born in 1941. Finding fame in the 1960s, she starred as Bonnie Parker in *Bonnie and Clyde* (1967) and opposite Steve McQueen in *The Thomas Crown Affair* (1968). Her other films include *Chinatown* (1974) and *Network* (1976) for which she won a Best Actress Oscar. More recently, she and *Bonnie and Clyde* co-star Warren Beatty were the presenters when *La La Land* (2016) was incorrectly announced as the winner of Best Picture at the 2017 Academy Awards. **Character:** The hapless police detective played by Leslie Nielsen in the three *Naked Gun* movies (1988–1994). The character first appeared in the 1982 ABC series *Police Squad!* (1982).

ROUND 4

1. BRAINSTORM

Complete the lists and spot the links – a point for each correct answer.

a) What word is missing from these titles: *The ________ of Comedy* for Robert De Niro (1982), *________ of New York* for Christopher Walken (1990) and *The ________ of Staten Island* for Pete Davidson (2020)?

b) Which character has been played by Peter Dinklage, Gérard Depardieu and Steve Martin?

c) What connects writer Dudley Nichols in 1935, actor George C. Scott in 1970 and actor Marlon Brando in 1973?

d) What connects Ian Holm in 1979, Lance Henriksen in 1986 and 1992, Winona Ryder in 1997, Michael Fassbender in 2012 and 2017, and David Jonsson in 2024?

e) Which 1999 film has a sequel with the word *Returns* in it (2001) and a third film with the subtitle *Tomb of the Dragon Emperor* (2008)?

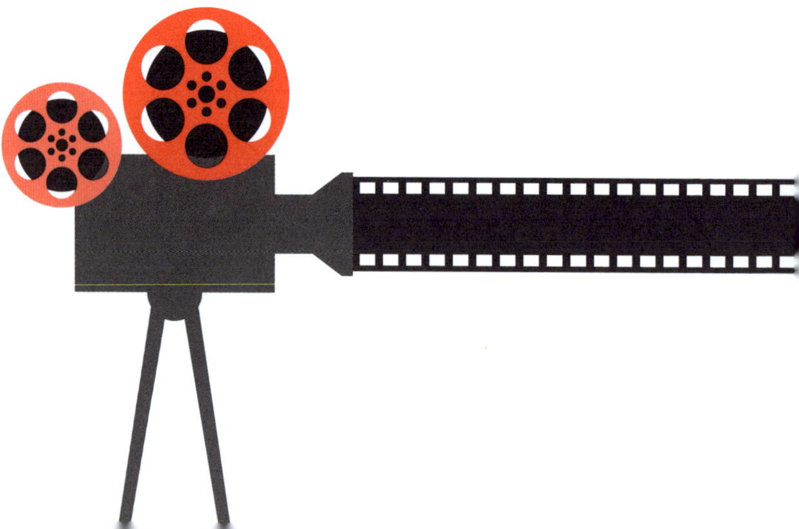

2. IT FOLLOWS

The first letter of each answer follows the first letter of the last. So, if the answer to c) is “Apple”, the answer to d) will begin with “B”. If you get to Z, go to A. Each question is worth one point.

a) What car was first driven by James Bond in the film *Goldfinger* (1964)?

b) In 1995, Martin Landau won his only Oscar for playing which classic horror movie star?

c) In *Being There* (1979), what was the name of the gardener portrayed by Peter Sellers?

d) Kathy Bates has starred in two films based on books by Stephen King, *Misery* (1990) and which other?

e) Which singer songwriter appeared in *Tommy* (1975) as the Pinball Wizard?

ROUND 5

THE LAST PICTURE SHOW

Say what you see! Can you identify the films from these picture clues? Each picture is worth a point.

1

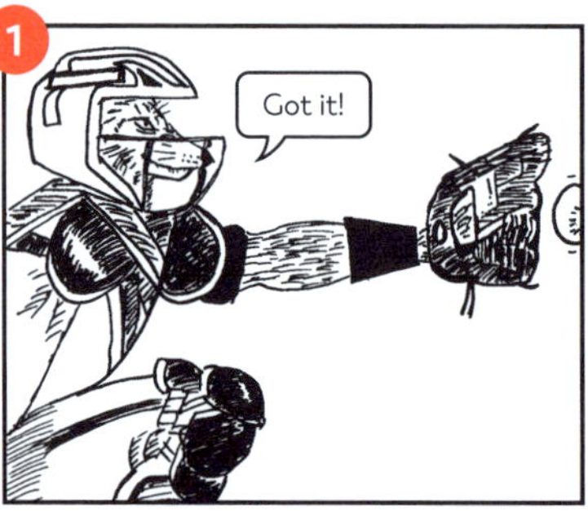

2

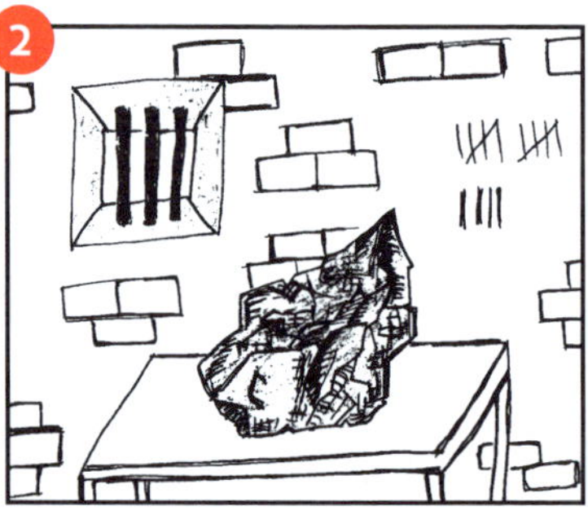

3

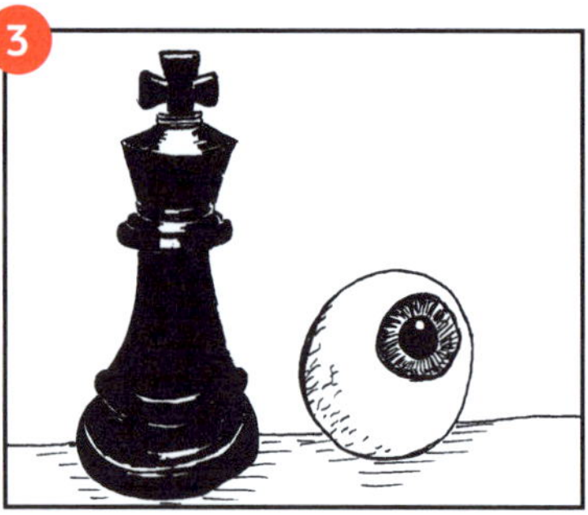

4

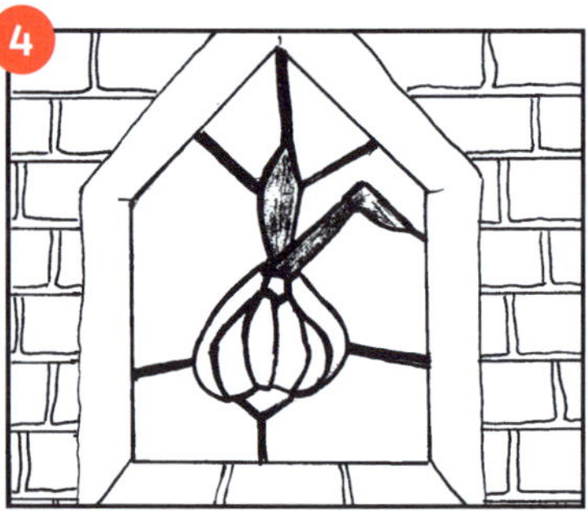

5

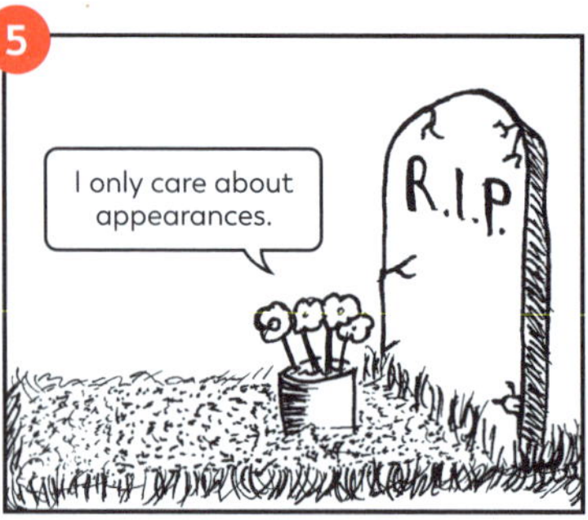

6

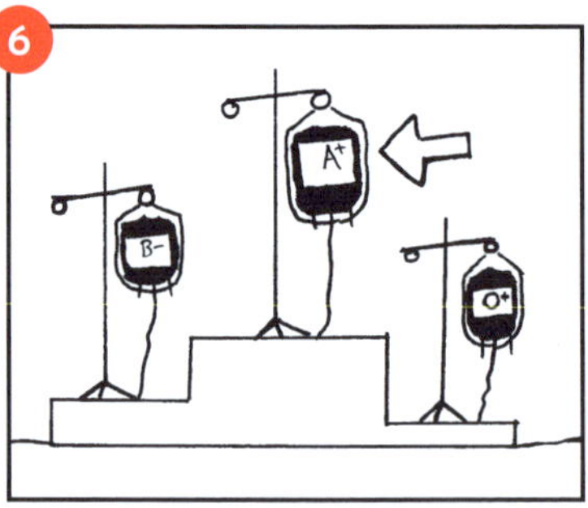

ANSWERS

ROUND 1

1. c) Tom Hanks (1956). Tom Cruise was born in 1962 and Tom Hardy in 1977.

2. Harrison Ford

3. c) *The Apartment*

4. b) *Pulp Fiction*

5. a) *Frida* by Julie Taymor.

6. *Empire of Light* and *In the Heat of the Night*.

7 a) While filming *The Lord of the Rings*, Sean Bean would spend 2 hours climbing to film the mountain scenes as he hates flying.

> **A poll for Yorkshire Day in 2018 saw Bean ranked as the "2nd Greatest Yorkshireman". He was beaten to the top spot by *Monty Python* legend Michael Palin.**

8. a) Mrs Robinson

9. 1990

> **Albert Finney enjoyed himself so much making *Miller's Crossing* that once he had finished filming his scenes he came back and appeared in the background of a scene in a ladies' toilet in drag.**

10. *Carry on Constable* (1960), *Carry on Cruising* (1962), *Carry on Cabby* (1963), *Carry on Cleo* (1964), *Carry on Cowboy* (1965), *Follow that Camel* (1967), *Carry on Camping* (1969), *Carry on Columbus* (1992).

ROUND 2

1. a) *The Goonies*

1. b) *The Usual Suspects*

1. c) *The Ladykillers*

1. d) *Lock, Stock and Two Smoking Barrels*

1. e) *Spaceballs*

2. a) *Father*

2. b) *Brother*

2. c) *Mother*

2. d) *Daughter*

2. e) *Uncle*

ROUND 3

1. a) *The Running* **Man** *on Fire*

1. b) *Some Like It* **Hot** *Tub Time Machine*

1. c) *The Longest* **Day** *of the Dead*

1. d) *Singin' in the* **Rain** *Man*

1. e) *That Thing You* **Do** *the Right Thing*

2. a) Paul Bettany and Patrick Bateman.

2. b) Lana Turner and Lydia Tár.

2. c) Rose Byrne and Roy Batty.

2. d) Léa Seydoux and Lisbeth Salander.

2. e) Faye Dunaway and Frank Drebin.

Police Squad! features one of my favourite jokes. Drebin (undercover) appears in a villain's office. "Who are you and how did you get in here?" snarls the villain. "I'm a locksmith. And I'm a locksmith." Drebin replies (Nielsen, as ever, perfectly straight-faced).

ROUND 4

1. a) "King". *The King of Comedy*, *King of New York* and *The King of Staten Island*.

1. b) Cyrano de Bergerac – Gerard Depardieu in *Cyrano de Bergerac* (1990), Peter Dinklage in *Cyrano* (2021) and Steve Martin in *Roxanne* (1987), though in *Roxanne*, when played by Steve Martin, he is renamed Charlie "C. D." Bales.

1. c) They all refused Oscars in those years. Nichols was on strike, Scott stated performances cannot be measured, and Brando was protesting against the treatment of Native Americans by Hollywood.

1. d) They play androids/synthetics in the *Alien* films (1979–present day) from those years.

1. e) *The Mummy*

2. a) Aston Martin DB5

2. b) Bela Lugosi – Best Supporting Actor in Tim Burton's *Ed Wood* (1994).

2. c) Chance (Chauncey Gardiner)

2. d) *Dolores Claiborne* (1995)

2. e) Elton John

ROUND 5

1. *Foxcatcher* (2014)
2. *Jailhouse Rock* (1957)
3. *The King and I* (1956)
4. *Glass Onion: A Knives Out Mystery* (2022)
5. *Shallow Grave* (1994)
6. *First Blood* (1982)

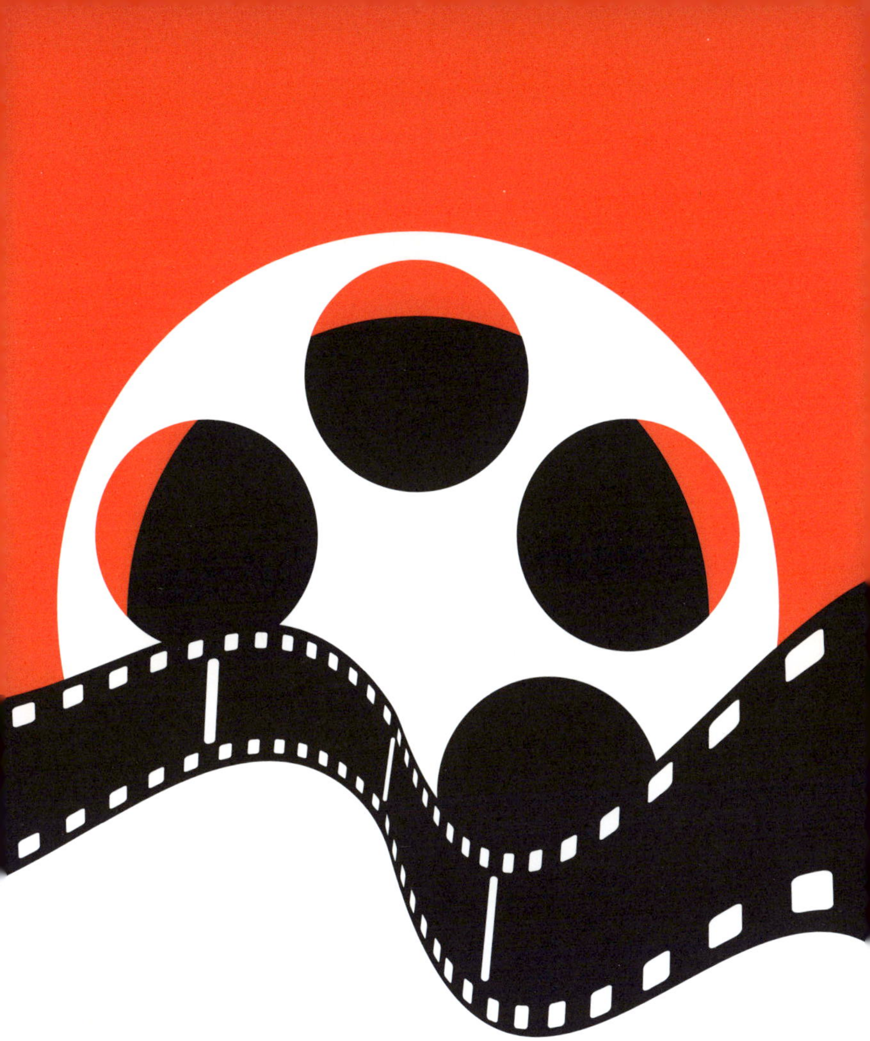

QUIZ 6

ROUND 1

STARTER FOR 10

Ten questions to begin!

1. THE FIRST QUESTION

Which of these "Bad" movies was released first?

a) *Bad Teacher*

b) *Bad Boys*

c) *Bad Taste*

2. THE ANAGRAM

Unscramble the actor's name: NO PLAYING OUT

3. FILM QUOTE

What film is the following quote from?

"In the meantime, I got this plan. It's called 'Save Ass'. And the way it works is this – I slip outta one of these windows and I run like a bastard!"

a) *Assault on Precinct 13* (1976)

b) *Butch Cassidy and the Sundance Kid* (1969)

c) *Young Guns* (1988)

d) *The Great Escape* (1963)

4. THUMBS DOWN

What film is this the one-star review of?

"CGI is used everywhere... absolutely everywhere. Nothing's real! It's not even well-crafted CGI, some of it is really shonky work."

a) *Indiana Jones and the Kingdom of the Crystal Skull* (2008)

b) *The Meg* (2018)

c) *The Dark Crystal* (1982)

5. ODD ONE OUT

Which of these films was not directed by Kathryn Bigelow? Bonus point if you know who it was directed by.

a) *Zero Dark Thirty* (2012)

b) *The Hurt Locker* (2008)

c) *Three Kings* (1999)

6. RHYMING FILMS

I'll give you the initials of two films whose titles rhyme with each other. I'll also give you one of the stars and the years they were released, just name the films for a point each.

TROTD, Anthony Hopkins (1993) and FAA, Tom Cruise (1992).

7. CELLULOID OR CELLULIED?

Which of the following is true about Ben Affleck?

a) Ben Affleck shut down the filming of *Gone Girl* (2014) for days because the catering crew could not find his favourite brand of macaroni cheese.

b) Ben Affleck shut down the filming of *Gone Girl* (2014) for days because he refused to wear a New York Yankees baseball cap.

c) Ben Affleck shut down the filming of *Gone Girl* (2014) for days after falling from his skateboard and twisting his ankle.

8. WHAT MIGHT HAVE BEEN

Which of these roles did Halle Berry turn down?

a) Leeloo (*The Fifth Element* – 1997)

b) Mary Jensen (*There's Something About Mary* – 1998)

c) Annie Porter (*Speed* – 1994)

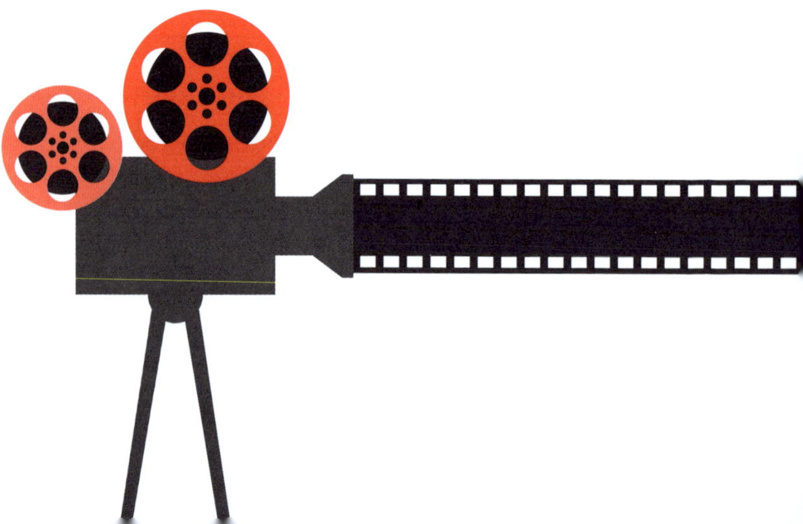

9. WHAT YEAR?

In what year did the following things happen?

Films released this year include: *Thunderball, Doctor Zhivago, Cat Ballou, Doctor Who and the Daleks, Help!, The Knack... and How to Get It*, and *Those Magnificent Men in Their Flying Machines. The Sound of Music* is the most successful film of the year and it later goes on to win the Best Picture Oscar the following year. Robert Downey Jr, Martin Lawrence, Sam Mendes, Viola Davis and Mads Mikkelsen are born. Stan Laurel, Clara Bow and David O. Selznick pass away. Robert de Niro makes his screen debut in the French film *Three Rooms in Manhattan*. But what was the year?

10. GIVE ME FIVE

A chance for five points! Name me five people who (up to 2024) have hosted (or co-hosted) the Oscars more than once. There are 23 possible answers.

ROUND 2

1. THE HIDDEN

The titles of these classic sci-fi films can be found in capital letters within the descriptions. Unscramble them to name the film for a point.

a) This film centres on a killer from the future that Sarah Connor and her son probably wish they had RATHER NOT MET I think. (1984)

b) When Dr Mark Watney joined the crew of the Ares III, he did not realize he would, one day, be a HERMIT AT AN improbable level. (2015)

c) The alien drives around picking up men to consume. She sees a swimmer on whom she will DINE. TRUNKS HE had are left on the beach. (2013)

d) These young soldiers are up against giant aliens but sometimes the SHOOTERS' TRAP RIPS the bugs apart. (1997)

e) Rick Deckard must hunt down escaped "replicants". These are not kids out on a LUNAR BENDER; they are dangerous. (1982)

2. ONE OF OUR ______ IS MISSING!

Just fill in the missing word – there's always a theme, and this time it's... shapes.

a) ________ *of Sadness* (2022)
b) *Dark* ________ (1974)
c) ________ *of Friends* (1995)
d) ________ *of Iron* (1977)
e) *Blood* ________ (2006)

ROUND 3

1. WICKED LITTLE LETTERS

There are five film titles below that are acronyms, can you tell me what they stand for? A point for each.

a) *RED* (2010)

b) *M*A*S*H* (1970)

c) *D.A.R.Y.L.* (1985)

d) *R.I.P.D.* (2013)

e) *WALL-E* (2008)

2. THE ODD COUPLE II

This time I'll describe a film character and a director that share the same initials. A point for each you can name.

a) **Character:** The daughter of Gomez and Morticia, sister of Pugsley. She is known for her pale skin, black hair and her brilliant if macabre mind. She was played in two films (that feature the character's surname in the title) by Christina Ricci (1991 and 1993). **Director:** American director born in 1969. He is known for a very distinctive style and for often using the same actors. His first film was *Bottle Rocket* (1996), others include *The Royal Tenenbaums* (2001), *The Life Aquatic with Steve Zissou* (2004), *Fantastic Mr. Fox* (2009) and *The Grand Budapest Hotel* (2014).

b) **Character:** Portrayed by Simon Pegg, this character fights zombies in North London with his best friend Ed (Nick Frost) and girlfriend Liz (Kate Ashfield). Together they take refuge in their local pub, the Winchester. **Director:**

American director born in 1959. Found fame with his horror classic *The Evil Dead* (1981), which he later made two sequels to. He is also well known for directing the 2002–2007 *Spider-Man* films and 2022's *Doctor Strange in the Multiverse of Madness.*

c) **Character:** The main antagonist from *No Country for Old Men* (2007), he is portrayed by Javier Bardem. This killer-for-hire is relentless and psychopathic. He often decides his victim's fate by flipping a coin and his weapons of choice include a bolt stunner. **Director:** British director born in 1935. He tended to make films focused on social realism, such as *Scum* (1979) and *Rita, Sue and Bob Too* (1987). He was responsible for early roles for actors such as Gary Oldman, Tim Roth and Ray Winstone.

d) **Character:** One of two hitmen working for Marsellus Wallace (Ving Rhames) in *Pulp Fiction* (1994), the other being Vincent Vega (John Travolta), he is portrayed by Samuel L. Jackson, who received a Best Supporting Actor Oscar nomination. **Director:** American director born in 1946. His first works were transgressive underground films such as *Multiple Maniacs* (1970), *Pink Flamingos* (1972) and *Female Trouble* (1974). *Hairspray* (1988) and *Cry-Baby* (1990) saw a move towards more mainstream fare. At time of writing (2024), his last film was *A Dirty Shame* (2004) but there is hope that a new movie, *Liarmouth* (based on his own novel), may be his next project.

e) **Character:** One of the original *Ghostbusters* (1984), portrayed by Bill Murray, he is a cynical wise-cracking parapsychologist. The role was originally written for John Belushi, with Murray brought in after Belushi's death. **Director:** Dutch director born in 1938. Spent the 1970s and early 1980s directing successful Dutch films before moving to the USA and having hits such as *RoboCop* (1987), *Total Recall* (1990), *Basic Instinct* (1992) and *Starship Troopers* (1997). His last film, at time of writing, was *Benedetta* (2021).

ROUND 4

1. BRAINSTORM

Complete the lists and spot the links – a point for each correct answer.

a) What day of the week appears in the title of films starring Bob Hoskins, Ice Cube and Billy Bob Thornton?

b) What name connects the character played by Lee Marvin in *Point Blank* (1967), the actor who portrayed Brian O'Conner in the *Fast & Furious* films (2001–present day) and the title of a film by Alex Cox from 1987?

c) In reference to the Academy Awards, what specifically connects Kevin Costner (1991), Clint Eastwood (1993 and 2005), Robert Redford (1980) and Warren Beatty (1982)?

d) Which character connects the actors Ron Perlman, David Harbour and Jack Kesy?

e) What ice cream brand connects *Shaun of the Dead* (2004), *Hot Fuzz* (2007) and *The World's End* (2013)?

2. IT FOLLOWS

The first letter of each answer follows the first letter of the last. So, if the answer to c) is "Apple", the answer to d) will begin with "B". If you get to Z, go to A. Each question is worth one point.

a) What is the name of the award-winning British cinematographer of films including *Fargo* (1996), *Skyfall* (2012), *Blade Runner 2049* (2017) and *1917* (2019)?

b) In a 1988 film, Steve Martin and Michael Caine were *Dirty Rotten* what?

c) Which actor won the Best Supporting Actress Oscar at the age of ten in 1974? (As of 2024, she remains the youngest person to win a competitive Oscar.)

d) In *The Odd Couple* (1968) and *The Odd Couple II* (1998), Walter Matthau plays Oscar Madison, while Jack Lemmon plays Felix who?

e) Which Greek musician and composer created the scores for *Blade Runner* (1982), *Chariots of Fire* (1981) and *Alexander* (2004)?

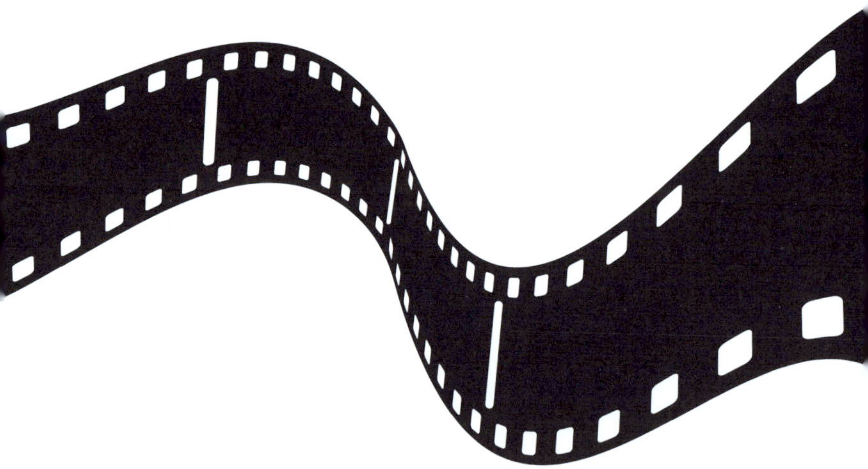

ROUND 5

THE LAST PICTURE SHOW

Say what you see! Can you identify the films from these picture clues? Each picture is worth a point.

1

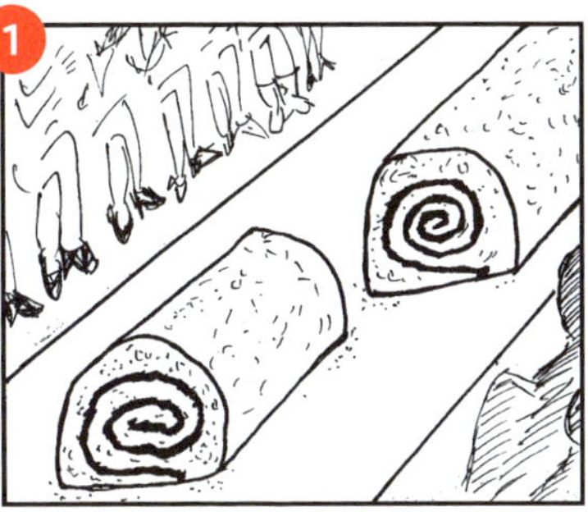

2

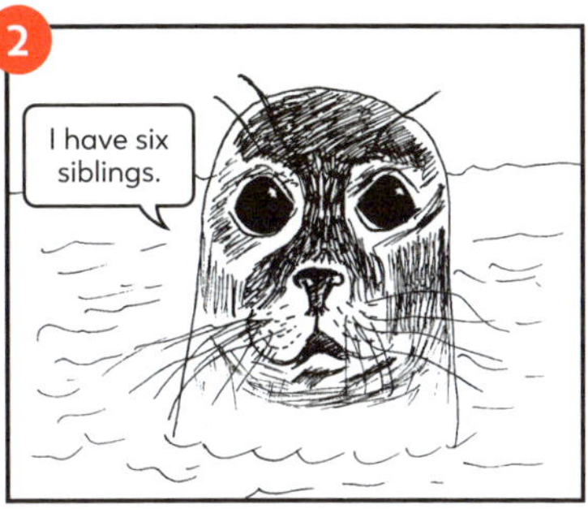

3

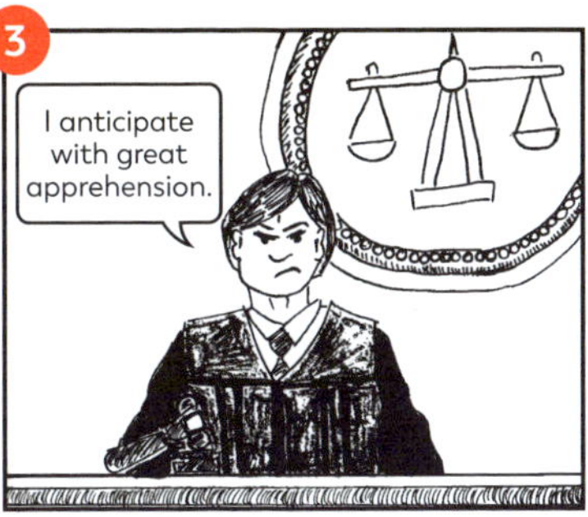

4

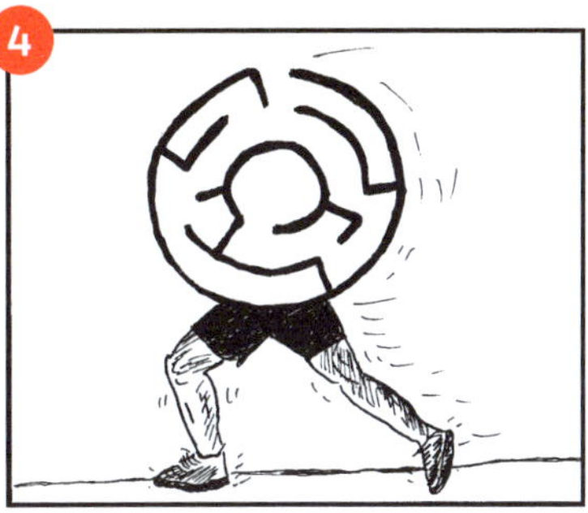

5

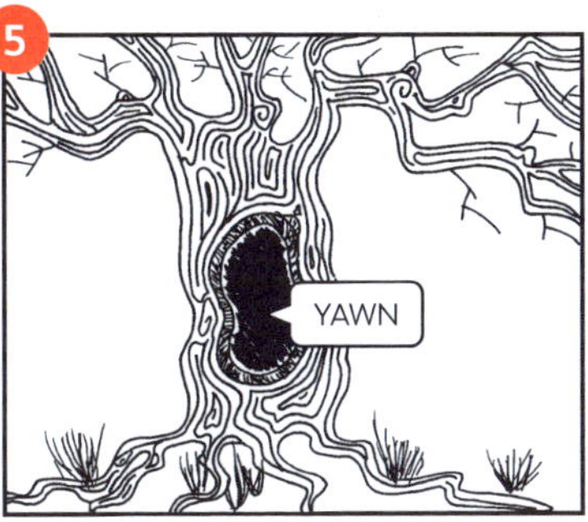

6

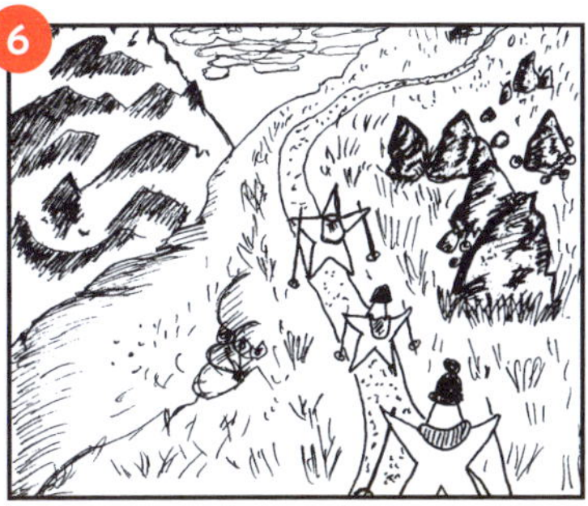

ANSWERS

ROUND 1

1. c) *Bad Taste* (1987). *Bad Boys* was 1995 and *Bad Teacher* was 2011.

2. Lupita Nyong'o

3. a) *Assault on Precinct 13*

4. a) *Indiana Jones and the Kingdom of the Crystal Skull*

Another review that made me laugh was: "Ray Winstone appears every 30 minutes to shout 'Jonesy!' then simply disappears."

5. c) *Three Kings* by David O. Russell.

6. *The Remains of the Day* and *Far and Away*.

7. b) Ben Affleck shut down the filming of *Gone Girl* for days because he refused to wear a New York Yankees baseball cap. (He feared the image would "become a thing".)

Ben Affleck and Matt Damon were extras at Fenway Park (home of the Red Sox) in *Field of Dreams* (1989).

8. c) Annie Porter

9. 1965

10. (In order of most appearances) Bob Hope (19), Billy Crystal (9), Johnny Carson (5), Whoopi Goldberg (4), Jimmy Kimmel (4), Jack Lemmon (4), Jerry Lewis (3), Steve Martin (3), Conrad Nagel (3), David Niven (3), Jack Benny (2), Chevy Chase (2), Sammy Davis

Jr (2), Ellen DeGeneres (2), William C. deMille (2), Jane Fonda (2), Goldie Hawn (2), Walter Matthau (2), Richard Pryor (2), Chris Rock (2), Frank Sinatra (2), James Stewart (2), Jon Stewart (2).

ROUND 2

1. a) *The Terminator*

1. b) *The Martian*

1. c) *Under the Skin*

1. d) *Starship Troopers*

1. e) *Blade Runner*

2. a) *Triangle*

2. b) *Star*

Dark Star (1974) was the first major film that sci-fi/horror legend Dan O'Bannon worked on. He co-wrote the script to this dark comedy (and helped create the "beachball with claws" alien) and went on to script *Alien* (1979). After seeing audiences failing to be amused by *Dark Star*, he said, "If I can't make them laugh, then maybe I can make them scream."

2. c) *Circle*

2. d) *Cross*

2. e) *Diamond*

ROUND 3

1. a) Retired, Extremely Dangerous.

1. b) Mobile Army Surgical Hospital.

1. c) Data-Analyzing Robot Youth Lifeform.

1. d) Rest In Peace Department.

1. e) Waste Allocation Load Lifter: Earth-class.

2. a) Wednesday Addams and Wes Anderson.

2. b) Shaun Riley and Sam Raimi.

2. c) Anton Chigurh and Alan Clarke.

2. d) Jules Winnfield and John Waters.

2. e) Peter Venkman and Paul Verhoeven.

ROUND 4

1. a) Friday. Bob Hoskins stars in *The Long Good Friday* (1980), Ice Cube in *Friday* (1995) and Billy Bob Thornton in *Friday Night Lights* (2004).

1. b) Walker (Paul Walker was the actor in *Fast & Furious*).

In the book that *Point Blank* is based on (the 1962 novel *The Hunter* by Donald E. Westlake), the character is called Parker. When the book was made into a film for a second time, *Payback*, in 1999, starring Mel Gibson, the character was called Porter.

1. c) They are actors/directors who, at the time of writing, have only won Oscars for directing (the years they won are in brackets).

1. d) Hellboy – Ron Pearlman: *Hellboy* (2004) and *Hellboy II: The Golden Army* (2008). David Harbour: *Hellboy* (2019). Jack Kesy: *Hellboy: The Crooked Man* (2024).

1. e) Cornetto

The trilogy is jokingly known as *The Cornetto* trilogy or *The Three Flavours Cornetto* trilogy as the ice cream is referenced in each film. The ice cream was used in the first film (*Shaun of the Dead*) as a hangover cure, which led to free ice cream at the after party for the creators (Edgar Wright and Simon Pegg), so they jokingly inserted a reference in *Hot Fuzz* and *The World's End*. No ice cream was forthcoming, but the idea stuck.

2. a) Roger Deakins

2. b) *Scoundrels*

2. c) Tatum O'Neal for *Paper Moon* (1973).

2. d) Ungar

The Odd Couple II is one of the longest gaps between sequels (with the same actors) at 30 years. Though Tom Cruise with *Top Gun: Maverick* (2022) pips it at 36 years after its predecessor, and *Beetlejuice Beetlejuice* (2024) and *Beetlejuice* (1988) also has a 36-year gap.

2. e) Vangelis

ROUND 5

1. *Role Models* (2008)
2. *The Seventh Seal* (1957)
3. *Judge Dredd* (1995)
4. *The Maze Runner* (2014)
5. *Sleepy Hollow* (1999)
6. *Star Trek* (1979)

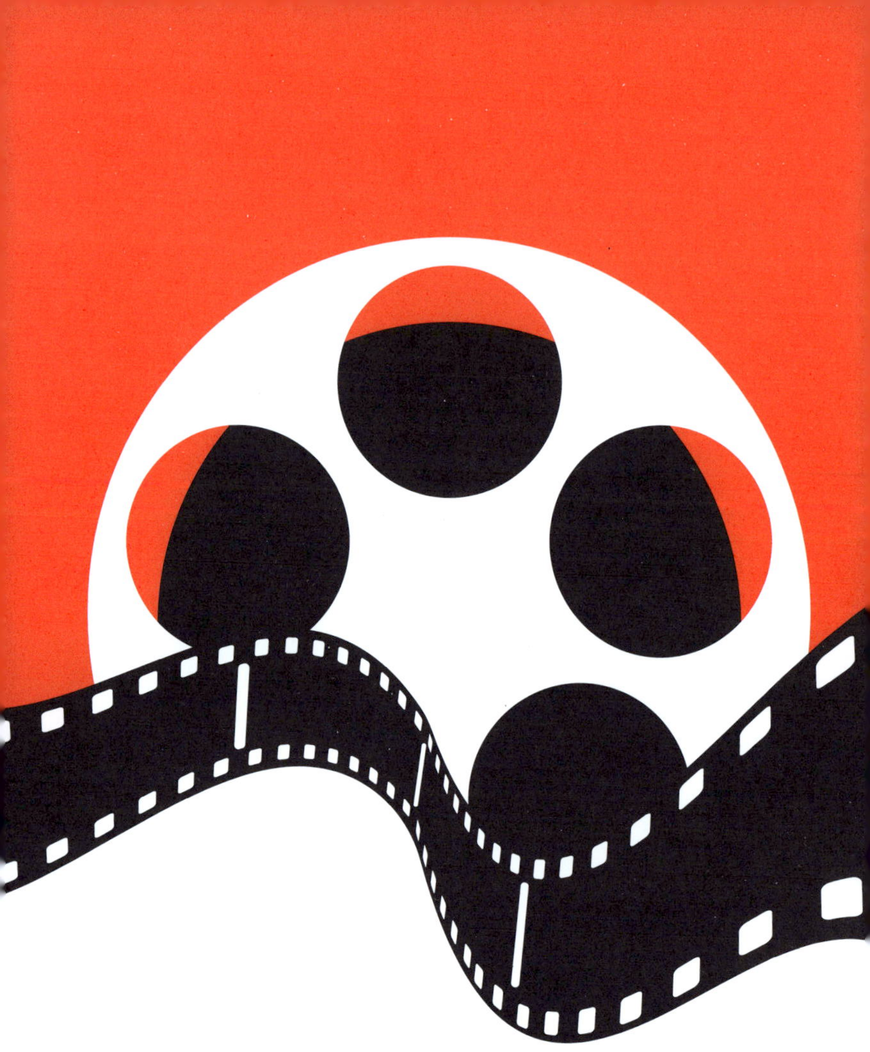

QUIZ 7

ROUND 1

STARTER FOR 10

Ten questions to begin!

1. THE FIRST QUESTION

Which of these school-based films was released first?

a) *The Breakfast Club*

b) *Napoleon Dynamite*

c) *Heathers*

2. THE ANAGRAM

Unscramble the actor's name: ENTERS LOST VALLEYS

3. FILM QUOTE

What film is the following quote from?

"As God is my witness, I'll never be hungry again."

a) *The Grapes of Wrath* (1940)

b) *Saltburn* (2023)

c) *Gone with the Wind* (1939)

d) *Pink Flamingos* (1972)

4. THUMBS DOWN

What film is this the one-star review of?

"Without giving too much away, the baddie – a trained assassin – visits a remote house to kill the occupant. But kills his wife instead – 'because he wasn't in'. Trained assassin? Reconnaissance? Good grief!"

a) *The Day of the Jackal* (1973)

b) *In Bruges* (2008)

c) *No Time to Die* (2021)

5. ODD ONE OUT

Which of these films was not directed by David Lynch? Bonus point if you know who it was directed by.

a) *Mulholland Drive* (2001)

b) *Lost Highway* (1997)

c) *The Road* (2009)

6. RHYMING FILMS

I'll give you the initials of two films whose titles rhyme with each other. I'll also give you one of the stars and the years they were released, just name the films for a point each.

S&L, Brenda Blethyn (1996) and TNG, Ryan Gosling (2016).

7. CELLULOID OR CELLULIED?

Which of the following is true about Pierce Brosnan?

a) During his time as James Bond, Pierce Brosnan's contract stated he was not allowed to swear in any other film or TV appearance.

b) During his time as James Bond, Pierce Brosnan's contract stated he was not allowed to cry in any other film or TV appearance.

c) During his time as James Bond, Pierce Brosnan's contract stated he was not allowed to wear a tuxedo in any other film or TV appearance.

8. WHAT MIGHT HAVE BEEN

Which of these roles did Michael Keaton turn down?

a) Peter Venkman (*Ghostbusters* – 1984)

b) Michael Dorsey/Dorothy Michaels (*Tootsie* – 1982)

c) Axel Foley (*Beverly Hills Cop* – 1984)

9. WHAT YEAR?

In what year did the following things happen?

Films released this year include: *Avatar, Up, The Hangover, 2012, Harry Potter and the Half-Blood Prince, Fast & Furious* and *The Damned United. Star Trek* is rebooted, with Chris Pine taking the role of Captain Kirk – the film also sees the movie debut of Chris Hemsworth. Exactly one year after his death, Heath Ledger is nominated for Best Supporting Actor (for his portrayal of the Joker in *The Dark Knight*) at the forthcoming Oscars (an award he will win). Karl Malden, John Hughes, Patrick Swayze and Edward Woodward pass away. Austin Butler makes his film debut in *Aliens in the Attic*. But what was the year?

10. GIVE ME FIVE

A chance for five points! Name five films (up to the end of 2024) that Tom Hanks has appeared in with one-word titles. There are 15 possible answers.

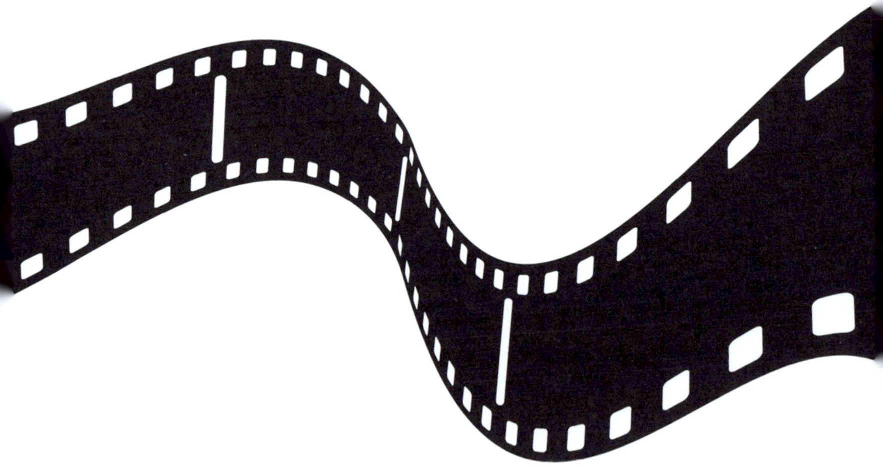

ROUND 2

1. PICTURE PERFECT

I am going to describe five movie posters – can you name the films? A point for each one you recognize.

a) A man wearing a hat and carrying a leather bag in his left hand, stands at the gate of a property. He looks up at the bright light emanating from an upstairs window.

b) A drawing of a bottle on its side pointing to the right. Within are two men with their hands pressed up to the glass. One man has a small goatee beard. Neither look happy.

c) On a grass lawn in front of a building, a man stands with his arms by his sides. In front of him is a pair of naked legs (cut at the thighs). Behind him two people are on loungers. Next to them is a man in a doorway. Everyone is looking at the camera. Everyone has lines across their eyes. In front of the loungers is a beach ball.

d) At the bottom right of the picture is a Volkswagen T2 Microbus. The middle door is open, and a man is sat inside; there is also a man in the driving seat. Two adults and a child are running in a line alongside the van (up to the open door) and one person seems to be pushing it. The driver of the van and the man inside are looking back.

e) A young man stands in front of a closed slatted door; he is staring at a leg that is having a stocking pulled on. Of the owner of the leg, only one leg and one hand are visible.

2. ONE OF OUR _____ IS MISSING!

Just fill in the missing word – there's always a theme, and this time it's... the body.

a) *Snake* ________ (1998)

b) *Angel* ________ (1987)

c) *The* ________ *of an Architect* (1987)

d) *The Man with Two* ________ (1983)

e) *Eyes Without a* ________ (1960)

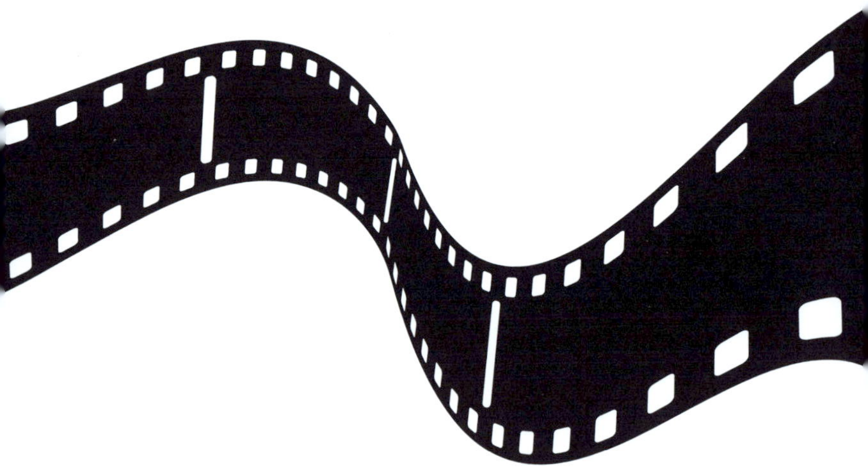

ROUND 3

1. AMERICAN MADE

A question about US remakes of international films – I'll tell you the original; tell me the remake for a point.

a) *Seven Samurai* (dir. Akira Kurosawa – 1954)

b) *Infernal Affairs* (dir. Andrew Lau and Alan Mak – 2002)

c) *Wings of Desire* (dir. Wim Wenders – 1987)

d) *La Femme Nikita* (dir. Luc Besson – 1990)

e) *La Cage aux Folles* (dir. Édouard Molinaro – 1978)

2. THE ODD COUPLE

I'll describe an actor and a film character that share the same initials. A point for each you can name.

a) **Actor:** English, born in 1950. Her first major film role was Susan "Rita" White in *Educating Rita* (1983). She went on to appear in films such as *Buster* (1988), *Billy Elliot* (2000) and the *Harry Potter* series (2001–2011), in which she plays Molly Weasley. **Character:** Portrayed by Keanu Reeves, who, in the first film of the series (2014) seeks revenge on the men who killed his puppy. Unfortunately for his targets, the character is an ex-hitman, and one of the best there is.

b) **Actor:** Danish actor born in 1965. Made his debut playing Tonny in *Pusher* (1996) by Nicolas Winding Refn and found international fame as Le Chiffre in *Casino Royale* (2006). Other roles include Galen Erso in *Rogue One: A Star Wars Story* (2016) and Martin in *Another Round* (2020), which won the Best International Feature Film Oscar in 2021.

Character: The real name of the central character in *Spider-Man: Into the Spider-Verse* (2018) and its sequels. These films are animated entries in the Spider-verse, in which the titular character is a New York teenager voiced by Shameik Moore.

c) **Actor:** American actor born in 1924. She made her debut in *To Have and Have Not* (1944) starring opposite her future husband Humphrey Bogart. Other noir hits included *The Big Sleep* (1946), *Dark Passage* (1947) and *Key Largo* (1948). She later appeared in comedies such as *How to Marry a Millionaire* (alongside Marilyn Monroe – 1953) and *Sex and the Single Girl* (1964). **Character:** Jake Gyllenhaal plays this unhinged "stringer" in the 2014 film *Nightcrawler.* A "stringer" is a freelance photojournalist that sells footage to news stations. In his efforts to make more and more money, Gyllenhaal's character makes increasingly dubious moral decisions.

d) **Actor:** English actor born in 1927. Often played tough characters, most famously Quint in *Jaws* (1975), Doyle Lonnegan in *The Sting* (1973) and Donald Grant – who has a memorable fight on a train with Sean Connery as James Bond – in *From Russia with Love* (1963). The actor was also an author; he wrote four novels and two plays. **Character:** One of the original *Ghostbusters* (1984), played by Dan Aykroyd (who also co-wrote the script). Memorably, Aykroyd's character accidently conjures up the enormous Marshmallow Man at the end of the first film.

e) **Actor:** American actor born in 1975. Best known for portraying Spider-Man in the Sam Raimi trilogy (2002–2007), he returned to the role in 2021 in *Spider-Man: No Way Home*. Some of his other film appearances include *Seabiscuit* (2003), *The Great Gatsby* (2013) and *Babylon* (2022). **Character:** The central character from *Scarface* (1983), portrayed by Al Pacino. The character arrives penniless in the USA from Cuba and becomes a powerful drug lord.

ROUND 4

1. BRAINSTORM

Complete the lists and spot the links – a point for each correct answer.

a) What word precedes ________ *draft* (1991), ________ *beat* (1994) and ________ *fire* (1987) to complete those film titles?

b) What connects Halle Berry in 2002 and 2005, Jared Leto in 2014 and 2022, and Sandra Bullock in 2010 and again in 2010?

c) In *The Shawshank Redemption* (1994), Andy (Tim Robbins) uses three different posters of actresses to hide his tunnel. Rita Hayworth, Marilyn Monroe and which other?

d) Which character connects Michael Gough, Michael Caine, Jeremy Irons and Andy Serkis?

e) Which country is the birthplace of Dan Aykroyd, William Shatner, Martin Short and Evangeline Lilly?

2. IT FOLLOWS

The first letter of each answer follows the first letter of the last. So, if the answer to c) is "Apple", the answer to d) will begin with "B". If you get to Z, go to A. Each question is worth one point.

a) Which character in *Gremlins* (1984) did Howie Mandel provide the voice for?

b) What was the name of the first African American actor to win an Oscar? She was awarded the Best Supporting Actress award for the role of Mammy in *Gone with the Wind* (1939).

c) In 1989, which character did River Phoenix play a younger version of at the beginning of the third movie in the series?

d) *Lost in Translation* (2003), *The Wolverine* (2013), *Black Rain* (1989) and *Kill Bill Vol. 1* (2003) are all set in which country?

e) What first name is shared by actors Basinger, Novak and Cattrall (and is Nicolas Cage's middle name)?

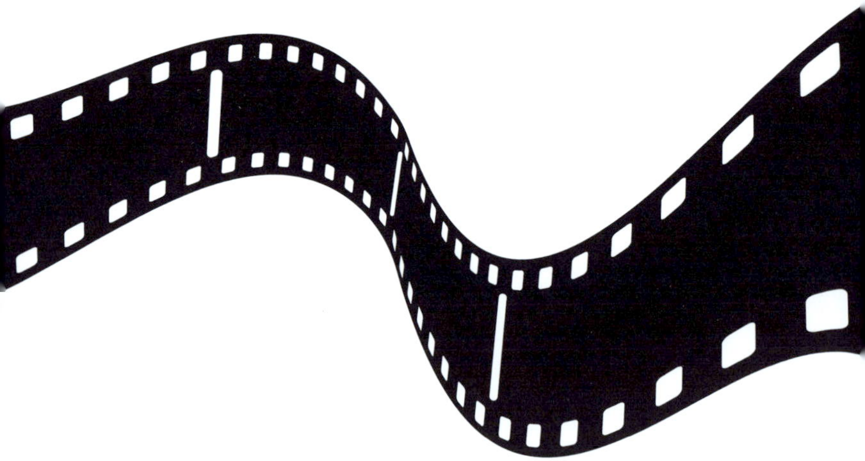

ROUND 5

THE LAST PICTURE SHOW

Say what you see! Can you identify the films from these picture clues? Each picture is worth a point.

1

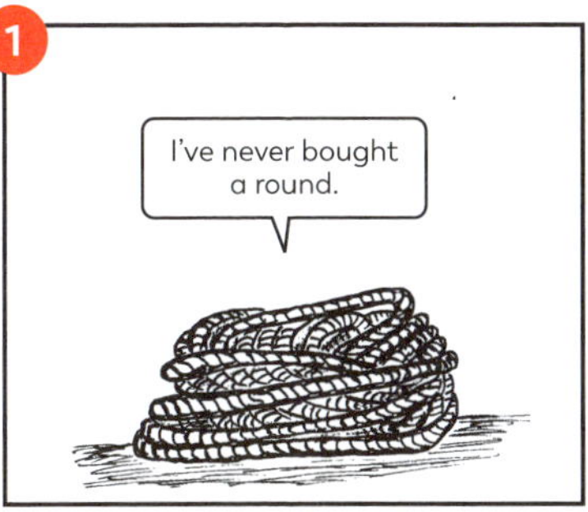

2

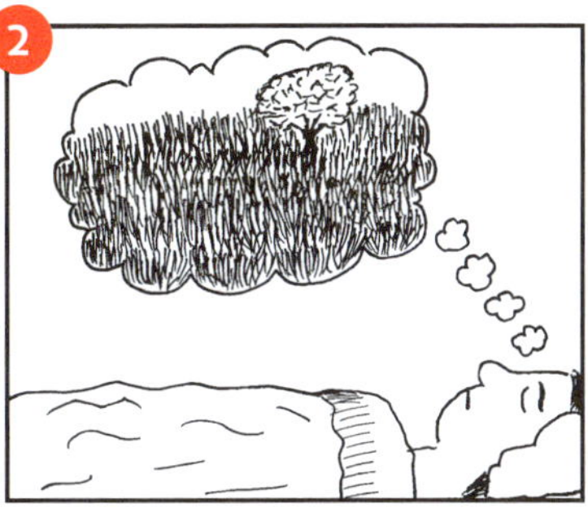

3

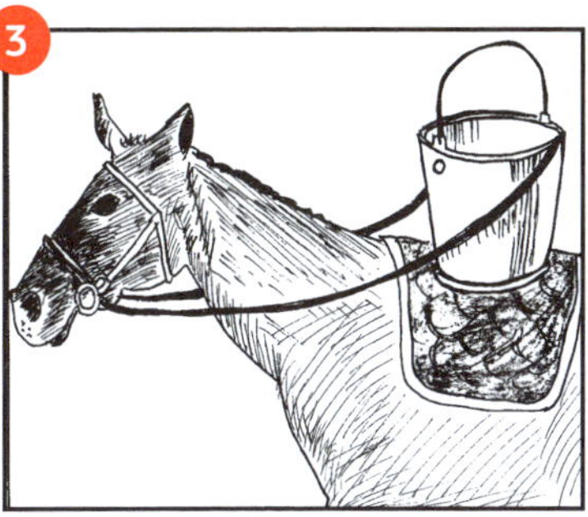

4

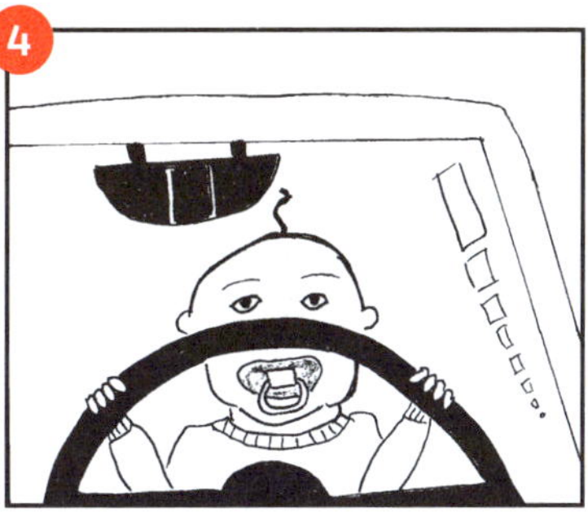

5

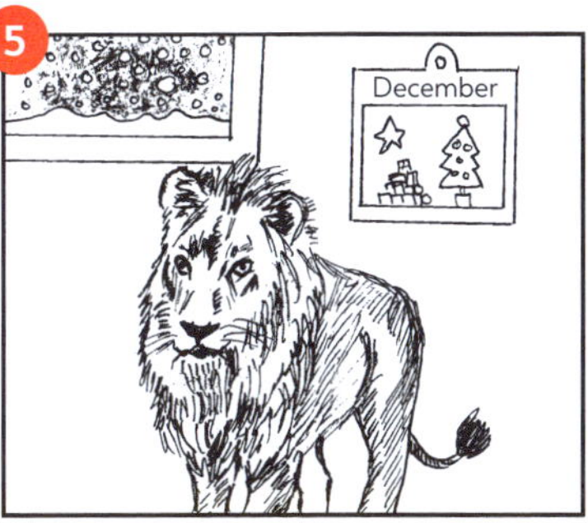

6

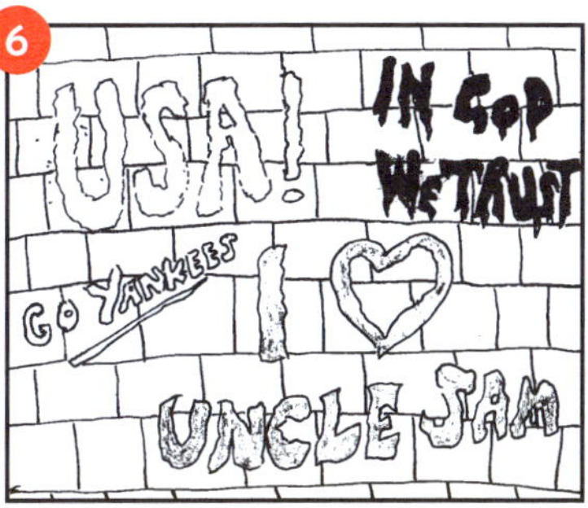

ANSWERS

ROUND 1

1. a) *The Breakfast Club* (1985). *Heathers* was 1988 and *Napoleon Dynamite* 2004.

2. Sylvester Stallone

3. c) *Gone with the Wind*

4. c) *No Time to Die*

Another one-star review that made me laugh was, "It's like an episode of Jeremy Kyle with an Aston Martin."

5. c) *The Road* by John Hillcoat.

6. *Secrets & Lies* and *The Nice Guys.*

7. c) During his time as James Bond, Pierce Brosnan was not allowed to wear a tuxedo in any other film or TV appearance.

When he filmed *The Thomas Crown Affair* (1999), the director ensured Brosnan left his shirt unbuttoned and bow tie untied.

8. a) Peter Venkman (*Ghostbusters*)

9. 2009

10. *Splash* (1984), *Volunteers* (1985), *Dragnet* (1987), *Big* (1988), *Punchline* (1988), *Philadelphia* (1993), *Cars* (2006 – voice performance), *Ithaca* (2015), *Sully* (2016), *Inferno* (2016), *Greyhound* (2020), *Finch* (2021), *Elvis* (2022), *Pinocchio* (2022), *Here* (2024).

ROUND 2

1. a) *The Exorcist* (1973)

1. b) *Sideways* (2004)

1. c) *Parasite* (2019)

1. d) *Little Miss Sunshine* (2006)

1. e) *The Graduate* (1967)

> The actor Linda Gray (Sue Ellen in *Dallas* – 1978–2014) has claimed the leg in the poster is hers, not the star of the film's (Anne Bancroft). She said Bancroft was absent that day and she was paid $25 for the shoot.

2. a) *Eyes*

2. b) *Heart*

2. c) *Belly*

2. d) *Brains*

2. e) *Face*

ROUND 3

1. a) *The Magnificent Seven* (1960)

1. b) *The Departed* (2006)

1. c) *City of Angels* (1998)

1. d) *Point of No Return* (1993)

1. e) *The Birdcage* (1996)

2. a) Julie Walters and John Wick.

2. b) Mads Mikkelsen and Miles Morales.

2. c) Lauren Bacall and Louis (Lou) Bloom.

2. d) Robert Shaw and Ray Stantz.

2. e) Tobey Maguire and Tony Montana.

ROUND 4

1. a) "Back". *Backdraft*, *Backbeat* and *Backfire*.

1. b) These actors have won both an Oscar (first year) and a Razzie (second year). Halle Berry won her Oscar for *Monster's Ball* and her Razzie for *Catwoman*, Jared Leto won his Oscar for *The Dallas Buyers Club* and his Razzie for *The House of Gucci* (he won another Razzie the following year, 2023, for *Morbius*), and Sandra Bullock won her Oscar for *The Blind Side* and her Razzie for *All About Steve*.

1. c) Raquel Welch

1. d) Alfred Pennyworth (Batman's butler) – Michael Gough in *Batman* (1989), *Batman Returns* (1992), *Batman Forever* (1995) and *Batman and Robin* (1997). Michael Caine in *Batman Begins* (2005), *The Dark Knight* (2008) and *The Dark Knight Rises* (2012). Jeremy Irons in *Batman vs Superman: Dawn of Justice* (2016) and *Justice League* (2017). Andy Serkis in *The Batman* (2022).

1. e) Canada

2. a) Gizmo

Originally, Gizmo, rather than give birth to the "Gremlins", was to transform into one (Spike). But executive producer Steven Spielberg suggested Gizmo should remain as a cute cuddly creature, as the audiences would warm to him.

2. b) Hattie McDaniel

McDaniel was not allowed to attend the Atlanta premiere of the film due to Georgia's segregation laws. Clark Gable threatened to boycott the event in support, but McDaniel persuaded him to attend. Despite winning an Academy Award, McDaniel was still forced to sit at a segregated table at the rear of the room.

2. c) Indiana Jones. In *Indiana Jones and the Last Crusade.*

2. d) Japan

2. e) Kim

ROUND 5

1. *Tightrope* (1984)
2. *Field of Dreams* (1989)
3. *Pale Rider* (1985)
4. *Baby Driver* (2017)
5. *The Lion in Winter* (1968)
6. *American Graffiti* (1973)

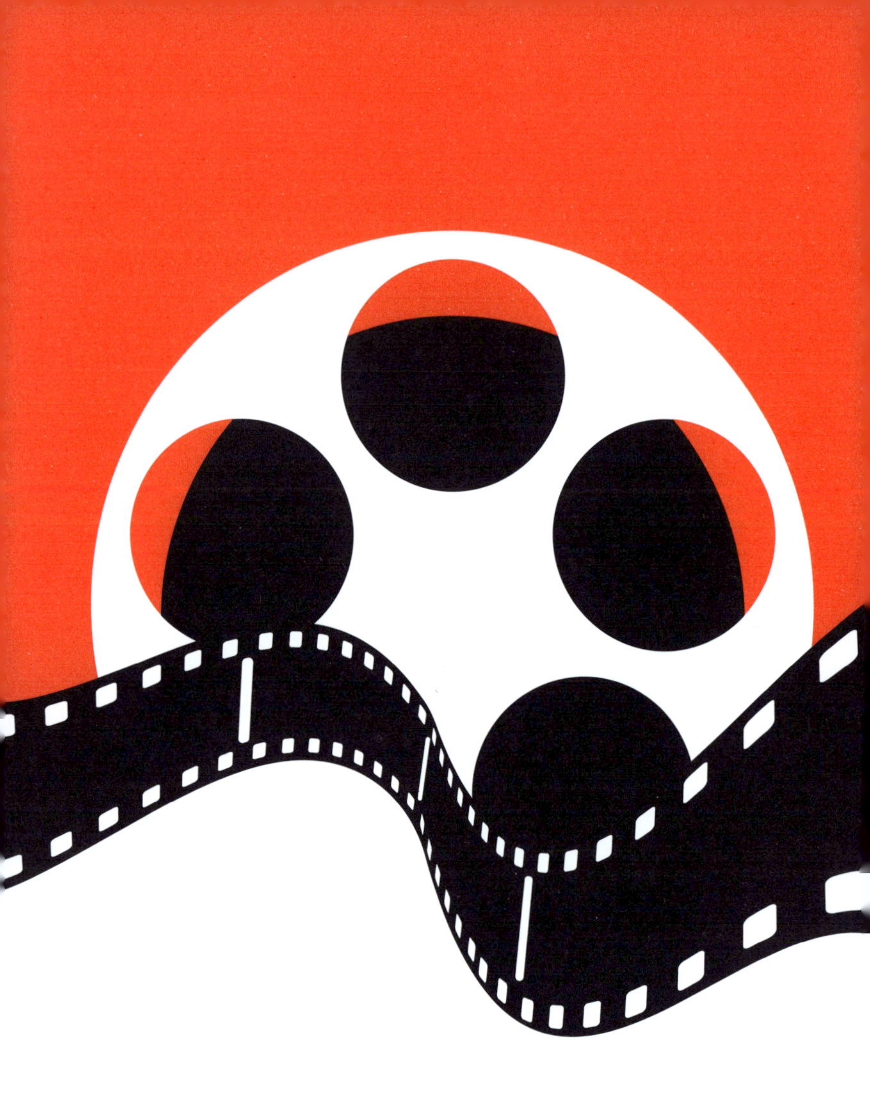

QUIZ 8

ROUND 1

STARTER FOR 10

Ten questions to begin!

1. THE FIRST QUESTION

Which of these directors was born first?

a) Steven Spielberg

b) Ridley Scott

c) James Cameron

2. THE ANAGRAM

Unscramble the actor's name: GEOLOGY ENCORE

3. FILM QUOTE

What film is the following quote from?

"Just keep swimming. Just keep swimming, swimming, swimming. What do we do? We swim, swim."

a) *The Swimmer* (1968)

b) *Finding Nemo* (2003)

c) *Life of Pi* (2012)

d) *Jaws* (1975)

4. THUMBS DOWN

What film is this the one-star review of?

"The worst sci-fi ever produced. Nothing happens for 3 hours. Hour 1: Pre-humans dancing around a monolith. Hour 2: Dude walks around a space station. Hour 3: Dude flies through space really fast. Did I miss anything?"

a) *Passengers* (2016)

b) *2001: A Space Odyssey* (1968)

c) *Solaris* (2002)

5. ODD ONE OUT

Which of these films was not directed by Pedro Almodóvar? Bonus point if you know who it was directed by.

a) *Body Heat* (1981)

b) *The Skin I Live In* (2011)

c) *Live Flesh* (1997)

6. RHYMING FILMS

I'll give you the initials of two films whose titles rhyme with each other. I'll also give you one of the stars and the years they were released, just name the films for a point each.

TQATD, Gene Hackman (1995) and PT, Daniel Day-Lewis (2017).

7. CELLULOID OR CELLULIED?

Which of the following is true about Robin Williams?

a) While filming *Mrs. Doubtfire* (1993), Robin Williams would browse sex shops in San Francisco, in full costume.

b) While filming *Mrs. Doubtfire* (1993), Robin Williams appeared on *Jeopardy* in full costume.

c) While filming *Mrs. Doubtfire* (1993), Robin Williams visited his mother in full costume and she didn't recognize him.

8. WHAT MIGHT HAVE BEEN

Which of these roles did Chevy Chase turn down?

a) Victor Fries/Mr Freeze (*Batman and Robin* – 1997)

b) Abraham Lincoln (*Lincoln* – 2012)

c) Forrest Gump (1994)

9. WHAT YEAR?

In what year did the following things happen?

Films released this year include: *Apocalypse Now, The Jerk, Kramer vs. Kramer, Quadrophenia, Alien, Being There* and *The Tin Drum*. The crew of the Starship Enterprise hit the screen for the first time in *Star Trek: The Motion Picture*, as do Jim Henson's Muppets in *The Muppet Movie*. Jordan Peele, Heath Ledger, James McAvoy, Mindy Kaling and Diego Luna are born. John Wayne, Mary Pickford and Merle Oberon pass away. The film studio Allied Artists files for bankruptcy, one year after they distribute their last film, *The Wild Geese*. But what was the year?

10. GIVE ME FIVE

A chance for five points! Name me five films where the composer John Williams was nominated for an Academy Award for Best Original Score (or scoring). There are 49 possible answers, as of 2024. Or if you want something a little trickier – name the five films he won for.

ROUND 2

1. NEXT

A round about sequels. I'll give you a film, you tell me the name of the sequel.

a) *Saturday Night Fever* (1977)

   i) *Jive Talking*

   ii) *Staying Alive*

   iii) *You Should be Dancing*

b) *The Blues Brothers* (1980)

   i) *The Return of the Blues Brothers*

   ii) *The Twos Brothers*

   iii) *Blues Brothers 2000*

c) *Bean* (1997)

   i) *Mr. Bean's Holiday*

   ii) *Mr. Bean Speaks!*

   iii) *Bean and Gone*

d) *Legally Blonde* (2001)

   i) *Legally Blonde 2: Out of the Woods*

   ii) *Legally Blonde 2: The Hair Apparent*

   iii) *Legally Blonde 2: Red, White & Blonde*

e) *Garfield: The Movie* (2004)

   i) *Garfield: A Tail of Two Kitties*

   ii) *Garfield: The Prince and the Pawper*

   iii) *Garfield: Double Indemkitty*

2. ONE OF OUR ______ IS MISSING!

Just fill in the missing word – there's always a theme, and this time it's... colours.

a) ________ *Velvet* (1986)

b) ________ *Card* (1990)

c) ________ *Heat* (1988)

d) *The* ________ *Rose of Cairo* (1985)

e) *Jackie* ________ (1997)

ROUND 3

1. TOMBSTONE

Here are five famous quotes from headstones, can you tell me who is buried beneath them? A point for each.

a) "I'm a writer but then nobody's perfect"

b) "I told you I was ill"

c) "That's all folks"

d) "She did it the hard way"

e) "[name of person] in"

2. THE ODD COUPLE

I'll describe an actor and a film character that share the same initials. A point for each you can name.

a) **Actor:** American actor born in 1970. Her first major role was Nadine in *Drugstore Cowboy* (1989). She found fame as Brandy/Rollergirl in *Boogie Nights* (1997) and as Felicity Shagwell in *Austin Powers: The Spy Who Shagged Me* (1999).
Character: The central character in *Breakfast at Tiffany's* (1961), as portrayed by Audrey Hepburn in her iconic black dress with her cat that didn't have a name, being adored by her neighbour Paul (George Peppard).

b) **Actor:** American actor born in 1967. As of 2024, he has been nominated four times for Best Supporting Actor (without winning) for *The Kids Are All Right* (2010), *Foxcatcher* (2014), *Spotlight* (2015) and *Poor Things* (2023). But he is perhaps generally best known for portraying The Hulk/Bruce Banner in the Marvel Cinematic Universe, beginning with a cameo at the end of *Iron Man 3* (2013). **Character:** The name of the road warrior and title character in four films (at time of writing). All directed by George Miller, he was portrayed in the first three films by Mel Gibson and in the fourth by Tom Hardy. He also appears in a cameo in the prequel *Furiosa* (2024) played by Jacob Tomuri.

c) **Actor:** American actor born in 1943. A character actor, playwright and screenwriter, he is probably best known for playing Vizzini in the cult classic *The Princess Bride* (1987). He also played Mr Hall in *Clueless* (1995), John Lahr in *Prick Up Your Ears* (1987) and he provided the voice of Rex the neurotic Tyrannosaurus rex in the *Toy Story* series of films (1995–2019). **Character:** A Vietnam veteran, friend and bowling companion of "the Dude" (Jeff Bridges) in *The Big Lebowski* (1998). The character is involved in a scuffle outside the bowling alley in which their other friend Donny (Steve Buscemi) passes away. He and the Dude's attempts to scatter Donny's ashes do not go well.

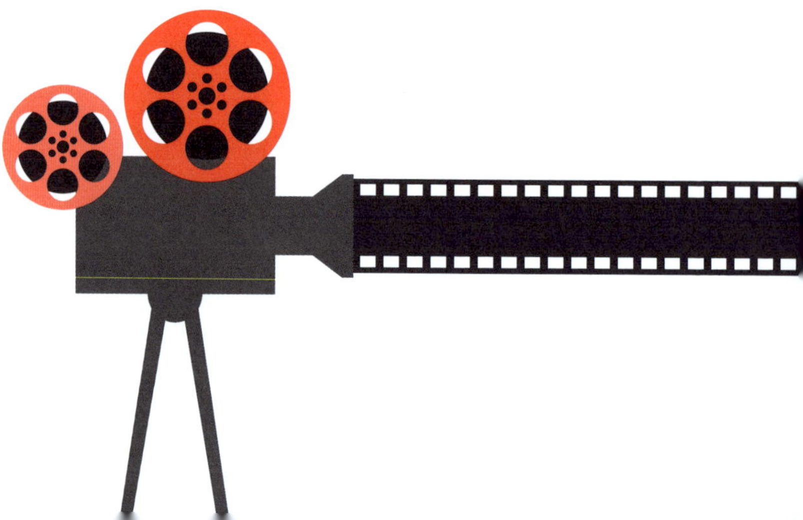

d) **Actor:** American actor born in 1977. The daughter of the lead singer of Aerosmith and Bebe Buell (but raised by Buell and Todd Rundgren), she first found fame in a series of 1990s films, including *Empire Records* (1995), *Stealing Beauty* (1996), *That Thing You Do!* (1996) and *Armageddon* (1998). She also starred as Arwen Undómiel in Peter Jackson's *The Lord of the Rings* trilogy (2001–2003). **Character:** The real name of the character known as the Wolf Man. He has been portrayed by Lon Chaney Jr (for the first time in 1941) and Benicio del Toro in 2010.

e) **Actor:** American actor born in 1958. Her first lead role was in *Grease 2* (1982), and she soon found fame in lead roles in movies such as *Scarface* (1983), *The Witches of Eastwick* (1987), *The Fabulous Baker Boys* (1989) and *Batman Returns* (1992). She reduced her workload over the next 30 years but joined the Marvel Cinematic Universe in 2018 playing Janet Van Dyne in *Ant-Man and the Wasp* (2018) and *Ant-Man and the Wasp: Quantumania* (2023). **Character:** The editor-in-chief of top fashion magazine *Runway*, portrayed by Meryl Streep in *The Devil Wears Prada* (2006).

ROUND 4

1. BRAINSTORM

Complete the lists and spot the links – a point for each correct answer.

a) How are the films *Freaky Friday* (1976), *The Change-Up* (2011), *All of Me* (1984) and *The Hot Chick* (2002) linked?

b) What connects Bill Murray in *Zombieland* (2009), Nicolas Cage in *The Unbearable Weight of Massive Talent* (2022) and Peter Falk in *Wings of Desire* (*Der Himmel über Berlin*) (1987)?

c) What comes next in this list? *Close Encounters of the Third Kind* (1977), *Jaws* (1975), *The Sugarland Express* (1974), ______ (1971).

d) What is the connection between Paul Newman in 1962 and 1987, Cate Blanchett in 1999 and 2008, and Al Pacino in 1973 and 1975?

e) Which historical figure was portrayed by Vivien Leigh in 1945, Elizabeth Taylor in 1963 and Amanda Barrie in 1964?

2. IT FOLLOWS

The first letter of each answer follows the first letter of the last. So, if the answer to c) is "Apple", the answer to d) will begin with "B". If you get to Z, go to A. Each question is worth one point.

a) Which actor was number one in the music charts (in the UK) for three weeks with "Wand'rin' Star" in 1970?

b) Which 1969 film directed by John Schlesinger and starring Dustin Hoffman and Jon Voight was the first X-rated film to win an Oscar?

c) In 2021, at the 93rd Academy Awards, Chloé Zhao became the first Asian woman (and second woman ever) to win the Best Director Oscar. What film did she win for?

d) The actor that plays Winona Ryder's daughter in the 2024 *Beetlejuice* sequel (*Beetlejuice Beetlejuice*) is Jenna who?

e) What is the name of the 2014 film starring Bill Nighy and Imelda Staunton that retells the story of the lesbian and gay activists that raised money for striking miners in the UK in 1984?

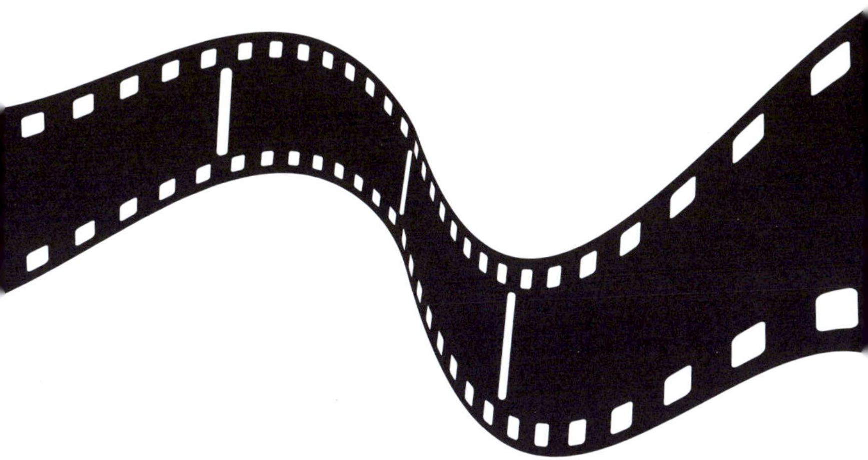

ROUND 5

THE LAST PICTURE SHOW

Say what you see! Can you identify the films from these picture clues? Each picture is worth a point.

1

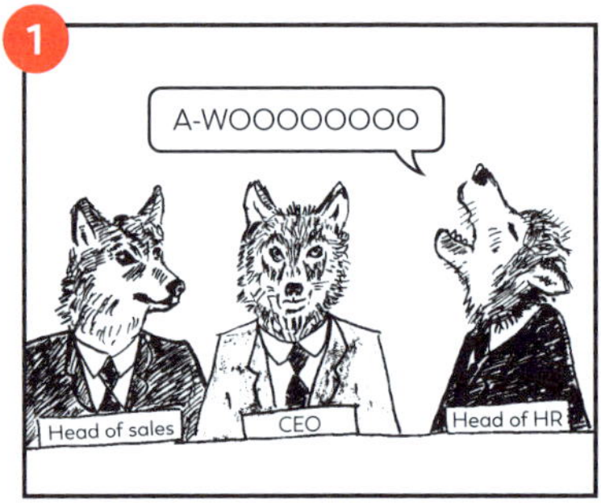

2

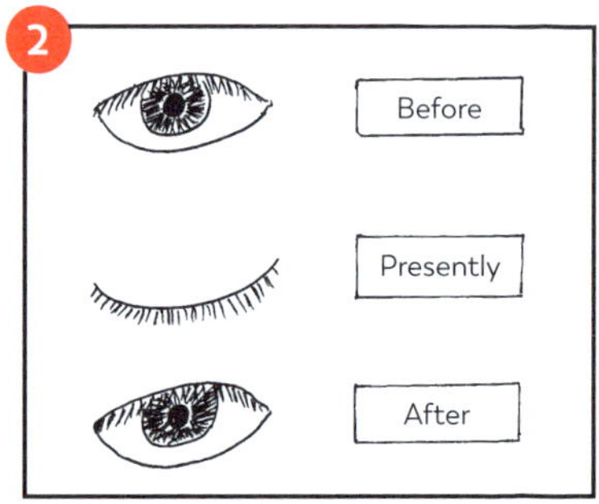

3

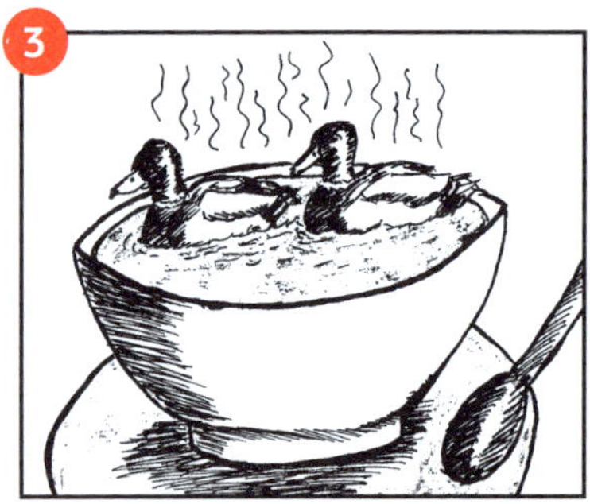

4

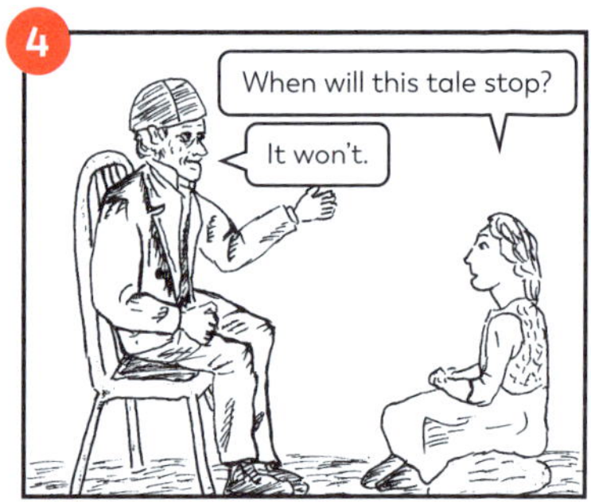

5

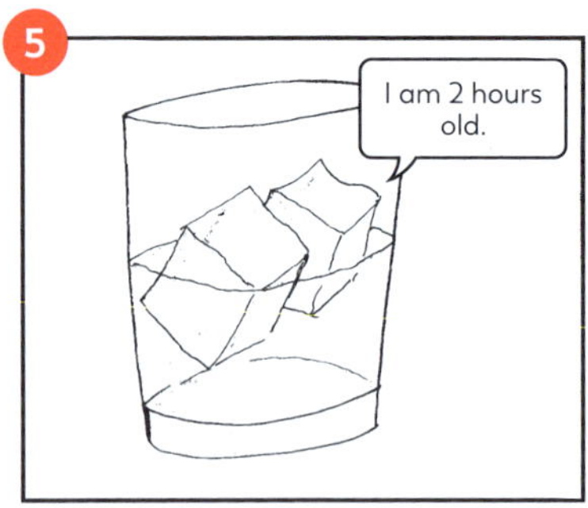

6

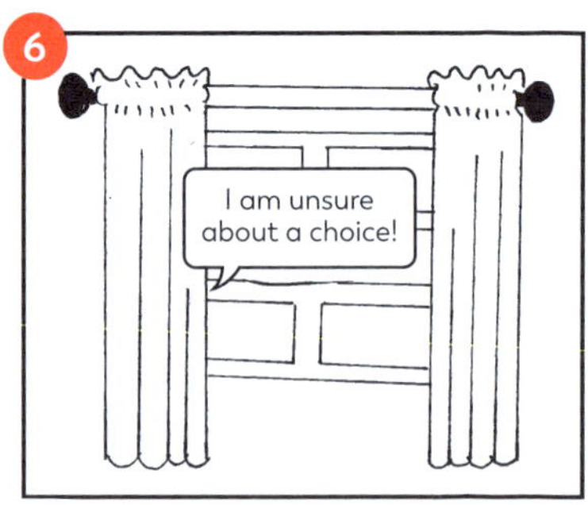

ANSWERS

ROUND 1

1. b) Ridley Scott (1937). Stephen Spielberg was born in 1946 and James Cameron was born in 1954.

2. George Clooney

3. b) *Finding Nemo*

4. b) *2001: A Space Odyssey*

5. a) *Body Heat* by Lawrence Kasdan.

6. *The Quick and the Dead* and *Phantom Thread.*

7. a) While filming *Mrs. Doubtfire* (1993), Robin Williams would browse sex shops in San Francisco, in full costume.

8. c) Forrest Gump

9. 1979

The Jerk was one of Stanley Kubrick's favourite films. Kubrick liked it so much he invited Steve Martin to his house in England and pitched the idea of *Eyes Wide Shut* to him. Kubrick would eventually make the movie nearly 20 years later (1999) with Tom Cruise.

10. *Valley of the Dolls* (1967), *Goodbye, Mr. Chips* (1969), *The Reivers* (1969), ***Fiddler on the Roof* (won – 1971)**, *Images* (1972), *The Poseidon Adventure* (1972), *Cinderella Liberty* (1973), *Tom Sawyer* (1973), *The Towering Inferno* (1974), ***Jaws* (won – 1975)**, ***Star Wars: Episode IV – A New Hope* (won – 1977)**, *Close Encounters of the Third Kind* (1977), *Superman* (1978), *Star Wars: Episode V – The Empire Strikes Back* (1980), *Indiana Jones and the Raiders of*

the Lost Ark (1981), ***E.T. the Extra-Terrestrial* (won – 1982)**, *Star Wars: Episode VI – Return of the Jedi* (1983), *Indiana Jones and the Temple of Doom* (1984), *The River* (1984), *Empire of the Sun* (1987), *The Witches of Eastwick* (1987), *The Accidental Tourist* (1988), *Born on the Fourth of July* (1989), *Indiana Jones and the Last Crusade* (1989), *Home Alone* (1990), *JFK* (1991), ***Schindler's List* (won – 1993)**, *Sabrina* (1995), *Nixon* (1995), *Sleepers* (1996), *Amistad* (1997), *Saving Private Ryan* (1998), *Angela's Ashes* (1999), *The Patriot* (2000), *A.I. Artificial Intelligence* (2001), *Harry Potter and the Philosopher's Stone* (*Sorcerer's Stone* in the US – 2001), *Catch Me if You Can* (2002), *Harry Potter and the Prisoner of Azkaban* (2004), *Memoirs of a Geisha* (2005), *Munich* (2005), *The Adventures of Tintin* (2011), *War Horse* (2011), *Lincoln* (2012), *The Book Thief* (2013), *Star Wars: Episode VII – The Force Awakens* (2015), *Star Wars: Episode VIII – The Last Jedi* (2017), *Star Wars: Episode IX – The Rise of Skywalker* (2019), *The Fabelmans* (2022), *Indiana Jones and the Dial of Destiny* (2023).

ROUND 2

1. a) ii) *Staying Alive* (1983)

1. b) iii) *Blues Brothers 2000* (1998)

1. c) i) *Mr. Bean's Holiday* (2007)

1. d) iii) *Legally Blonde 2: Red, White & Blonde* (2003)

1. e) i) *Garfield: A Tail of Two Kitties* (2006)

2. a) *Blue*

2. b) *Green*

2. c) *Red*

2. d) *Purple*

2. e) *Brown*

ROUND 3

1. a) Billy Wilder

1. b) Spike Milligan

1. c) Mel Blanc

1. d) Bette Davis

1. e) Jack Lemmon

Other good ones include: "There goes the neighbourhood", Rodney Dangerfield, "Let 'er rip", Leslie Nielsen. Also, magicians Penn and Teller already have a joint headstone prepared – it states, "Is this your card?"

2. a) Heather Graham and Holly Golightly.

2. b) Mark Ruffalo and Max Rockatansky.

2. c) Wallace Shawn and Walter Sobchak.

2. d) Liv Tyler and Larry Talbot.

2. e) Michelle Pfeiffer and Miranda Priestly.

ROUND 4

1. a) They are all body-swap comedies; films where two people's consciousnesses switch bodies.

1. b) They are all playing fictionalized versions of themselves. Falk is credited as "Der Filmstar".

1. c) *Duel* – these are films directed by Steven Spielberg going backwards to his first major work. Although a TV film, it was later given a theatrical release. (He also directed *Firelight* in 1964 when he was 17.)

In *Jaws*'s death scene, Spielberg added a sample of a dinosaur taken from the 1957 film *The Land Unknown*. He had already used that sample in *Duel* and wanted to give his first success a hat tip.

1. d) They were nominated for Oscars for playing the same role in two films. Paul Newman played "Fast Eddie" Felson in *The Hustler* (1961) and *The Color of Money* (1986), Cate Blanchett played Queen Elizabeth I in *Elizabeth* (1998) and *Elizabeth: The Golden Age* (2007), and Al Pacino was Michael Corleone in *The Godfather* (1972) and *The Godfather Part II* (1974). At the time of writing, this has only happened six times, the other actors being Sylvester Stallone, Peter O'Toole and Bing Crosby.

1. e) Cleopatra (*Caesar and Cleopatra*, *Cleopatra* and *Carry on Cleo*).

2. a) Lee Marvin

2. b) *Midnight Cowboy*

Andy Warhol had agreed to make an appearance at the loft party scene in *Midnight Cowboy* but was shot in an assassination attempt by radical feminist Valerie Solanas the week before the scene was due to be filmed.

2. c) *Nomadland* (2020)

> Frances McDormand became the first person to win Oscars for both acting in and producing the same film.

2. d) Ortega

2. e) *Pride*

ROUND 5

1. *The Company of Wolves* (1984)
2. *Don't Look Now* (1973)
3. *Duck Soup* (1933)
4. *The NeverEnding Story* (1984)
5. *Ice Age* (2002)
6. *Torn Curtain* (1966)

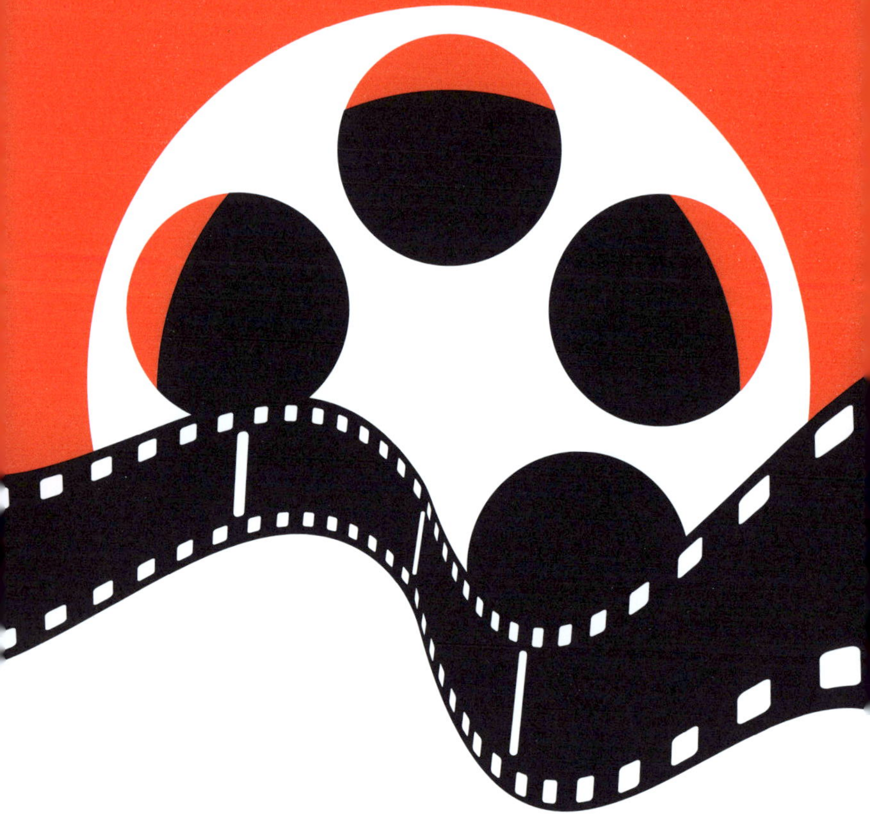

QUIZ 9

ROUND 1

STARTER FOR 10

Ten questions to begin!

1. THE FIRST QUESTION

Which of these Oscar-winning songs won the award first?

a) "Can You Feel the Love Tonight?"

b) "Flashdance... What a Feeling"

c) "My Heart Will Go On"

2. THE ANAGRAM

Unscramble the actor's name: GORY UNIVERSE AWE

3. FILM QUOTE

What film is the following quote from?

"We're all pretty bizarre. Some of us are just better at hiding it, that's all."

a) *The Breakfast Club* (1985)

b) *Miss Peregrine's Home for Peculiar Children* (2016)

c) *One Flew Over the Cuckoo's Nest* (1975)

d) *Psycho* (1960)

4. THUMBS DOWN

What film is this the one-star review of?

"It made no sense whatsoever. Putting someone with no legs in a machine, taking him to a planet where everyone is blue and now he has legs and he's blue."

a) *Star Trek III: The Search for Spock* (1984)

b) *Avatar* (2009)

c) *FernGully: The Last Rainforest* (1992)

5. ODD ONE OUT

Which of these films was not directed by Hayao Miyazaki? Bonus point if you know who it was directed by.

a) *Howl's Moving Castle* (2004)

b) *Princess Mononoke* (1997)

c) *The Tale of the Princess Kaguya* (1991)

6. RHYMING FILMS

I'll give you the initials of two films whose titles rhyme with each other. I'll also give you one of the stars and the years they were released, just name the films for a point each.

ITMFL, Maggie Cheung (2000) and TWOTD, Helena Bonham Carter (1997).

7. CELLULOID OR CELLULIED?

Which of the following is true about Dustin Hoffman?

a) When Dustin Hoffman auditioned for *Straw Dogs* (1971), Sam Peckinpah dismissed him as "too nice" so Hoffman punched him in the face.

b) When Dustin Hoffman auditioned for *The Graduate* (1967), he was mistaken for a window cleaner. So, he washed the window.

c) When Dustin Hoffman auditioned for *Midnight Cowboy* (1969), the casting agent thought he was a vagrant and threw him out.

8. WHAT MIGHT HAVE BEEN

Which of these roles did Michelle Pfeiffer turn down?

a) Clarice Starling (*The Silence of the Lambs* – 1991)

b) Erin Brockovich (2000)

c) Annie Wilkes (*Misery* – 1990)

9. WHAT YEAR?

In what year did the following things happen?

Films released this year include: *Some Like It Hot*, *Ben-Hur*, *North by Northwest*, *Anatomy of a Murder*, *Sleeping Beauty*, *Look Back in Anger* and *Rio Bravo*. In April, *The 400 Blows* by François Truffaut opens the Cannes Film Festival, bringing the French New Wave to wider attention. The Three Stooges release their 190th (and final) short film, *Sappy Bull Fighters*. Matthew Modine, Catherine Keener, Emma Thompson, Sean Bean and Val Kilmer are born.

Errol Flynn, Lou Costello and Cecil B. DeMille pass away. Rock Hudson and Doris Day appear on screen together for the first time in *Pillow Talk*. But what was the year?

10. GIVE ME FIVE

A chance for five points! Name five feature-length films (up to the end of 2024) directed by Martin Scorsese and starring Robert De Niro. There are ten possible answers.

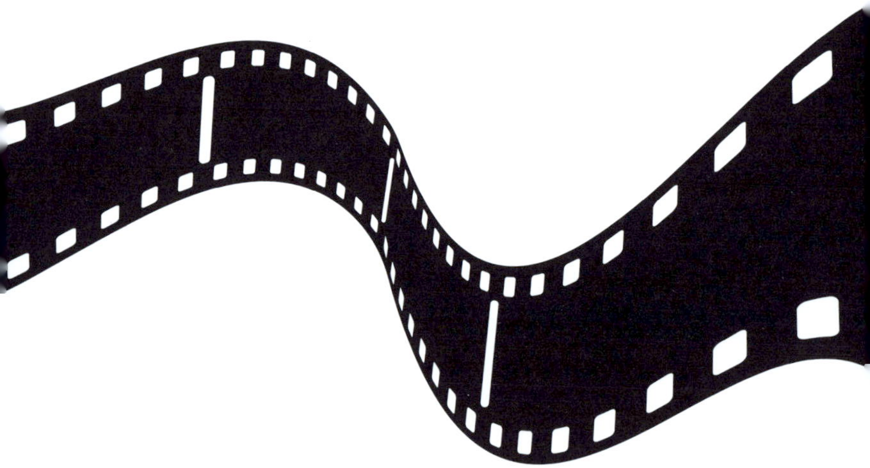

ROUND 2

1. LINK

I will give you a word that ends one film title and begins another, plus the star and the year – name both for two points.

a) The link is "Far". Film one – Sean Connery (1977). Film two – Tom Cruise (1992).

b) The link is "Run". Film one – Michael York (1976). Film two – Simon Pegg (2007).

c) The link is "Dead". Film one – Bruce Campbell (1981). Film two – Nicole Kidman (1989).

d) The link is "Baby". Film one – Hilary Swank (2004). Film two – Ansel Elgort (2017).

e) The link is "War". Film one – Kirsten Dunst (2024). Film two – Jeremy Irvine (2011).

2. ONE OF OUR ________ IS MISSING!

Just fill in the missing word – there's always a theme, and this time it's... insects and arachnids.

a) *Along Came a* ________ (2001)

b) *Blue* ________ (2023)

c) *The Human* ________ (2009)

d) *The* ________ *Effect* (2004)

e) ________ *Me to the Moon* (2024)

ROUND 3

1. TOTAL RECALL

Can you fill in the missing words from these famous Arnold Schwarzenegger quotes? A point for each one you know.

a) "Get to the ________!"

b) "I'm not into politics, I'm into ________."

c) "If it ________, we can kill it."

d) "Come with me if you want to ________."

e) "Consider that a ________."

2. THE ODD COUPLE

I'll describe an actor and a film character that share the same initials. A point for each you can name.

a) **Actor:** American actor born in Hawaii in 1979. He is probably best known for portraying the DC character Aquaman (2017–2023) and Khal Drogo in the TV series *Game of Thrones* (2011–2019). He has also appeared in *Dune* (2021) playing Duncan Idaho and the 2011 version of *Conan the Barbarian*, playing Conan. **Character:** Bruce Willis began playing this New York detective in *Die Hard* (1988) and continued until 2013's *A Good Day to Die Hard*.

b) **Actor:** American actor born in 1968. The son of famous actor James (his stepmother was Barbra Streisand), he found fame early in *The Goonies* (1985), but his career faltered until the 2000s when he saw a resurgence in films, including *No Country for Old Men* (2007), *Milk* (2008) and *True Grit* (2010). He played Thanos in the Marvel Cinematic

Universe and Gurney Halleck in *Dune* (2021) and *Dune: Part 2* (2024). **Character:** The main protagonist in John Carpenter's 1986 cult classic *Big Trouble in Little China*. Portrayed by Kurt Russell, he is a truck driver who gets involved in a battle between David Lo Pan (James Hong) and Wang Chi (Dennis Dun).

c) **Actor:** Australian actor born in 1979. A body of only 20 films in total, including *A Knight's Tale* (2001), *Monster's Ball* (2001), *Brokeback Mountain* (2005) and *The Dark Knight* (2008) for which he won the Best Actor Oscar – awarded posthumously. He died while filming Terry Gilliam's *The Imaginarium of Doctor Parnassus* (2009). **Character:** The main antagonist in Quentin Tarantino's *Inglourious Basterds* (2009). Portrayed by Christoph Waltz, he is an SS Colonel nicknamed "the Jew Hunter".

d) **Actor:** Swedish actor born in 1988. She won an Oscar for Best Supporting Actress for her performance as Gerda Wegener in *The Danish Girl* (2015). Other starring roles include Ava, an android in *Ex Machina* (2014) and Lara Croft in the 2018 version of *Tomb Raider*. She met her husband Michael Fassbender on the film *The Light Between Oceans* (2016). **Character:** The "pet detective" portrayed by Jim Carrey in two films, the first in 1994 and again in a sequel in 1995, subtitled *When Nature Calls*.

e) **Actor:** American actor born in 1980. Best known as a child star whose roles included Kevin McCallister in the first two *Home Alone* movies (1990–1992), Thomas J. Sennett in *My Girl* (1991) and the title role in *Richie Rich* (1994). **Character:** The criminal who holds an obsessive grudge against the attorney that sent him to prison in *Cape Fear* (1962). He was played by Robert Mitchum in the 1962 version and by Robert De Niro in the 1991 Martin Scorsese remake.

ROUND 4

1. BRAINSTORM

Complete the lists and spot the links – a point for each correct answer.

a) What colour connects films starring Isabella Rossellini, Brooke Shields, Léa Seydoux and Béatrice Dalle?

b) What connects Mike Myers in the *Austin Powers* films (1997–2002), Leonardo DiCaprio in *The Man in the Iron Mask* (1998), Lee Marvin in *Cat Ballou* (1965) and Lupita Nyong'o in *Us* (2019)?

c) What connects *American Beauty* (1999), *Sunset Boulevard* (1950), *Shallow Grave* (1994) and *Menace II Society* (1993)?

d) What attribute connects the characters in these films? Ferris Bueller in *Ferris Bueller's Day Off* (1986), Alfie Elkins in *Alfie* (1966), Alvy Singer in *Annie Hall* (1977) and Deadpool in *Deadpool* (2016)?

e) Which character has been played by Donald Pleasence, Telly Savalas, Charles Gray, Max von Sydow and Christoph Waltz?

2. IT FOLLOWS

The first letter of each answer follows the first letter of the last. So, if the answer to c) is "Apple", the answer to d) will begin with "B". If you get to Z, go to A. Each question is worth one point.

a) In 1951, Ronald Reagan made a film starring a chimp which was called *Bedtime for* ________?

b) What word follows *First* ________ in a Kelly Reichardt film title (2019), *Funny* ________ in a 2017 film starring Maxine Peake by Adrian Shergold, and *Poor* ________ in Ken Loach's 1967 film starring Terence Stamp?

c) In which 2010 animated film do we first meet the Minions?

d) What was the last film Bruce Lee completed in his lifetime?

e) In 1966 and 1967 James Coburn played a parody of James Bond in two films; the character's name was Derek what?

ROUND 5

THE LAST PICTURE SHOW

Say what you see! Can you identify the films from these picture clues? Each picture is worth a point.

1

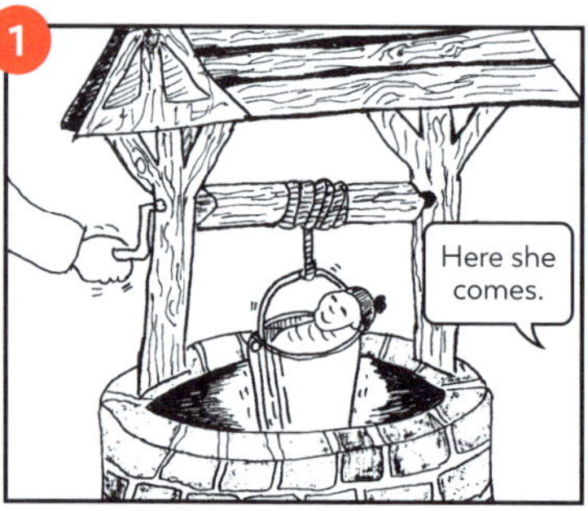

2

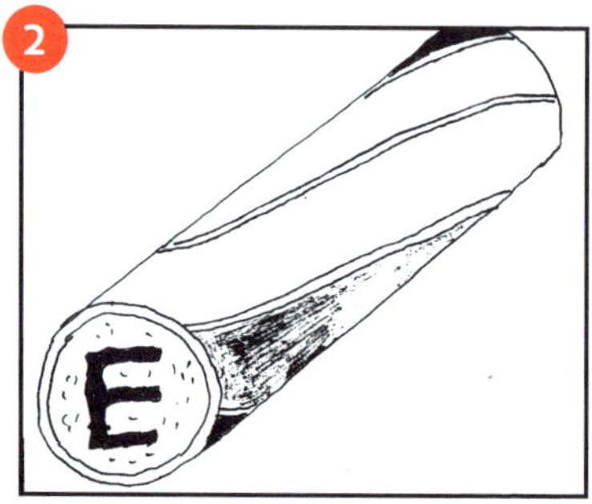

3

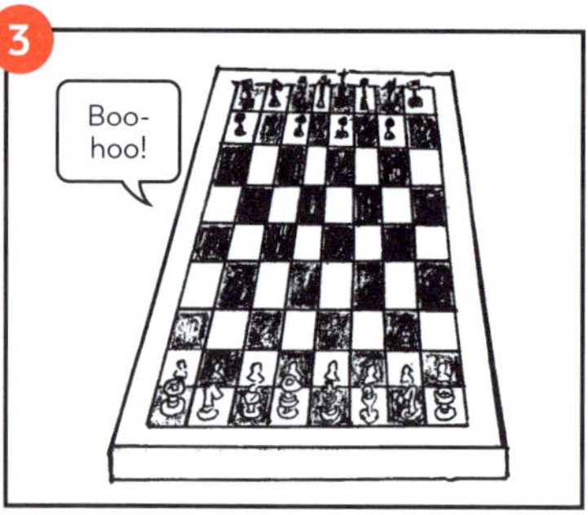

4

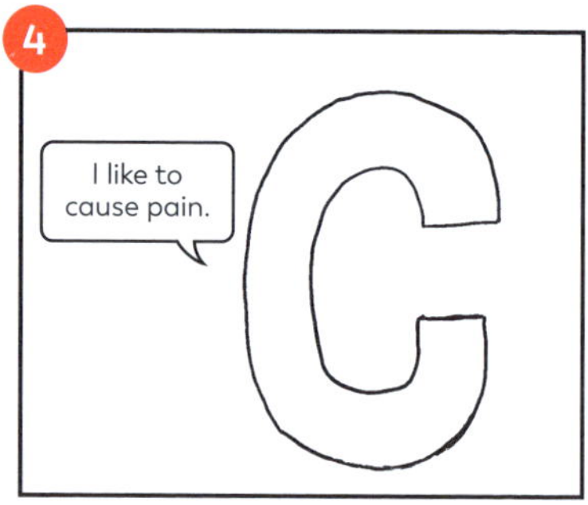

5

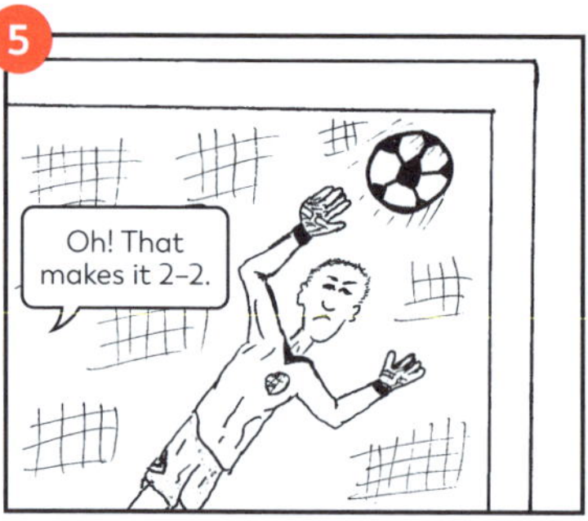

6

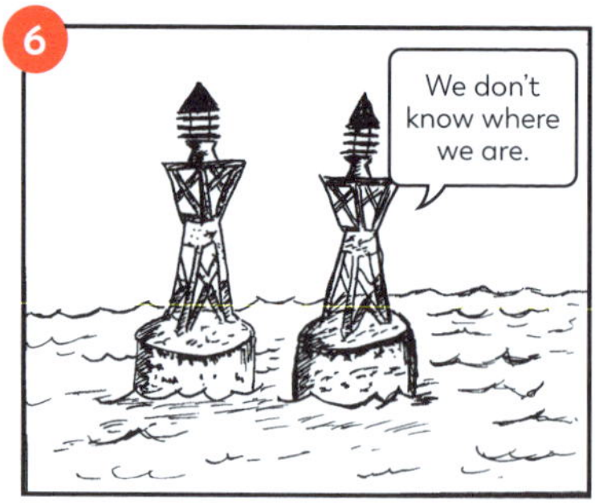

ANSWERS

ROUND 1

1. b) "Flashdance... What a Feeling" (won 1984) by Irene Cara for *Flashdance* (1983). "Can You Feel the Love Tonight?" by Elton John for *The Lion King* (1994) won in 1995. "My Heart Will Go On" by Celine Dion for *Titanic* (1997) won in 1998.

2. Sigourney Weaver

3. a) *The Breakfast Club*

4. b) *Avatar*

5. c) *The Tale of the Princess Kaguya* by Isao Takahata.

6. *In the Mood for Love* and *The Wings of the Dove.*

7. b) When Dustin Hoffman auditioned for *The Graduate* (1967), he was mistaken for a window cleaner. So, he washed the window.

8. a) Clarice Starling (*The Silence of the Lambs*)

It's quite tricky to find a major female role from the 80s and 90s that Michelle Pfeiffer didn't turn down. Among the many films she decided not to do are *Thelma & Louise* (1991), *Pretty Woman* (1990), *Splash* (1984), *Basic Instinct* (1992) and *Sleepless in Seattle* (1993).

9. 1959

10. *Mean Streets* (1973), *Taxi Driver* (1976), *New York, New York* (1977), *Raging Bull* (1980), *The King of Comedy* (1982), *Goodfellas* (1990), *Cape Fear* (1991), *Casino* (1995), *The Irishman* (2019), *Killers of the Flower Moon* (2023). (There is also a short called *The Audition* – 2015.)

ROUND 2

1. a) *A Bridge Too* ***Far*** *and Away*

1. b) *Logan's* ***Run*** *Fatboy Run*

1. c) *The Evil* ***Dead*** *Calm*

1. d) *Million Dollar* ***Baby*** *Driver*

1. e) *Civil* ***War*** *Horse*

2. a) *Spider*

2. b) *Beetle*

2. c) *Centipede*

2. d) *Butterfly*

2. e) *Fly*

ROUND 3

1. a) Chopper – *Predator* (1987).

1. b) Survival – *The Running Man* (1987).

1. c) Bleeds – *Predator* (1987).

1. d) Live – *Terminator 2: Judgment Day* (1991).

1. e) Divorce – *Total Recall* (1990).

2. a) Jason Momoa and John McClane.

2. b) Josh Brolin and Jack Burton.

2. c) Heath Ledger and Hans Landa.

2. d) Alicia Vikander and Ace Ventura.

2. e) Macaulay Culkin and Max Cady.

ROUND 4

1. a) Blue (*Blue Velvet* – 1986, *Blue Lagoon* – 1980, *Blue Is the Warmest Colour* – 2013, *Betty Blue* – 1986).

1. b) In those films they play both the "hero" and the "villain".

1. c) Dead narrators. All these films feature narration from characters who are dead by the end of the film.

1. d) They all break the fourth wall (i.e. speak directly to the audience).

1. e) Ernst Stavro Blofeld

2. a) *Bonzo*

2. b) "Cow". *First Cow*, *Funny Cow* and *Poor Cow*.

2. c) *Despicable Me*

2. d) *Enter the Dragon* (1973)

2. e) Flint. *Our Man Flint* (1966) and *In Like Flint* (1967).

> ***Our Man Flint*** **features a villain named Hans Gruber. Twenty-two years later, that name would appear in *Die Hard* (1988), again for a villainous character played by Alan Rickman.**

ROUND 5

1. *Bringing Up Baby* (1938)
2. *Rocky* (1976)
3. *The Crying Game* (1992)
4. *The Cruel Sea* (1953)
5. *The Equalizer* (2014)
6. *The Lost Boys* (1987)

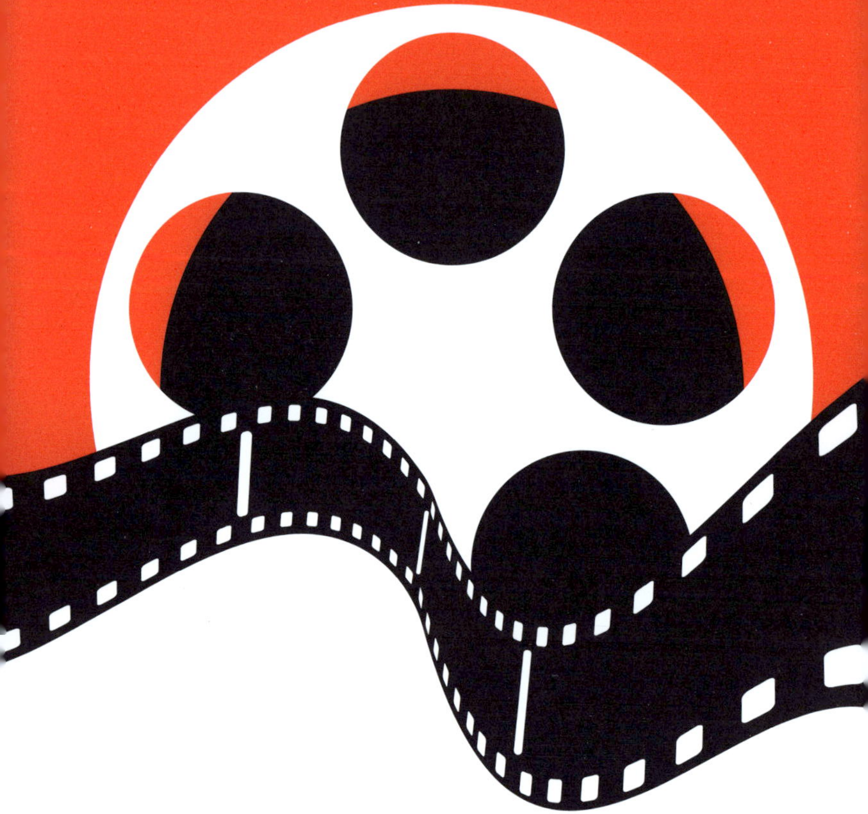

QUIZ 10

ROUND 1

STARTER FOR 10

Ten questions to begin!

1. THE FIRST QUESTION

Which of these sequels was released first?

a) *Star Wars: Episode V – The Empire Strikes Back*

b) *Terminator 2: Judgment Day*

c) *Aliens*

2. THE ANAGRAM

Unscramble the actor's name: URGE A RHYTHM BOP

3. FILM QUOTE

What film is the following quote from?

"I find it amusing. Men are supposed to be made out of steel or something."

a) *Good Will Hunting* (1997)

b) *Brokeback Mountain* (2005)

c) *Steel Magnolias* (1989)

d) *Man of Steel* (2013)

4. THUMBS DOWN

What film is this the one-star review of?

"... it is without doubt the most pompous, pretentious and ridiculously 'God bless America' film it has ever been my misfortune to endure. The characters are two-dimensional wooden caricatures; not a single one inspires you with the slightest amount of empathy, while the plot is thin and extremely shaky."

a) *Top Gun* (1986)

b) *Team America: World Police* (2004)

c) *Full Metal Jacket* (1987)

5. ODD ONE OUT

Which of these films was not directed by Billy Wilder? Bonus point if you know who it was directed by.

a) *The Post* (2017)

b) *Ace in the Hole* (1951)

c) *The Front Page* (1974)

6. RHYMING FILMS

I'll give you the initials of two films whose titles rhyme with each other. I'll also give you one of the stars and the years they were released, just name the films for a point each.

AQP, Emily Blunt (2018) and SOG, Sean Penn (1990).

7. CELLULOID OR CELLULIED?

Which of the following is true about Johnny Depp?

During the filming of *Finding Neverland* (2004) to make the children laugh:

a) Depp used a remote-control fart machine placed under Julie Christie's chair.

b) Depp would make rabbit ears behind director Marc Forster's head.

c) Depp would refer to J. M. Barrie's famous character as "Peter Pants".

8. WHAT MIGHT HAVE BEEN

Which of these roles did Lee Marvin turn down?

a) Reuben J. "Rooster" Cogburn (*True Grit* – 1969)

b) Quint (*Jaws* – 1975)

c) Obi-Wan Kenobi (*Star Wars: Episode IV – A New Hope* – 1977)

9. WHAT YEAR?

In what year did the following things happen?

Films released this year include: *2001: A Space Odyssey*, *Rosemary's Baby*, *Planet of the Apes*, *Bullitt*, *The Odd Couple*, *Barbarella*, *The Thomas Crown Affair* and *Night of the Living Dead*. Spencer Tracy and Katharine Hepburn pick up best Actor/Actress Baftas for *Guess Who's Coming to Dinner* (released the year previously). Daniel Craig, Robert Rodriguez, Guy Ritchie, Will Smith, Hugh Jackman and Naomi Watts are born. Tony Hancock and Tallulah

Bankhead pass away. The Monkees release the psychedelic, satirical film *Head*, a box office and critical failure that signals the end of their career as a band (though now regarded as a cult classic). But what was the year?

10. GIVE ME FIVE

A chance for five points! It's a great ensemble cast but can you name five actors credited as appearing in Rian Johnson's *Knives Out* (2019)? There are 24 possible answers.

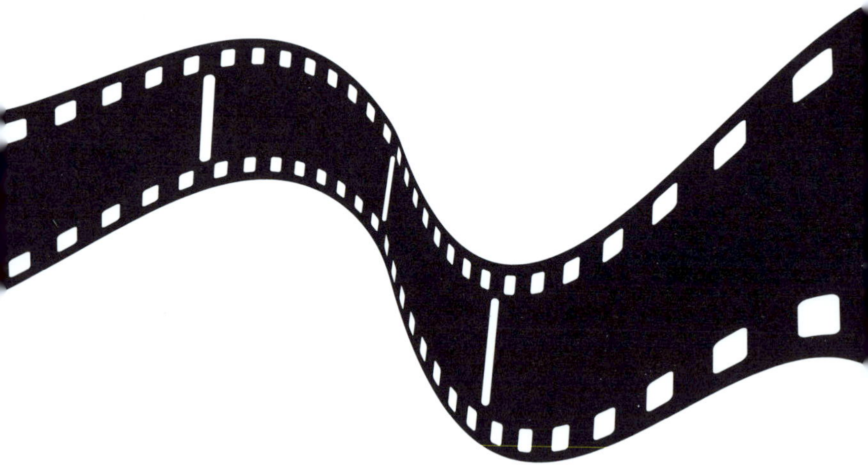

ROUND 2

1. THE HIDDEN

The titles of these classic children's films can be found in capital letters within the descriptions. Unscramble them to name the film for a point.

a) The story begins when this ICON WANDERED, IN ALL good faith, after a departing white rabbit. (1951)

b) When lawsuits stop these superheroes wanting to intervene, THE DISCERNIBLE affect is that they disappear for 15 years... (2004)

c) Wait, thinks Larry Daley, seeing Christopher Columbus, is THE STATUE HUMMING? Is Theodore Roosevelt smiling? (2006)

d) In the warren, General Woundwort WANTED WORSHIP but Bigwig defeats him. (1978)

e) If you'll pardon the pun, this is A TAIL TO LURE you to the finest restaurants in France. (2007)

2. ONE OF OUR ________ IS MISSING!

Just fill in the missing word – there's always a theme, and this time it's... American states.

a) *Paris,* ________ (1984)

b) *The* ________ *Project* (2017)

c) ________ *Grind* (2015)

d) *The* ________ *Fried Movie* (1977)

e) *My Own Private* ________ (1991)

ROUND 3

1. THE PERFECT SCORE

I will give you the titles of three pieces of music (and their length) from a film score – just tell me the name of the film they are taken from for a point.

a) "Flight from Peru" (2:23), "The Well of The Souls" (4:57), "Marion's Theme" (3:10)

b) "Rock Hammer" (1:51), "Brooks Was Here" (5:06), "So Was Red" (2:44)

c) "We Built Our Own World" (1:55), "Dream Within a Dream" (5:04) "Paradox" (3:25)

d) "Sam" (5:33), "Ditto" (3:19), "Molly" (6:17)

e) "Attack on Murron" (3:00), "The Battle of Stirling" (5:57), "Freedom / The Execution / Bannockburn" (7:24)

2. THE ODD COUPLE

I'll describe an actor and a film character that share the same initials. A point for each you can name.

a) **Actor:** American actor and comedian born in 1940. Began his career as a groundbreaking stand-up comedian before moving to movies and finding fame initially with Gene Wilder (*Silver Streak* – 1976 and *Stir Crazy* – 1980) and then with roles in *Superman III* (1983) and *Harlem Nights* (1989). **Character:** Portrayed by Robert De Niro in the Martin Scorsese movie *The King of Comedy* (1982). An aspiring (but delusional) stand-up comedian who, after failing to find the fame he believes he deserves, kidnaps Jerry Langford (a successful comedian, played by Jerry Lewis) in an attempt to force the network to grant him a TV spot.

b) **Actor:** Irish actor born in 1983. Son of famous actor Brendan, he first found fame as Bill Weasley in the final two *Harry Potter* movies (2010–2011). He also appeared in the *Star Wars* universe as General Armitage Hux in the sequel trilogy (2015–2019). Other key roles include Tim Lake in *About Time* (2013), Caleb Smith in *Ex Machina* (2014) and A. A. Milne in *Goodbye Christopher Robin* (2017). **Character:** The young girl whisked away from Kansas by a tornado, who appears to land, with her dog Toto, "over the rainbow" in the land of Oz. Portrayed by Judy Garland in *The Wizard of Oz* (1939) and subsequently by Diana Ross (*The Wiz* – 1978) and Fairuza Balk (*Return to Oz* – 1985).

c) **Actor:** English actor born in 1990. After beginning his career on British television soap opera *Eastenders* (2007–2016), this actor found fame in Danny Boyle and Richard Curtis' *Yesterday* (2019) in which he plays the central role of Jack Malik. He has also appeared in *Tenet* (2020) and *Don't Look Up* (2021). **Character:** The "preacher" with LOVE tattooed on the knuckles of one hand and HATE on the other from *The Night of the Hunter* (1955) directed by Charles Laughton. Portrayed by Robert Mitchum, the preacher is searching for $10,000 dollars and will murder to attain it.

d) **Actor:** Swedish actor born in 1951. This actor has appeared many times for Danish film maker Lars von Trier, in films including *Dogville* (2003) and *Melancholia* (2011). He has also appeared in many American movies, such as *Mamma Mia!* (2008), *Dune* (2021) and *Dune: Part Two* (2024) portraying Baron Harkonnen. In 2011 he appeared in *Thor* playing Dr Erik Selvig and he has returned to this role five times. **Character:** The professor of Potions at Hogwarts School of Witchcraft and Wizardry, portrayed by Alan Rickman in the *Harry Potter* series of films (2001–2011).

e) **Actor:** English actor born in 1933. A legend of British cinema, this actor first rose to stardom in 1964 in *Zulu*. A string of hits followed, including *The Ipcress File* (1965), *Alfie* (1966), *The Italian Job* (1969), *Get Carter* (1971) and *Sleuth* (1972). More recently he has become Christopher Nolan's "lucky charm", making a string of appearances in his films until the actor's retirement in 2023. **Character:** The character portrayed by Bette Davis in *All About Eve* (1950). She is a well-established and respected Broadway star who meets Eve (Anne Baxter), an ambitious young fan. Eve's attempts to gain fame will disrupt Davis's character's life dramatically.

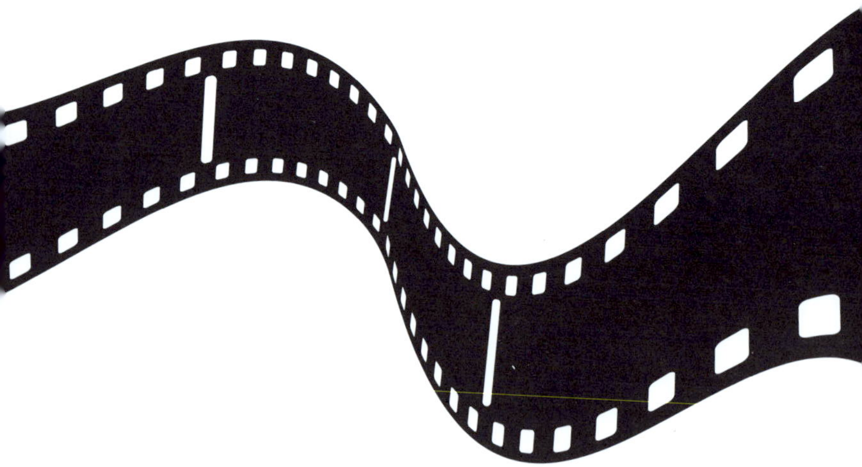

ROUND 4

1. BRAINSTORM

Complete the lists and spot the links – a point for each correct answer.

a) What four words go before Jackal, Locust and Dolphin in three films from the 1970s?

b) What is next in the list? *A Clockwork Orange* (1971), *Barry Lyndon* (1975), *The Shining* (1980), *Full Metal Jacket* (1987)...

c) Which singer and actor played characters called Vince Everett, Chadwick "Chad" Gates, Clint Reno and Lucky Jackson?

d) Which character has been portrayed by Albert Finney, Peter Ustinov and Kenneth Branagh?

e) Which film has sequels subtitled *2½: The Smell of Fear* (1991) and *33⅓: The Final Insult* (1994)?

2. IT FOLLOWS

The first letter of each answer follows the first letter of the last. So, if the answer to c) is "Apple", the answer to d) will begin with "B". If you get to Z, go to A. Each question is worth one point.

a) What first name is shared by the guitarist in *This Is Spinal Tap* (1984 – played by Christopher Guest), Austin Powers' father in *Austin Powers in Goldmember* (2002 – played by Michael Caine) and the pelican from *Finding Nemo* (2003 – voiced by Geoffrey Rush)?

b) Can you name the Austrian/American director of the films *Laura* (1944), *The Man with the Golden Arm* (1955), *Bonjour Tristesse* (1958) and *Anatomy of a Murder* (1959)?

c) What is the name of the 2016 film by Jim Jarmusch, starring Adam Driver as the titular bus driver and poet? It is also the name of the city he lives in.

d) What word connects a 2008 *James Bond* film and a subatomic universe in the *Ant-Man* (2015–2023) films?

e) Which American punk band featured in the Roger Corman (executive producer) film *Rock 'n' Roll High School* (1979)?

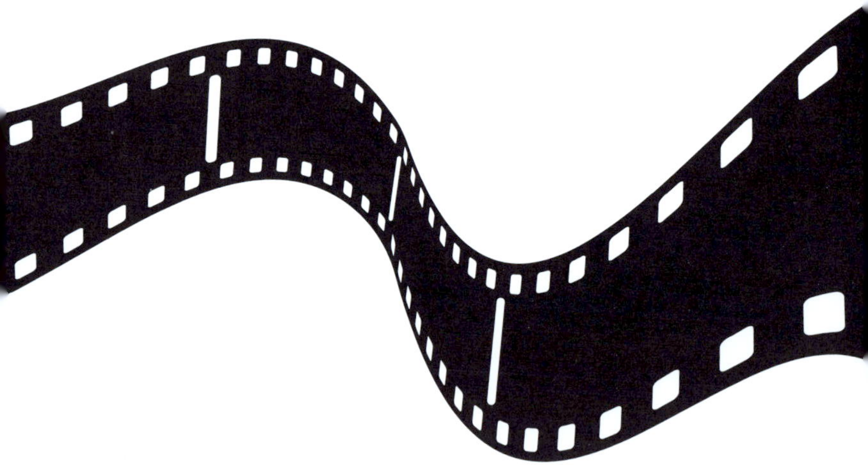

ROUND 5

THE LAST PICTURE SHOW

Say what you see! Can you identify the films from these picture clues? Each picture is worth a point.

1

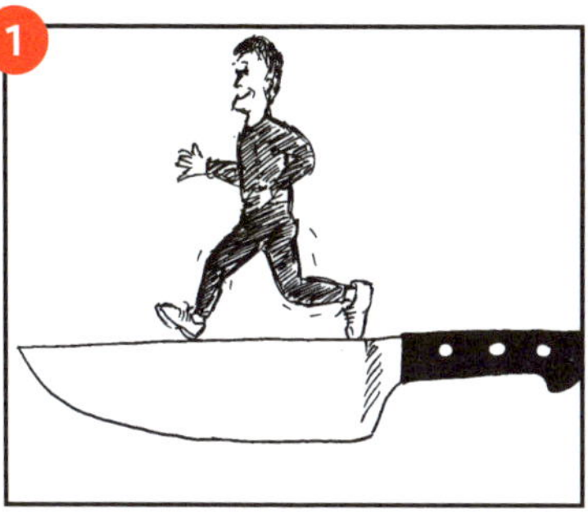

2

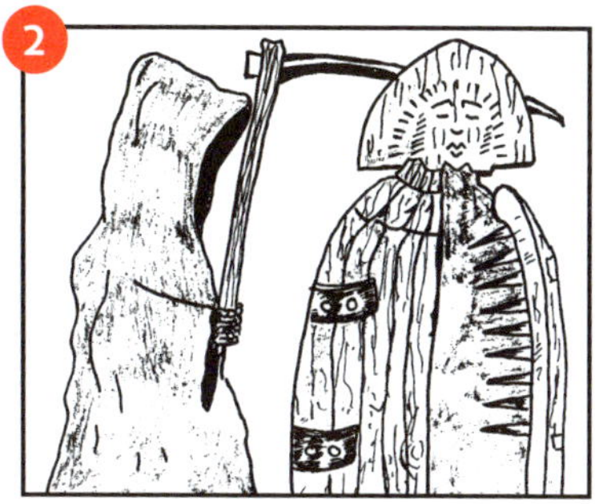

3

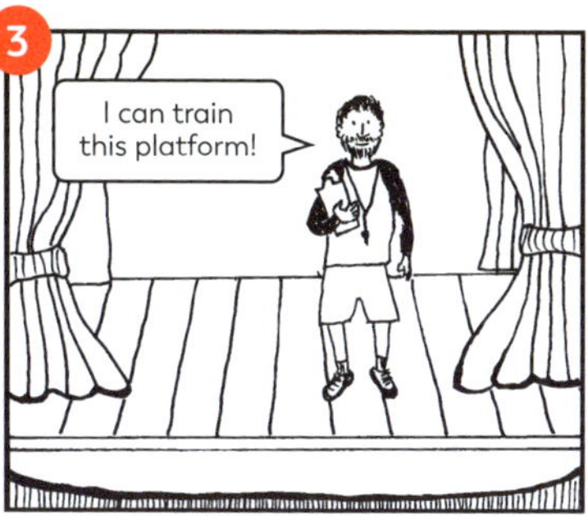

4

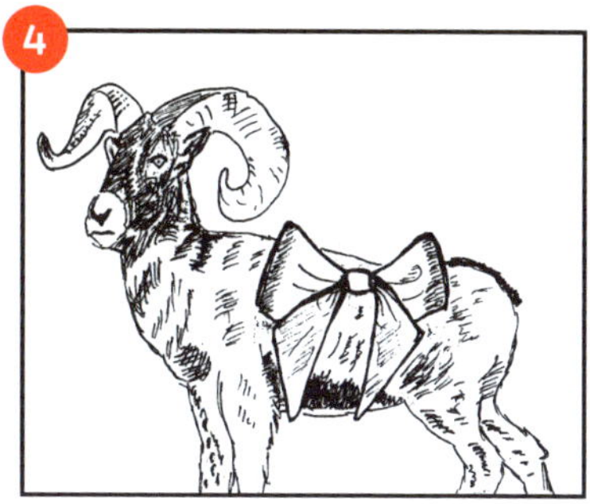

5

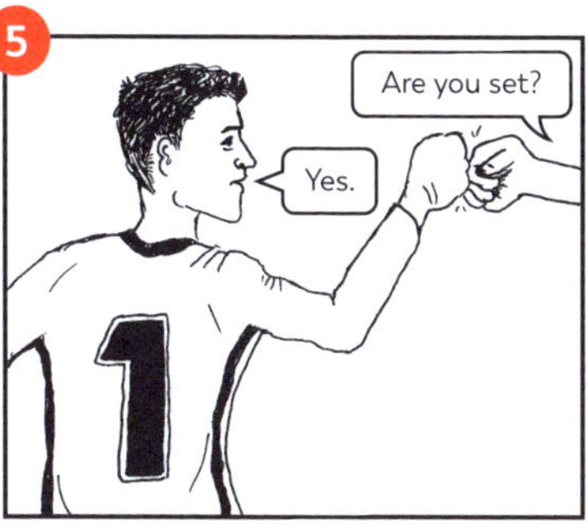

6

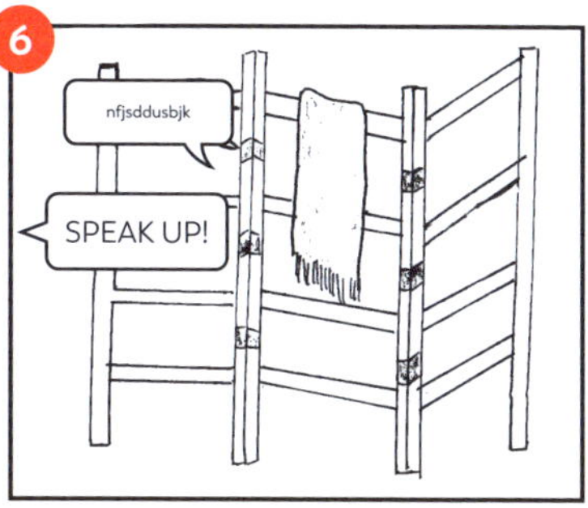

ANSWERS

ROUND 1

1. a) *Star Wars: Episode V – The Empire Strikes Back* (1980). *Aliens* was 1986 and *Terminator 2: Judgment Day* was 1991.

2. Humphrey Bogart

3. c) *Steel Magnolias*

4. a) *Top Gun*

5. a) *The Post* by Steven Spielberg.

6. *A Quiet Place* and *State of Grace*.

7. a) Depp used a remote-control fart machine placed under Julie Christie's chair.

8. b) Quint (*Jaws*)

> **Mark Hamill (on the set of *The Big Red One* – 1980) asked Lee why he turned Quint down. Marvin replied, "How was I supposed to know people would go see a movie about a f*cking fish?"**

9. 1968

10. Daniel Craig, Chris Evans, Ana de Armas, Jamie Lee Curtis, Michael Shannon, Don Johnson, Toni Collette, LaKeith Stanfield, Christopher Plummer, Katherine Langford, Jaeden Martell, Riki Lindhome, Edi Patterson, Frank Oz, K Callan, Noah Segan, M. Emmet Walsh, Marlene Forte, Raúl Castillo, Shyrley Rodriguez, Kerry Frances, Gary Tanguay, Octavia Chavez-Richmond, Joseph Gordon-Levitt (voice only).

ROUND 2

1. a) *Alice in Wonderland*

1. b) *The Incredibles*

1. c) *Night at the Museum*

1. d) *Watership Down*

1. e) *Ratatouille*

2. a) *Texas*

2. b) *Florida*

2. c) *Mississippi*

2. d) *Kentucky*

2. e) *Idaho*

ROUND 3

1. a) *Indiana Jones and the Raiders of the Lost Ark* (1981) by John Williams.

1. b) *The Shawshank Redemption* (1994) by Thomas Newman.

1. c) *Inception* (2010) by Hans Zimmer.

1. d) *Ghost* (1990) by Maurice Jarre.

1. e) *Braveheart* (1995) by James Horner.

2. a) Richard Pryor and Rupert Pupkin.

2. b) Domhnall Gleeson and Dorothy Gale.

2. c) Himesh Patel and Harry Powell.

2. d) Stellan Skarsgård and Severus Snape.

2. e) Michael Caine and Margo Channing.

ROUND 4

1. a) "*The Day of the...*" *Jackal* (1973), *Locust* (1975), *Dolphin* (1973).

1. b) *Eyes Wide Shut* (1999). These are the last five films directed by Stanley Kubrick in chronological order.

1. c) Elvis Presley (in *Jailhouse Rock* – 1957, *Blue Hawaii* – 1961, *Love Me Tender* – 1956, and *Viva Las Vegas* – 1964).

1. d) Hercule Poirot. Albert Finney in *Murder on the Orient Express* (1974). Peter Ustinov in *Death on the Nile* (1978), *Evil Under the Sun* (1982) and *Appointment with Death* (1988). Kenneth Branagh in *Murder on the Orient Express* (2017), *Death on the Nile* (2022) and *A Haunting in Venice* (2023).

1. e) *The Naked Gun: From the Files of Police Squad!* (1988)

2. a) Nigel. Nigel Tufnel, Nigel Powers and Nigel... the pelican.

2. b) Otto Preminger

Otto Preminger was also an actor and played Mr Freeze in two episodes of the 1960s *Batman* (1966–1968) TV series.

2. c) *Paterson*

2. d) "Quantum". *Quantum of Solace* and the Quantum Realm.

2. e) Ramones

ROUND 5

1. *Blade Runner* (1982)
2. *Death and the Maiden* (1994)
3. *Stagecoach* (1939)
4. *Rambo* (1982–2019)
5. *Ready Player One* (2018)
6. *The Horse Whisperer* (1998)

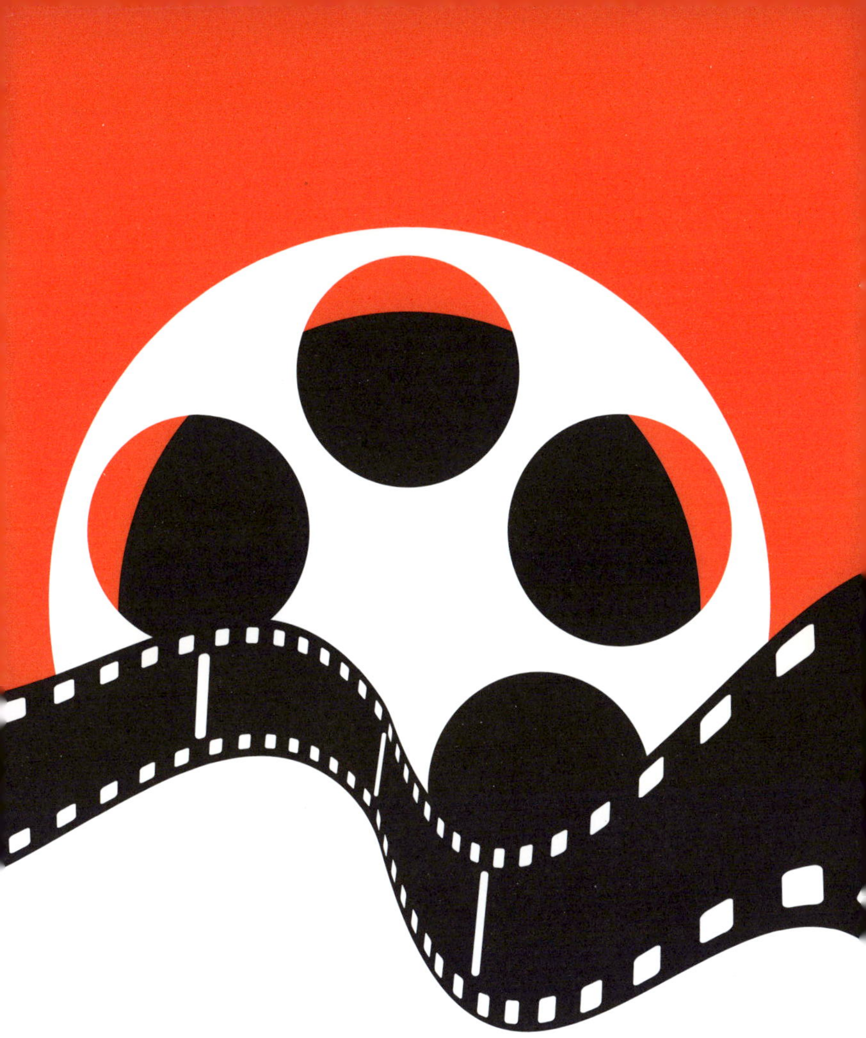

QUIZ 11

ROUND 1

STARTER FOR 10

Ten questions to begin!

1. THE FIRST QUESTION

Which of these "Good" films was released first?

a) *Good Morning, Vietnam*

b) *As Good as It Gets*

c) *Goodfellas*

2. THE ANAGRAM

Unscramble the actor's name: AND SOARS AS NUN

3. FILM QUOTE

What film is the following quote from?

"When I buy a new book, I read the last page first. That way, in case I die before I finish, I know how it ends."

a) *Naked* (1993)

b) *Barton Fink* (1991)

c) *When Harry Met Sally* (1989)

d) *The NeverEnding Story* (1984)

4. THUMBS DOWN

What film is this the one-star review of?

"Anyone who thinks this dated monstrosity is a good movie is either 100 years old, a pretentious film snob or recently had their eyeballs pecked out by hungry crows."

a) *The Blair Witch Project* (1999)

b) *The Omen* (1976)

c) *The Birds* (1963)

5. ODD ONE OUT

Which of these films was not directed by Akira Kurosawa? Bonus point if you know who it was directed by.

a) *Ran* (1985)

b) *Prospero's Books* (1991)

c) *Throne of Blood* (1957)

6. RHYMING FILMS

I'll give you the initials of two films whose titles rhyme with each other. I'll also give you one of the stars and the years they were released, just name the films for a point each.

LALD, Roger Moore (1973) and TTSS, Gary Oldman (2011).

7. CELLULOID OR CELLULIED?

Which of the following is true about David Niven?

a) David Niven is the only actor (at time of writing) to win an Oscar on the same night as hosting the ceremony.

b) David Niven is the only actor (at time of writing) to win an Oscar and also a Nobel prize for literature.

c) David Niven is the only actor (at time of writing) to play both James Bond and Ernst Stavro Blofeld in the same film.

8. WHAT MIGHT HAVE BEEN

Which of these roles did Warren Beatty turn down?

a) John Merrick (*The Elephant Man* – 1980)

b) Daniel Hillard/Mrs Doubtfire (*Mrs. Doubtfire* – 1993)

c) Butch Cassidy (*Butch Cassidy and the Sundance Kid* – 1969)

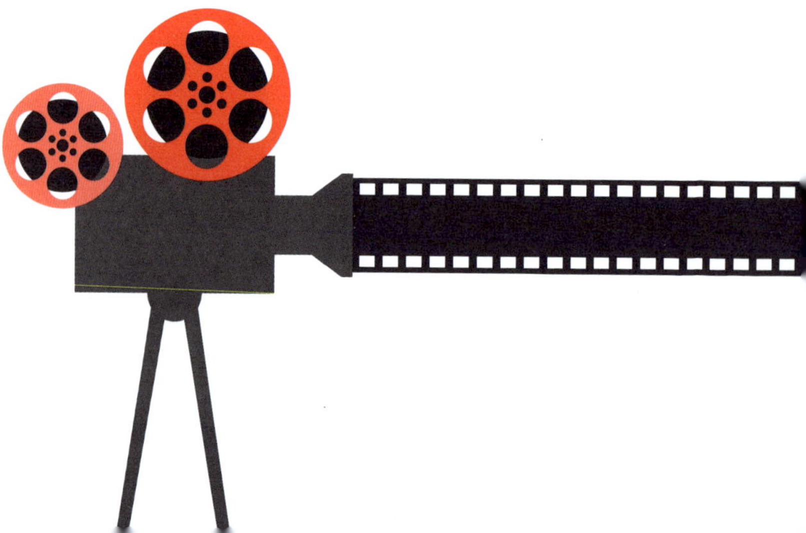

9. WHAT YEAR?

In what year did the following things happen?

Films released this year include: *The Sixth Sense*, *The Matrix*, *Notting Hill*, *The World Is Not Enough*, *Austin Powers: The Spy Who Shagged Me*, *Fight Club*, *Magnolia*, *American Pie* and *Toy Story 2*. Joey King is born. Stanley Kubrick dies six days after screening a final cut of *Eyes Wide Shut* for his family and the film's stars. Oliver Reed dies during a break from filming *Gladiator* after challenging a group of sailors to a drinking match in a bar in Valletta, Malta. Dirk Bogarde, Madeline Kahn and George C. Scott also pass away. And *Star Wars* begins a new era with the release of *Episode I – The Phantom Menace*. But what was the year?

10. GIVE ME FIVE

A chance for five points! Name five films directed by Clint Eastwood (up to the end of 2024) with one- or two-word titles. There are 28 possible answers.

ROUND 2

1. ONE OR THE OTHER

A 50–50 round. Just choose the correct option!

a) Which Ryan was born first: Ryan Reynolds or Ryan Gosling?

b) The 2002 *Spider-Man* film starring Tobey Maguire – in the scene where Peter Parker stops Mary Jane (Kirsten Dunst) falling and catches all her lunch items – was not a special effect but done in real time (yes, really). But how many takes did it take? 76 or 156?

c) How many cars were destroyed in the making of *The Blues Brothers* (1980)? 104 or 203?

d) How many costumes were created for the 1963 film *Cleopatra*? 8,000 or 26,000?

e) Who is taller, Kevin Hart or Tom Cruise?

2. ONE OF OUR ______ IS MISSING!

Just fill in the missing word – there's always a theme, and this time it's... days of the week.

a) *The Long Good* ________ (1980)

b) *Mr.* ________ *Night* (1992)

c) *Stormy* ________ (1988)

d) *Big* ________ (1978)

e) *Any Given* ________ (1999)

ROUND 3

1. THE LAST WORD

Here are five pairs of films where the title ends with the same word. I will give you that word, one actor from the film and the years they were released. Name both films – a point for each.

a) The word is "Run". Film one was released in 1998 starring Franka Potente. Film two was released in 2000 starring Julia Sawalha (voice performance).

b) The word is "Girl". Film one was released in 2015 starring Eddie Redmayne. Film two was released in 1991 starring Anna Chlumsky.

c) The word is "List". Film one was released in 2007 starring Jack Nicholson. Film two was released in 2011 starring Neil Maskell.

d) The word is "Blood". Film one was released in 2007 starring Daniel Day-Lewis. Film two was released in 1973 starring Vincent Price.

e) The word is "Boys". Film one was released in 1987 starring Jason Patric. Film two was released in 2006 starring Richard Griffiths.

2. THE ODD COUPLE

I'll describe an actor and a film character that share the same initials. A point for each you can name.

a) **Actor:** American actor born in 1950. Found early fame on TV in the US with *Saturday Night Live* (1977–1980) before switching to movie roles in *Caddyshack* (1980), *Stripes*

(1981), *Ghostbusters* (1984) and *Groundhog Day* (1993). Has since appeared in many films for Wes Anderson and was nominated for a Best Actor Oscar for *Lost in Translation* (2003). **Character:** The main protagonist from the *Taken* series of films (2008–2014) with "a very particular set of skills", portrayed by Liam Neeson.

b) **Actor:** American actor and director born in 1963. Starred opposite Jack Nicholson in *As Good as It Gets* (1997) and had a string of subsequent hits, including *Twister* (1996), *Cast Away* (2000) and *What Women Want* (2000). She made her directorial debut in 2007 with *Then She Found Me*. **Character:** "As far back as I can remember, I always wanted to be a gangster" – this character speaks this line to open the film *Goodfellas* (1990). Portrayed by Ray Liotta, we see the world of the mob through his eyes. The character was based on a real person – his life story taken from the book *Wiseguy* (1985) by Nicholas Pileggi.

c) **Actor:** American actor born in 1944. A character actor who became well known for tough guy roles (often with brief screen time) in the 1990s, including parts in *Desperado* (1995), *Heat* (1995), *From Dusk till Dawn* (1996) and *Con Air* (1997). He is perhaps best known for the character Isador "Machete" Cortez in the *Spy Kids* series (2001–2018) and two *Machete* features: *Machete* (2010) and *Machete Kills* (2013). **Character:** Portrayed by Vin Diesel in the *Fast & Furious* franchise (2001–present). The character is the patriarch of the street racers and plays a key part in each instalment.

d) **Actor:** American actor born in 1931. She made her breakthrough in the 1956 western *Gun the Man Down*, building on that with *Rio Bravo* (1959) in which she starred with John Wayne. Other films include the original *Ocean's 11* (1960), *The Killers* (1964), *Point Blank* (1967) and *Dressed to Kill* (1980). She also found fame on US TV in the *Police Woman* series (1974–1978). **Character:** In *The Shawshank*

Redemption (1994), a banker from Portland, Maine, arrives at Shawshank State Prison convicted of murdering his wife and her lover. The character, portrayed by Tim Robbins, insists that he is innocent. He is befriended by Ellis "Red" Redding, who is portrayed by Morgan Freeman.

e) **Actor:** American actor born in 1956. Possibly best known for two TV roles: the father on *Malcolm in the Middle* (2000–2006) and Walter White in *Breaking Bad* (2008–2013). This actor has had starring roles in films such as *Godzilla* (2014), *Trumbo* (2015), *Wakefield* (2016) and *Argylle* (2024). **Character:** The working-class boy from South Yorkshire who finds a kestrel and nurtures it – the bird providing the only real love and hope in the boy's difficult life. Played by David "Dai" Bradley in the film *Kes* (1969), which is directed by Ken Loach.

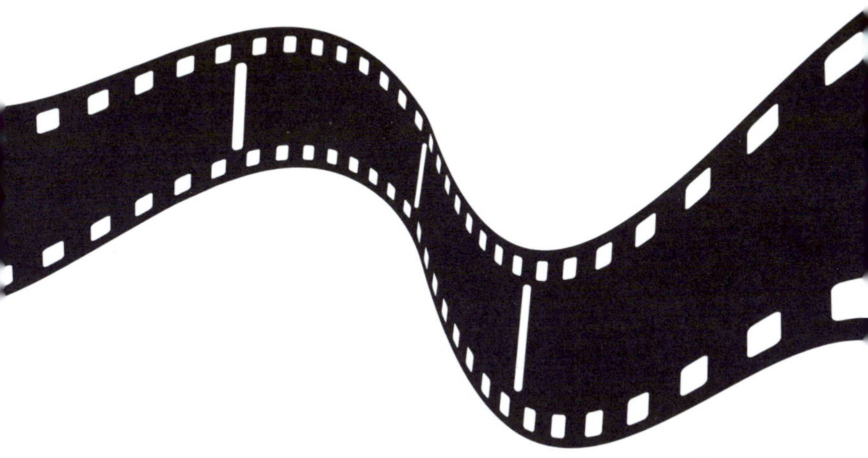

ROUND 4

1. BRAINSTORM

Complete the lists and spot the links – a point for each correct answer.

a) Which character connects John Wayne in 1969 and Jeff Bridges in 2010?

b) *Don't Look Now* (1973), *Casino Royale* (2006) and *Top Hat* (1935) all feature which Italian city as a primary location?

c) What word goes before the following to make three film titles: ________ *Things* (1998), ________ *Rose* (2018) and ____ *Orchid* (1989)?

d) What connects the final films in the original *Twilight* (2008–2012), *Harry Potter* (2001–2011) and *Hunger Games* (2012–2023) series?

e) What word connects the third *Blade* film (2004), Carrie-Anne Moss's character from the *Matrix* films (1999–2021) and two spaghetti westerns starring Terence Hill and Bud Spencer?

2. IT FOLLOWS

The first letter of each answer follows the first letter of the last. So, if the answer to c) is "Apple", the answer to d) will begin with "B". If you get to Z, go to A. Each question is worth one point.

a) The titular character of the 1989 comedy, written by Willy Russell and starring Pauline Collins, is Shirley who?

b) What location has been escaped to (twice), returned from, raced to and gone beyond in six Disney films from 1975 to 2009? The latest instalment featured Dwayne Johnson.

c) Which 1980 musical fantasy film starring Olivia Newton-John was the final film for Gene Kelly?

d) What word goes before ________ *Guns* (1988), ________ *Frankenstein* (1974) and ________ *Einstein* (1988) to complete the titles of those films?

e) What is the name of John Boorman's 1974 sci-fi flop (which has since become a cult favourite) starring Sean Connery in a (now notorious) red nappy?

ROUND 5

THE LAST PICTURE SHOW

Say what you see! Can you identify the films from these picture clues? Each picture is worth a point.

1

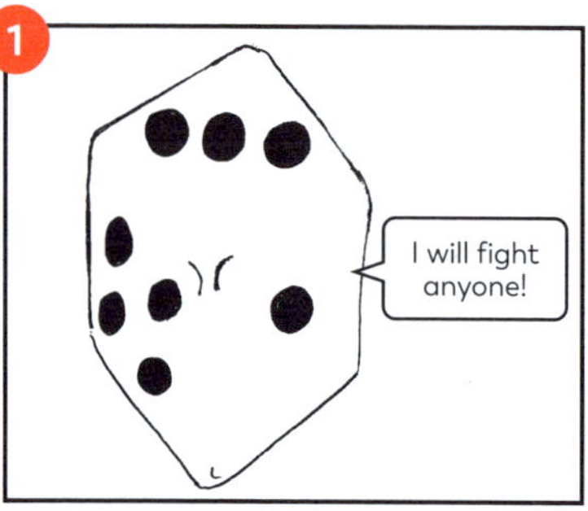

2

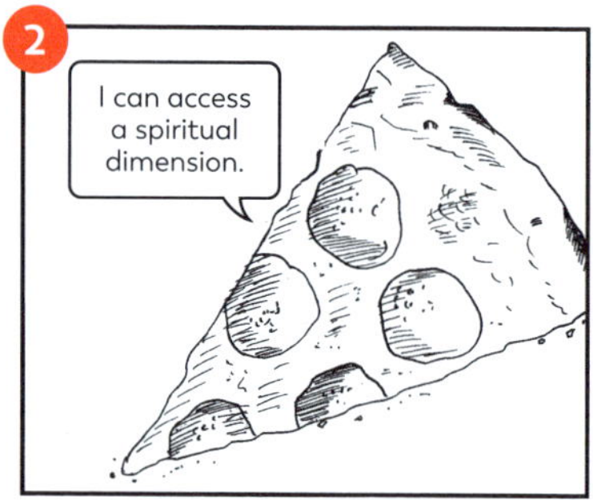

3

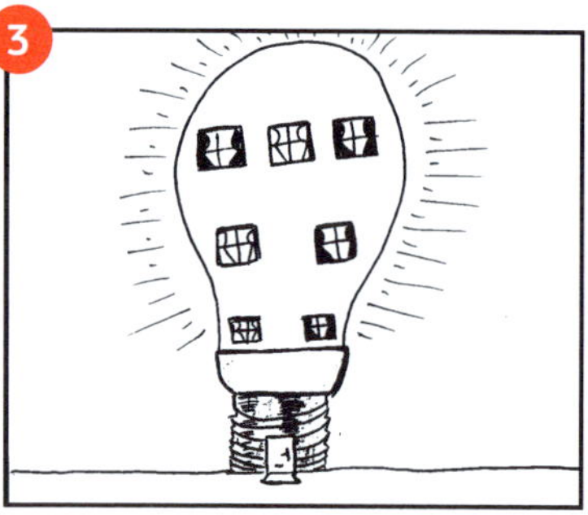

4

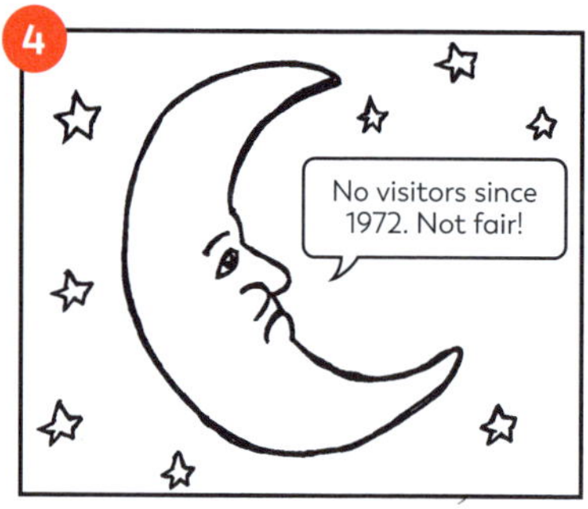

5

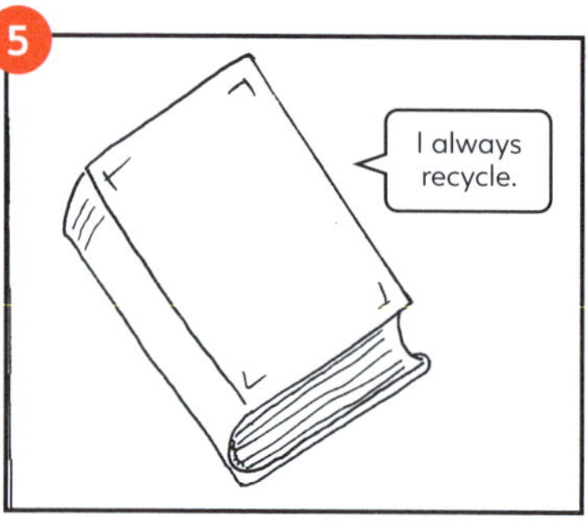

6

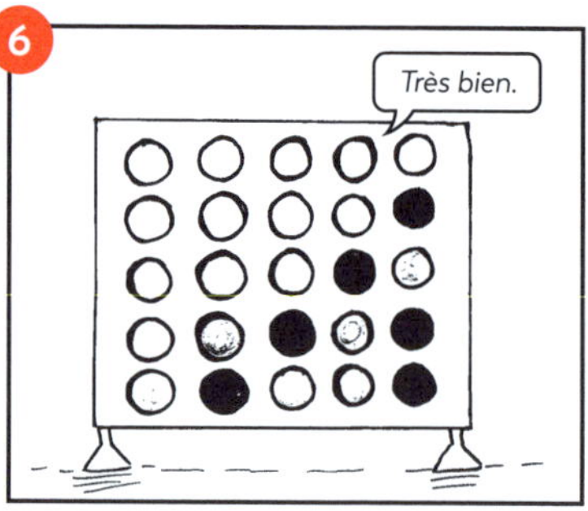

ANSWERS

ROUND 1

1. a) *Good Morning, Vietnam* (1987). *Goodfellas* was 1990 and *As Good as It Gets* was 1997.

2. Susan Sarandon

3. c) *When Harry Met Sally*

4. c) *The Birds*

5. b) *Prospero's Books* by Peter Greenaway (all three films are adaptations of Shakespeare plays).

6. *Live and Let Die* and *Tinker Tailor Soldier Spy*.

7. a) David Niven is the only actor (at time of writing) to win an Oscar on the same night as hosting the ceremony – for *Separate Tables* (1958).

> David Niven died in 1983. At his memorial service, there was a very large wreath from the porters at Heathrow airport. The card read, "To the finest gentleman who ever walked through these halls. He made a porter feel like a king."

8. b) Daniel Hillard/Mrs Doubtfire (*Mrs. Doubtfire*)

> Though Beatty didn't turn down the role of Butch Cassidy, he did turn down the role of the Sundance Kid. He also turned down *Superman* (1978) which I discovered when I wanted to use it as a red herring!

9. 1999

10. *Dirty Harry* (1971), *The Gauntlet* (1977), *Bronco Billy* (1980), *Firefox* (1982), *Honkytonk Man* (1982), *Sudden Impact* (1983), *Tightrope* (1984), *Pale Rider* (1985), *Heartbreak Ridge* (1986), *Bird* (1988), *The Rookie* (1990), *Unforgiven* (1992), *Absolute Power* (1997), *True Crime* (1999), *Space Cowboys* (2000), *Blood Work* (2002), *Mystic River* (2003), *Changeling* (2008), *Gran Torino* (2008), *Invictus* (2009), *Hereafter* (2010), *J. Edgar* (2011), *Jersey Boys* (2014), *American Sniper* (2014), *Sully* (2016), *The Mule* (2018), *Richard Jewell* (2019), *Cry Macho* (2021).

ROUND 2

1. a) Ryan Reynolds. He was born 23 October 1976; Gosling was born 12 November 1980.

1. b) 156 takes.

1. c) 104 cars.

1. d) 26,000 costumes (according to IMDb).

For a time, Elizabeth Taylor held the Guinness World Record for most costume changes in one film (65).

1. e) Tom Cruise – he is 5ft 7, Kevin Hart is 5ft 5.

2. a) *Friday*

2. b) *Saturday*

2. c) *Monday*

2. d) *Wednesday*

2. e) *Sunday*

ROUND 3

1. a) *Run Lola Run* and *Chicken Run.*

1. b) *The Danish Girl* and *My Girl.*

1. c) *The Bucket List* and *Kill List.*

1. d) *There Will Be Blood* and *Theatre of Blood.*

1. e) *The Lost Boys* and *The History Boys.*

2. a) Bill Murray and Bryan Mills.

2. b) Helen Hunt and Henry Hill.

2. c) Danny Trejo and Dominic Toretto.

2. d) Angie Dickinson and Andy Dufresne.

2. e) Bryan Cranston and Billy Casper.

ROUND 4

1. a) Reuben J. "Rooster" Cogburn (in *True Grit*).

1. b) Venice

1. c) "Wild". *Wild Things, Wild Rose* and *Wild Orchid.*

1. d) They all split the final book in the series into two films – *The Twilight Saga: Breaking Dawn – Part 1* (2011) and *Part 2* (2012), *Harry Potter and the Deathly Hallows Part 1* (2010) and *Part 2* (2011) and *The Hunger Games: Mockingjay Part 1* (2014) and *Part 2* (2015).

1. e) "Trinity". The third *Blade* film is called *Blade: Trinity* (2004) and the two spaghetti westerns are called *They Call Me Trinity* (1970) and *Trinity Is Still My Name* (1971).

2. a) Valentine

2. b) Witch Mountain. *Escape to Witch Mountain* (1975 and 1995), *Return from Witch Mountain* (1978), *Beyond Witch Mountain* (1982), *Race to Witch Mountain* (2009).

2. c) *Xanadu*

2. d) "Young". *Young Guns*, *Young Frankenstein* and *Young Einstein*.

The star of *Young Einstein* (1988) was called Yahoo Serious (born Greg Pead), and in the year 2000 he sued the search engine Yahoo for trademark infringement. The case was thrown out.

2. e) *Zardoz*

ROUND 5

1. *Die Hard* (1988)
2. *Mystic Pizza* (1988)
3. *The Lighthouse* (2019)
4. *Bitter Moon* (1992)
5. *Green Book* (2018)
6. *The French Connection* (1971)

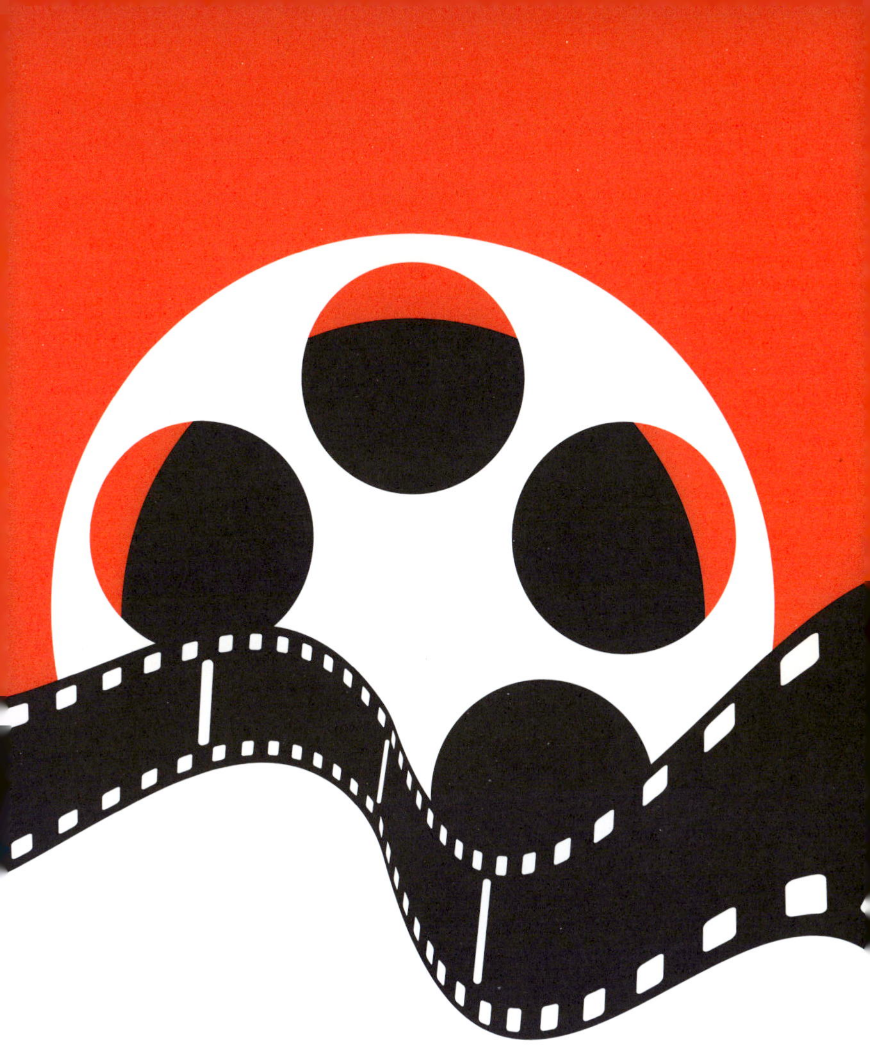

QUIZ 12

ROUND 1

STARTER FOR 10

Ten questions to begin!

1. THE FIRST QUESTION

Which of these "Red" films was released first?

a) *The Hunt for Red October*

b) *Red Sonja*

c) *Red Dragon*

2. THE ANAGRAM

Unscramble the actor's name: JOCK SAUNA SMELL

3. FILM QUOTE

What film is the following quote from?

"Oh yeah? Who's the only one here who knows secret ninja moves from the government?"

a) *Napoleon Dynamite* (2004)

b) *Austin Powers: International Man of Mystery* (1997)

c) *Iron Man* (2008)

d) *Skyfall* (2012)

4. THUMBS DOWN

What film is this the one-star review of?

"Allison's makeover was terrible: she definitely looked much better before than after; I guess that's the 80s for ya!"

a) *Grease* (1978)

b) *The Breakfast Club* (1985)

c) *Clueless* (1995)

5. ODD ONE OUT

Which of these films was not directed by Alfred Hitchcock? Bonus point if you know who it was directed by.

a) *The Lady Vanishes* (1938)

b) *Woman of the Year* (1942)

c) *The Man Who Knew Too Much* (1956)

6. RHYMING FILMS

I'll give you the initials of two films whose titles rhyme with each other. I'll also give you one of the stars and the years they were released, just name the films for a point each.

S, Daryl Hannah (1984) and W, Miles Teller (2014).

7. CELLULOID OR CELLULIED?

Which of the following is true about *Police Academy* (1984) star Steve Guttenberg?

a) Steve Guttenberg's memoir from 2012 is called *More than Mahoney.*

b) Steve Guttenberg's memoir from 2012 is called *Blame the Stonecutters.*

c) Steve Guttenberg's memoir from 2012 is called *The Guttenberg Bible.*

8. WHAT MIGHT HAVE BEEN

Which of these roles did Leonardo DiCaprio turn down?

a) Captain Jack Sparrow (*Pirates of the Caribbean: The Curse of the Black Pearl* – 2003)

b) Dirk Diggler (*Boogie Nights* – 1997)

c) The Joker (*The Dark Knight* – 2008)

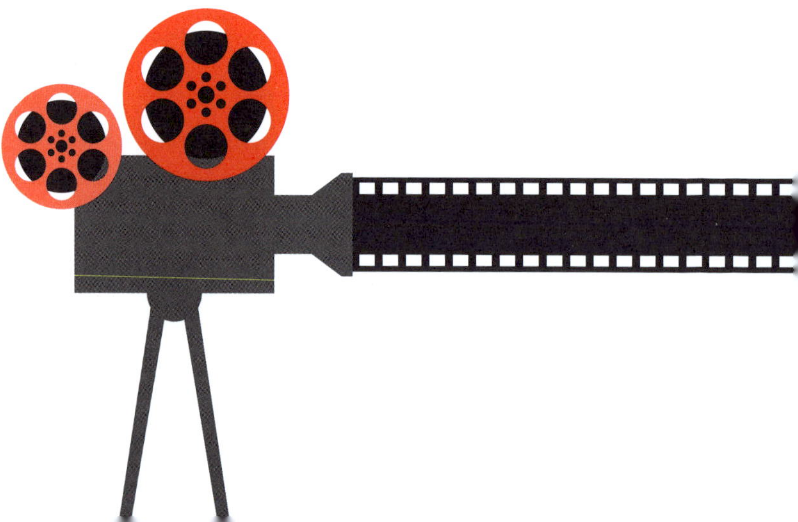

9. WHAT YEAR?

In what year did the following things happen?

Films released this year include: *Sunset Boulevard, All About Eve, Cinderella, Rashomon, Father of the Bride* (the original) and *Rio Grande*. Walt Disney Studios releases its first completely live action film, *Treasure Island. All the King's Men* wins the Best Picture Oscar. Julie Walters, Neil Jordan, William H. Macy, Robbie Coltrane, John Landis, Bill Murray and Ed Harris are born. Al Jolson passes away. Marlon Brando makes his film debut in *The Men*. The hit film of the year is *King Solomon's Mines* starring Deborah Kerr and Stewart Granger. But what was the year?

10. GIVE ME FIVE

A chance for five points! Name five Bafta Rising Star winners (up to 2024). There are 19 possible answers.

ROUND 2

1. SPY HARD

Are these female characters in *James Bond* films or types of melon?

a) Solitaire

b) Autumn Sweet

c) Mini Love

d) Bonita

e) Honey Ryder

2. ONE OF OUR ______ IS MISSING!

Just fill in the missing word – there's always a theme, and this time it's... ranks in the military.

a) ________ *Corelli's Mandolin* (2001)

b) *A ________ Function* (1984)

c) ________ *York* (1941)

d) ________ *League* (1989)

e) *Bad ________* (1992)

ROUND 3

1. TRUE STORIES

These questions are about biopics. I will tell you the subject, the actor who played them and the year of release. Just name the film.

a) John Nash played by Russell Crowe in 2001.

b) Martin Luther King Jr played by David Oyelowo in 2014.

c) Edith Piaf played by Marion Cotillard in 2007.

d) Andy Kaufman played by Jim Carrey in 1999.

e) Johnny Cash played by Joaquin Phoenix in 2005.

2. THE ODD COUPLE II

This time I'll describe a film character and a director that share the same initials. A point for each you can name.

a) **Character:** This character from *A Streetcar Named Desire* (1947) by Tennessee Williams has been portrayed many times on screen, though the most well-known performance is from Marlon Brando in the film of the same name in 1951. The character is a factory-parts salesman living in New Orleans with his wife, Stella, whose lives are disrupted when her sister, Blanche DuBois, moves in. **Director:** American director born in 1928. Widely regarded as one of the greatest directors of all time. He was notorious for his perfectionism and his insistence on a huge number of takes. He directed only 13 films over a 47-year period. They include this run of films: *Dr. Strangelove* (1964), *2001: A Space Odyssey* (1968), *A*

Clockwork Orange (1971), *Barry Lyndon* (1975), *The Shining* (1980) and *Full Metal Jacket* (1987).

b) Character: The titular character of two films (1992 and 1993), written and performed by Mike Myers, he is a heavy-metal-obsessed cable-access-show host who lives with his parents. His ever-present sidekick (Garth) is portrayed by Dana Carvey. The character is known for his catchphrases such as "Schwing!" and "Party on!" **Director:** American director born in 1939. Best known as a horror director, his first film was *The Last House on the Left* (1972), and his second was *The Hills Have Eyes* (1977). In 1984, he wrote and directed the first in the Freddy Krueger series, *A Nightmare on Elm Street*. He also directed the first four *Scream* movies (1996–2011).

c) Character: The young boy who wishes to be "Big" in the 1988 film. Played by Tom Hanks, he gets his wish after visiting a local fair and making the request to an (unplugged) fortune teller machine called Zoltar. **Director:** English director, screenwriter and producer born in 1933. He has received five Academy Awards nominations for his work, including: *Point Blank* (1967), *Deliverance* (1972), *Excalibur* (1981) and *Hope and Glory* (1987). In 2024, at the age of 91, he began work on a new project – the animated film *The Honey Wars*.

d) Character: This character was created by author Helen Fielding and portrayed by Renée Zellweger. By 2025, she will have appeared in four films (that all feature her name). The films follow the character's trials and tribulations with her love interests (Colin Firth and Hugh Grant). **Director:** American director, writer and producer born in 1979. He won Best Picture and Best Adapted Screenplay for his 2016 film *Moonlight* and was nominated for his adapted screenplay of *If Beale Street Could Talk* (2018). In 2024, he directed the musical *Mufasa: The Lion King*.

e) **Character:** Leonardo DiCaprio's character from *Titanic* (1997) who falls in love with a passenger from a higher deck (and social class), Rose DeWitt Bukater, played by Kate Winslet. **Director:** American director born in 1946. Probably best known for his films *Gremlins* (1984) and *Gremlins 2: The New Batch* (1990). His other work includes *The 'Burbs* (1989), *Small Soldiers* (1998) and early horror outings *Piranha* (1978) and *The Howling* (1981).

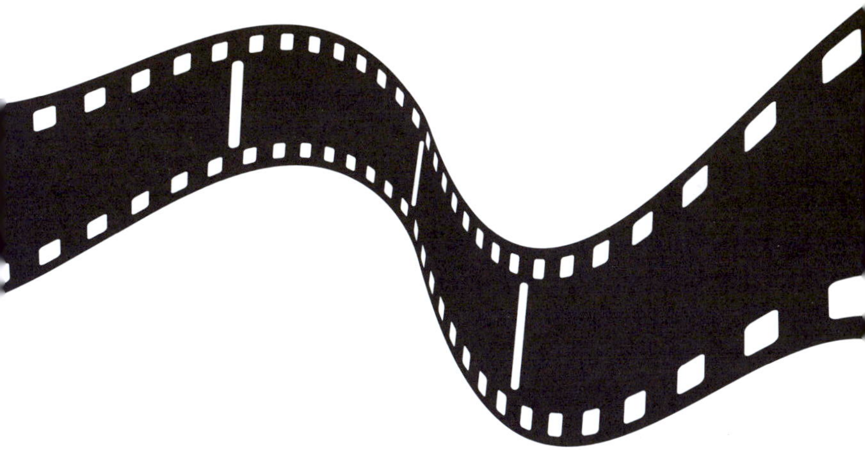

ROUND 4

1. BRAINSTORM

Complete the lists and spot the links – a point for each correct answer.

a) What word goes before ________ *Fiction* (2023), ________ *Hustle* (2013) and ________ *Gangster* (2007) to complete these film titles?

b) What comes next in this list: *Reloaded* (2003), *Revolutions* (2003)...?

c) James Earl Jones, Sebastian Shaw and David Prowse all contribute to the same character in a single film – but which character? And for a bonus point, which film?

d) What did Emma Stone, Jodie Foster, Bette Davis and Hilary Swank all do before they were 35 that (by 2024) no male actor had ever done?

e) What number connects a 1995 film by Terry Gilliam and starring Bruce Willis, a 1957 film by Sydney Lumet starring Henry Fonda and a 2013 film by Steve McQueen starring Chiwetel Ejiofor?

2. IT FOLLOWS

The first letter of each answer follows the first letter of the last. So, if the answer to c) is "Apple", the answer to d) will begin with "B". If you get to Z, go to A. Each question is worth one point.

a) What is the name of the lead protagonist, played by Jack Nicholson, in *Chinatown* (1974)?

b) Which actor is the only female to appear on the classic white-and-orange *Trainspotting* (1996) poster?

c) What 1993 horror comedy, starring Warwick Davis and Jennifer Aniston, has, at time of writing, produced seven sequels?

d) What is the name of Rocky Balboa's (Sylvester Stallone) head trainer, played by Burgess Meredith, in the first three *Rocky* films (1976–1982)?

e) What is the name of the only film (as of 2024) directed by Gary Oldman? It stars Ray Winstone and Kathy Burke.

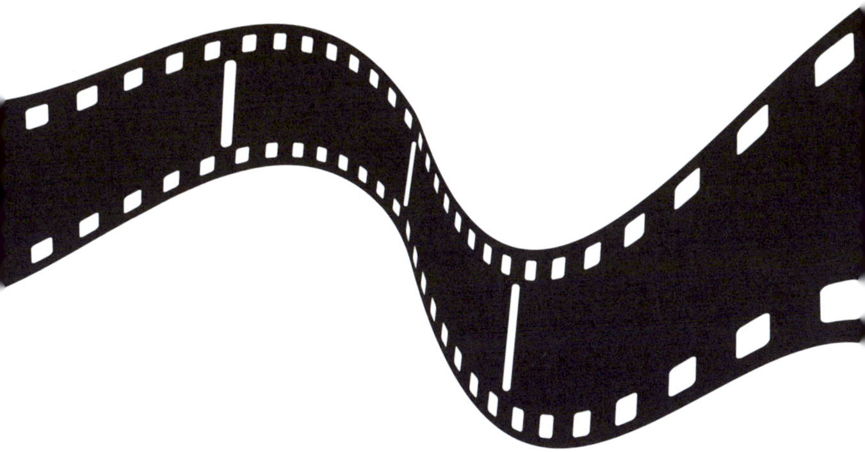

ROUND 5

THE LAST PICTURE SHOW

Say what you see! Can you identify the films from these picture clues? Each picture is worth a point.

1

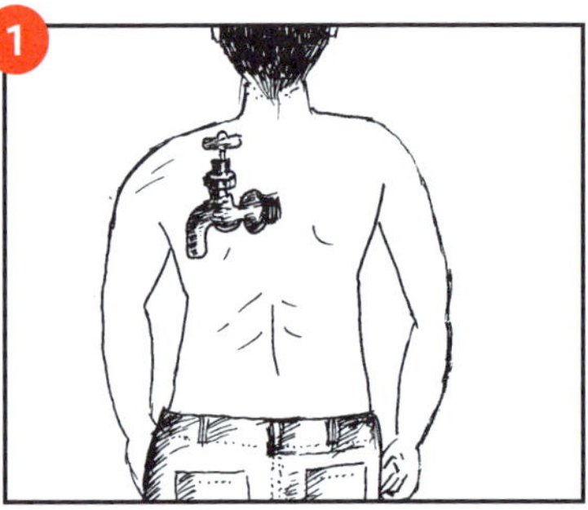

2

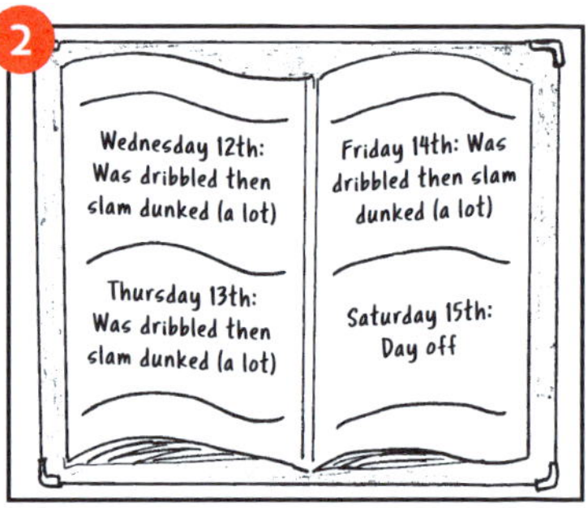

3

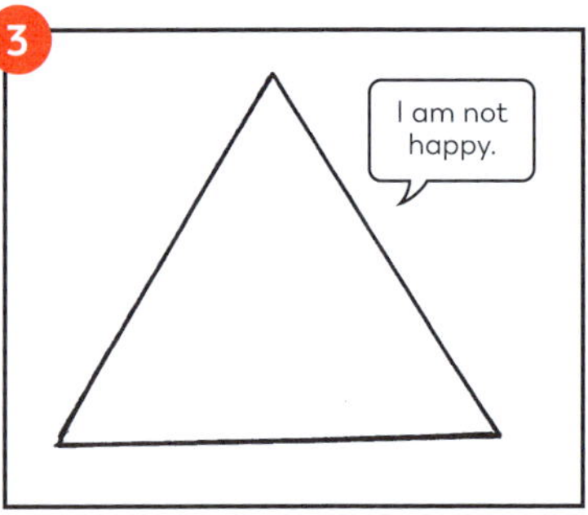

4

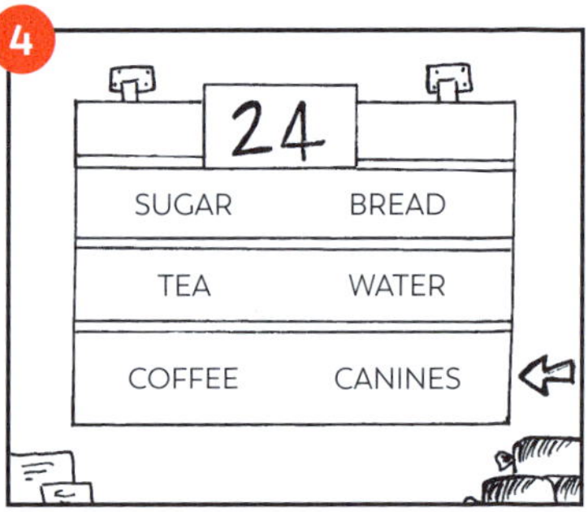

5

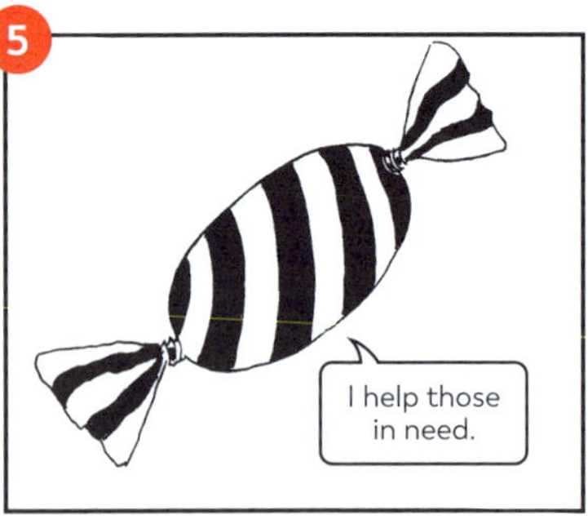

6

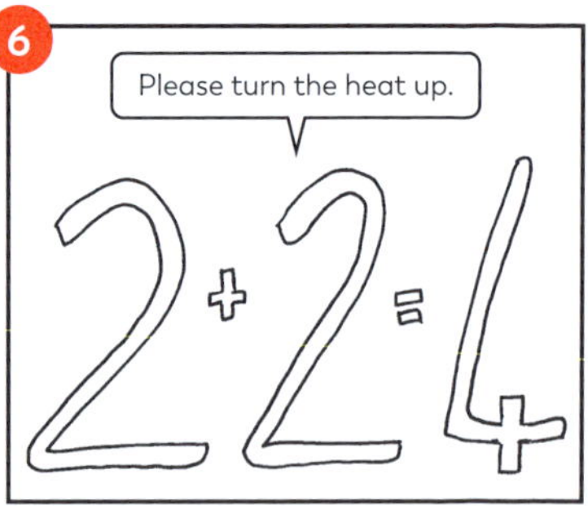

ANSWERS

ROUND 1

1. b) *Red Sonja* (1985). *The Hunt for Red October* was 1990 and *Red Dragon* was 2002.

2. Samuel L. Jackson

3. a) *Napoleon Dynamite*

4. b) *The Breakfast Club*

5. b) *Woman of the Year* by George Stevens.

6. *Splash* and *Whiplash*.

7. c) Steve Guttenberg's memoir from 2012 is called *The Guttenberg Bible*.

Woody Harrelson begins his review, "*The Guttenberg Bible* is better than the original! More compelling reading anyway..."

8. b) Dirk Diggler (*Boogie Nights*)

Rather than playing Dirk Diggler, DiCaprio instead made *Titanic* (1997).

9. 1950

10. James McAvoy, Eva Green, Shia LaBeouf, Noel Clarke, Kristen Stewart, Tom Hardy, Adam Deacon, Juno Temple, Will Poulter, Jack O'Connell, John Boyega, Tom Holland, Daniel Kaluuya, Letitia Wright, Michael Ward, Bukky Bakray, Lashana Lynch, Emma Mackey, Mia McKenna-Bruce.

ROUND 2

1. a) Bond girl (Jane Seymour in *Live and Let Die* – 1973).

1. b) Melon

1. c) Melon

1. d) Bond girl (Nadja Regin in *Goldfinger* – 1964).

1. e) Bond girl (Ursula Andress in *Dr. No* – 1962).

2. a) *Captain*

2. b) *Private*

2. c) *Sergeant*

2. d) *Major*

2. e) *Lieutenant*

ROUND 3

1. a) *A Beautiful Mind*

1. b) *Selma*

1. c) *La Vie En Rose*

Marion Cotillard is a fan of Leeds United Football Club; she began to follow the team when her countryman Eric Cantona played for them in the 1990s.

1. d) *Man on the Moon*

1. e) *Walk the Line*

2. a) Stanley Kowalski and Stanley Kubrick.

2. b) Wayne Campbell and Wes Craven.

2. c) Josh Baskin and John Boorman.

2. d) Bridget Jones and Barry Jenkins.

2. e) Jack Dawson and Joe Dante.

ROUND 4

1. a) "American". *American Fiction*, *American Hustle* and *American Gangster.*

Jeffrey Wright and Sterling K. Brown were both Oscar nominated for *American Fiction* (2023), marking the first time two black actors have been nominated in the lead and supporting categories for the same film.

1. b) *Resurrections* (2021). These are the subtitles of *The Matrix* sequels (2–4) in chronological order.

1. c) Darth Vader. *Star Wars: Episode VI – Return of the Jedi* (1983). Jones is the voice, Prowse is in the suit and Shaw is his face when they lift the mask off.

Though Shaw has been digitally replaced by Hayden Christensen in later home media versions.

d) They all won two Oscars by the age of 35. Others to do the same are Meryl Streep, Luise Rainer, Olivia de Havilland and Elizabeth Taylor.

e) 12. *12 Monkeys*, *12 Angry Men* and *12 Years a Slave.*

2. a) J. J. "Jake" Gittes

2. b) Kelly Macdonald

2. c) *Leprechaun* (1993)

> Subtitles in the series include *Leprechaun 4: In Space* (1996) and *Leprechaun in the Hood* (2000).

2. d) Mickey (Goldmill)

2. e) *Nil by Mouth* (1997)

ROUND 5

1. *This Is Spinal Tap* (1984)
2. *The Basketball Diaries* (1995)
3. *Triangle of Sadness* (2022)
4. *Isle of Dogs* (2018)
5. *Sweet Charity* (1969)
6. *Some Like It Hot* (1959)

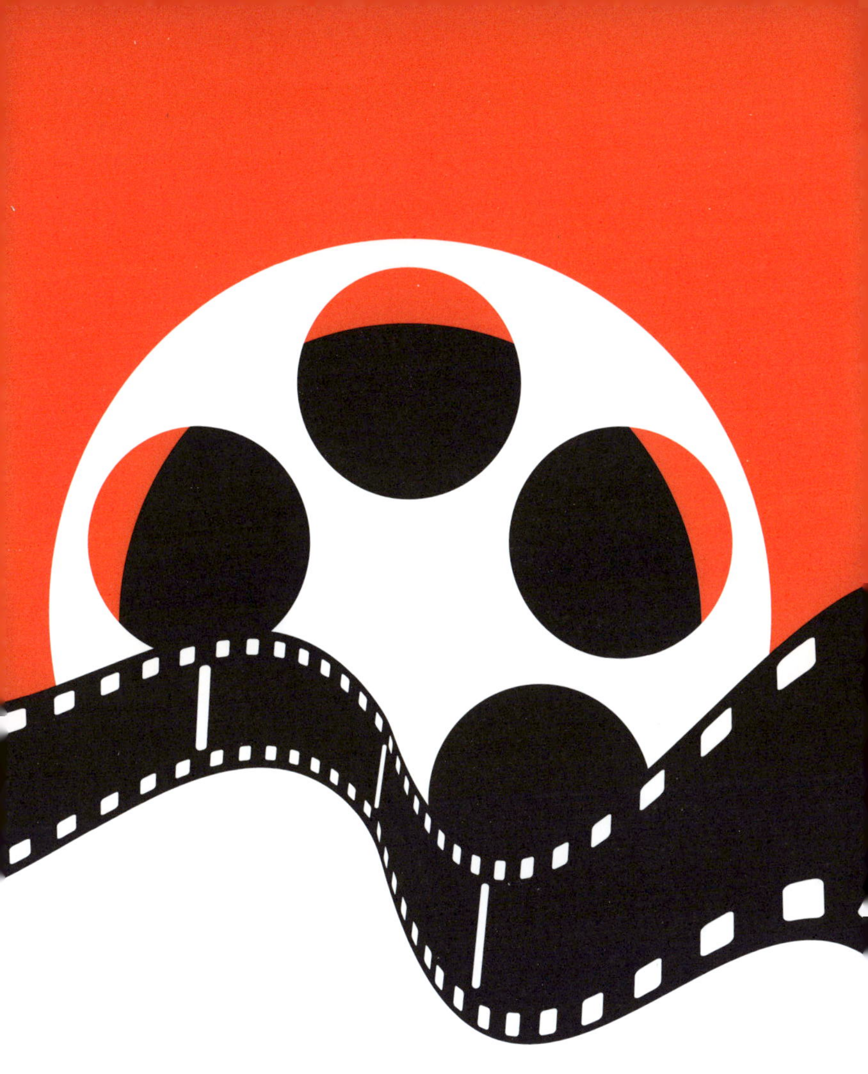

QUIZ 13

ROUND 1

STARTER FOR 10

Ten questions to begin!

1. THE FIRST QUESTION

Which of these actors called Julie was born first?

a) Julie Christie

b) Julie Walters

c) Julie Andrews

2. THE ANAGRAM

Unscramble the actor's name: STARKEST WINTER

3. FILM QUOTE

What film is the following quote from?

"You never really understand a person until you consider things from his point of view... Until you climb inside of his skin and walk around in it."

a) *12 Angry Men* (1957)

b) *To Kill a Mockingbird* (1962)

c) *Philadelphia* (1993)

d) *The Silence of the Lambs* (1991)

4. THUMBS DOWN

What film is this the one-star review of?

"I have seen ALL the *Marvel* films and loved most of them. But this, well... Wow, and not a good wow either. This is just a bad film from the off, no real coherent story line, bunch of characters no one cares about all shoved into an unnecessary film."

a) *The Eternals* (2021)

b) *Avengers: Endgame* (2019)

c) *Justice League* (2017)

5. ODD ONE OUT

Which of these films was not directed by Mel Brooks? Bonus point if you know who it was directed by.

a) *Blazing Saddles* (1974)

b) *High Anxiety* (1977)

c) *Airplane!* (1980)

6. RHYMING FILMS

I'll give you the initials of two films whose titles rhyme with each other. I'll also give you one of the stars and the years they were released, just name the films for a point each.

OTT, Gene Kelly (1949) and WD, John Hurt (voice performance) (1978).

7. CELLULOID OR CELLULIED?

Which of the following is true about Daniel Day-Lewis?

In the five-year period Daniel Day-Lewis first retired from acting (beginning in 1996), he spent a long time:

a) Learning to make shoes.

b) Writing a still-unpublished novel.

c) Sailing solo around the world.

8. WHAT MIGHT HAVE BEEN

Which of these roles did Denzel Washington turn down?

a) Michael Clayton (2007)

b) Andy Dufresne (*The Shawshank Redemption* – 1994)

c) John Wick (2014)

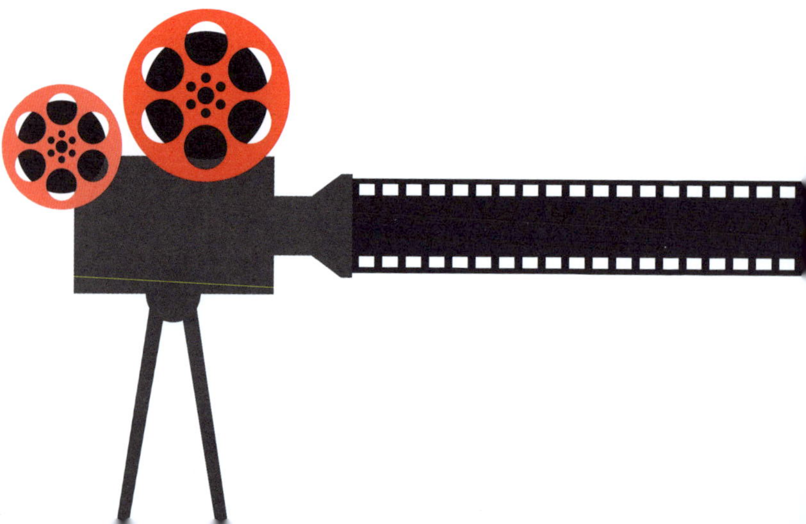

9. WHAT YEAR?

In what year did the following things happen?

Films released this year include: *Blue Velvet*, *Ferris Bueller's Day Off*, *Aliens*, *Platoon*, *Hannah and Her Sisters*, *Top Gun*, *Stand by Me*, *Crocodile Dundee*, *Short Circuit*, *The Fly* and *Labyrinth*. Pixar studios are founded by Edwin Catmull and Alvy Ray Smith. Timothy Dalton is announced as the next actor to play James Bond. Gemma Arterton (who will appear in the later Bond film *Quantum of Solace* – 2008) is born, as are Jamie Bell, Lady Gaga and Robert Pattinson. James Cagney, Otto Preminger, Cary Grant, Donna Reed and Andrei Tarkovsky pass away. Disney have a hit with *The Great Mouse Detective* – which has been credited for saving Disney after the box office disaster of *The Black Cauldron* (1985). But what was the year?

10. GIVE ME FIVE

A chance for five points! Name five films that Audrey Hepburn appeared in. There are 27 possible answers.

ROUND 2

1. LINK

I will give you a word that ends one film title and begins another, plus the star and the year – name both for two points.

a) The link is "Down". Film one – Josh Hartnett (2001). Film two – Tom Waits (1986).

b) The link is "Time". Film one – Christopher Reeve (1980). Film two – David Rappaport (1981).

c) The link is "Black". Film one – Brad Pitt (1998). Film two – Deborah Kerr (1947).

d) The link is "Heaven". Film one – Steve Martin (1990). Film two – Warren Beatty (1978).

e) The link is "Bird". Film one – Saoirse Ronan (2017). Film two – Goldie Hawn (1990).

2. ONE OF OUR ________ IS MISSING!

Just fill in the missing word – there's always a theme, and this time it's... genres of music.

a) ________ *of Gucci* (2021)

b) *Brighton* ________ (1948)

c) *Biloxi* ________ 1988

d) *The Last Days of* ________ (1998)

e) *The Big* ________ (1958)

ROUND 3

1. THE SINGER, NOT THE SONG

Which musicians made a rare acting appearance in the films below? A point for each you know. I will give you the title of the film and the musician's initials.

a) *8 Mile* (2002) E.

b) *Dancer in the Dark* (2000) B.

c) *The Fastest Guitar Alive* (1967) R. O.

d) *Parting Shots* (1999) C. R.

e) *Glitter* (2001) M. C.

2. THE ODD COUPLE

I'll describe an actor and a film character that share the same initials. A point for each you can name.

a) **Actor:** Australian actor born in 1990. Her breakthrough role was in *The Wolf of Wall Street* (2013) playing Naomi Lapaglia. In a series of star roles, she is perhaps best known for *Barbie* (2023), in the titular role, or as Harley Quinn in the DC Extended Universe. She is also a producer who co-founded LuckyChap Entertainment with her husband Tom Ackerley in 2014. **Character:** Portrayed by Karen Allen, this character has appeared as the love interest of Indiana Jones in three films: *Indiana Jones and the Raiders of the Lost Ark* (1981), *Indiana Jones and the Kingdom of the Crystal Skull* (2008) and *Indiana Jones and the Dial of Destiny* (2023). She is the mother of their child, Mutt Williams (Shia LaBeouf).

b) **Actor:** American actor born in 1940. Best known for three roles: Elaine Robinson in *The Graduate* (1967), Etta Place in *Butch Cassidy and the Sundance Kid* (1969) and Joanna Eberhart in *The Stepford Wives* (1975). A notable later role was Dr Lilian Thurman in *Donnie Darko* (2001). **Character:** The son of Han Solo and Princess Leia Organa, and trained as a Jedi Knight by Luke Skywalker, he turns to the dark side and changes his name from Ben Solo to the answer of this question. Portrayed by Adam Driver in the *Star Wars* sequel trilogy (2015–2019).

c) **Actor:** American actor born in 1921. Born into extreme poverty, he became famous as a tough guy in films such as *The Magnificent Seven* (1960 – in which he played Bernardo O'Reilly), *Once Upon a Time in the West* (1968) and *The Dirty Dozen* (1967). In 1974, he played Paul Kersey in *Death Wish*, a character he would play in four more films. The fifth film, *Death Wish V: The Face of Death* (1994), marked his final screen appearance. **Character:** The titular character of a 1965 western comedy, portrayed by Jane Fonda. The character becomes an outlaw to avenge her murdered father. Lee Marvin also starred in it, winning the Best Actor Academy Award for playing the drunken gunslinger Kid Shelleen.

d) **Actor:** American-born actor (1983) who moved to Britain aged three. First came to prominence with two roles in 2010: Eduardo Saverin in *The Social Network* and Tommy D in *Never Let Me Go*, before finding international fame as Peter Parker/Spider-Man in *The Amazing Spider-Man* (2012) and *The Amazing Spider-Man 2* (2014) – he also appeared in *Spider-Man: No Way Home* (2021). **Character:** The main protagonist of the 1964 *James Bond* movie that uses his surname as its title. Portrayed by Gert Fröbe, the character wishes to raid Fort Knox with the aid of his henchman, Oddjob.

e) **Actor:** American actor born in 1933. Best known for his comedy roles in Mel Brooks' films, such as *The Producers* (1967), *Young Frankenstein* and *Blazing Saddles* (both 1974) and for his partnership with Richard Pryor in four films. He is also well remembered for his portrayal of Willy Wonka in *Willy Wonka and the Chocolate Factory* (1971). **Character:** An ambitious journalist who is the only character to appear in every film in the *Scream* series (1996–2023) so far. Portrayed by Courteney Cox.

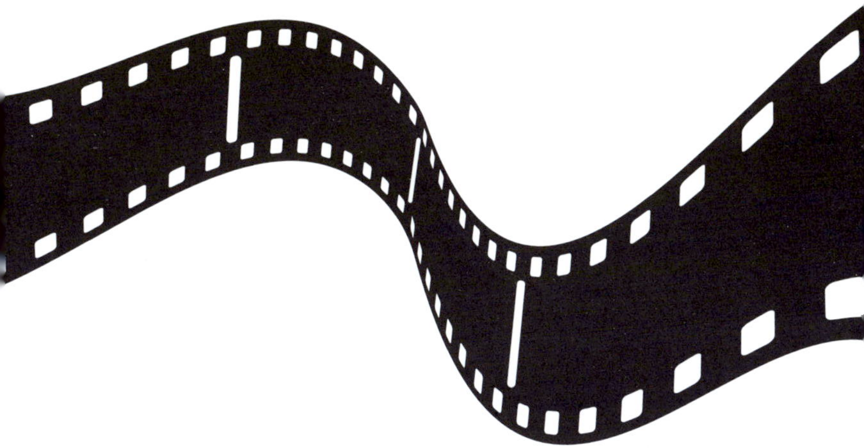

ROUND 4

1. BRAINSTORM

Complete the lists and spot the links – a point for each correct answer.

a) In the 2007 film *I'm Not There*, six actors represent aspects of Bob Dylan's life. They are Marcus Carl Franklin, Ben Whishaw, Christian Bale, Richard Gere, Heath Ledger and which other?

b) What title is shared by a 1974 film starring David Essex as troubled singer, Jim MacLaine, a 2007 fantasy starring Claire Danes and Charlie Cox, and a 2020 biopic of David Bowie starring Johnny Flynn?

c) What completes this list? *It Happened One Night* (1934), *One Flew Over the Cuckoo's Nest* (1975) and?

d) Which series of films has these subtitles: *Evolution* (2006), *Rise of the Lycans* (2009), *Awakening* (2012) and *Blood Wars* (2016)?

e) Which Shakespearean role connects Laurence Olivier in 1955 and Ian McKellen in 1995?

2. IT FOLLOWS

The first letter of each answer follows the first letter of the last. So, if the answer to c) is "Apple", the answer to d) will begin with "B". If you get to Z, go to A. Each question is worth one point.

a) In 2024, it was announced that a sequel was in development to which 1998 fantasy film starring Nicole Kidman and Sandra Bullock as sisters Sally and Gillian Owens?

b) In *Total Recall* (1990), Arnold Schwarzenegger's character is called Douglas what?

c) *Three Coins in the Fountain* (1954), *Bicycle Thieves* (1948) *Angels and Demons* (2009) and *The Belly of an Architect* (1987) are all set predominantly in which city?

d) What is the name of the red crab in *The Little Mermaid* (1989)?

e) Which singer portrayed the Acid Queen in *Tommy* (1975), Aunty Entity in *Mad Max Beyond Thunderdome* (1985) and the Mayor in *Last Action Hero* (1993)?

ROUND 5

THE LAST PICTURE SHOW

Say what you see! Can you identify the films from these picture clues? Each picture is worth a point.

1

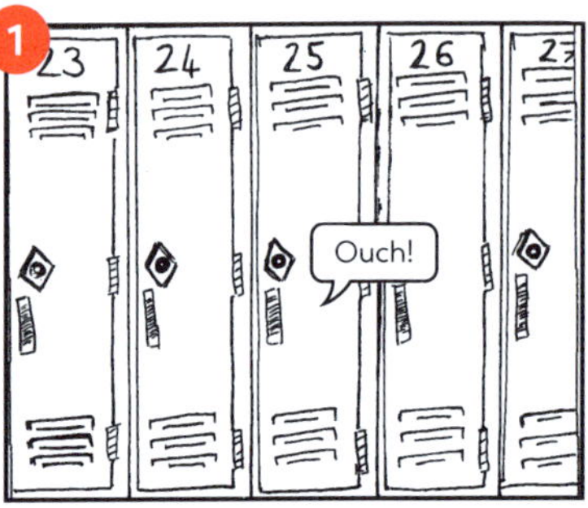

2

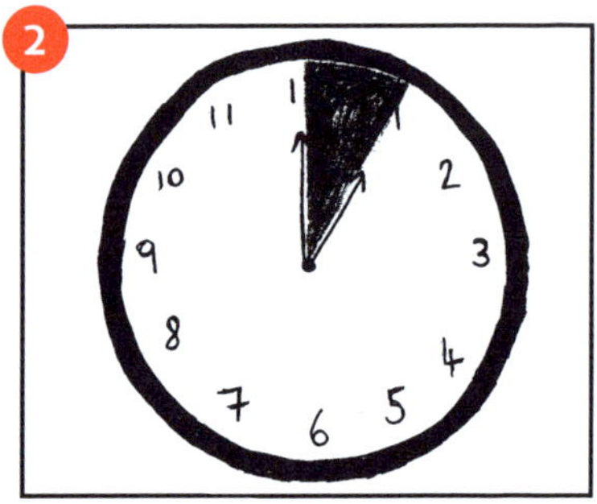

3

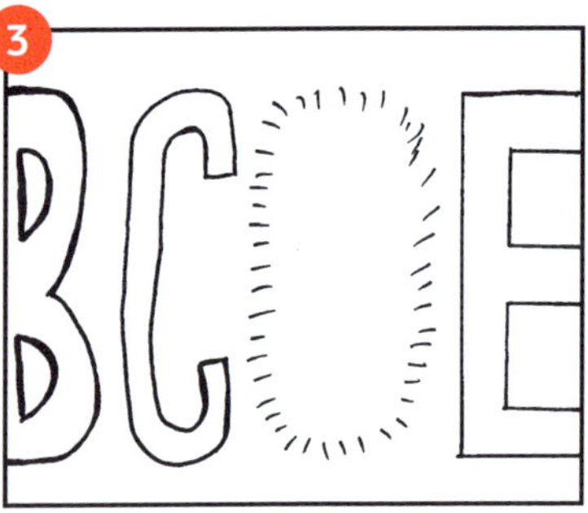

4

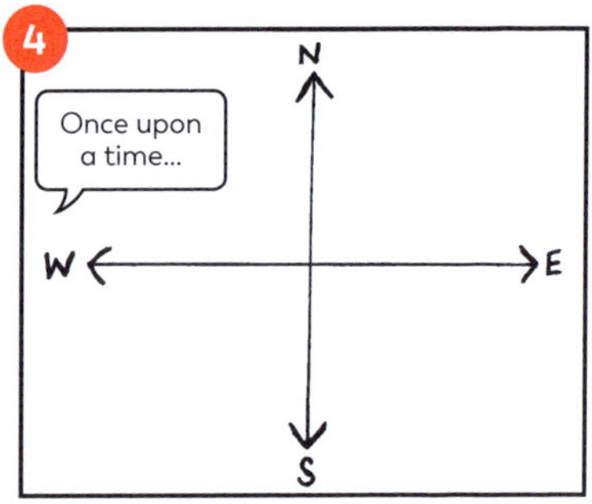

5

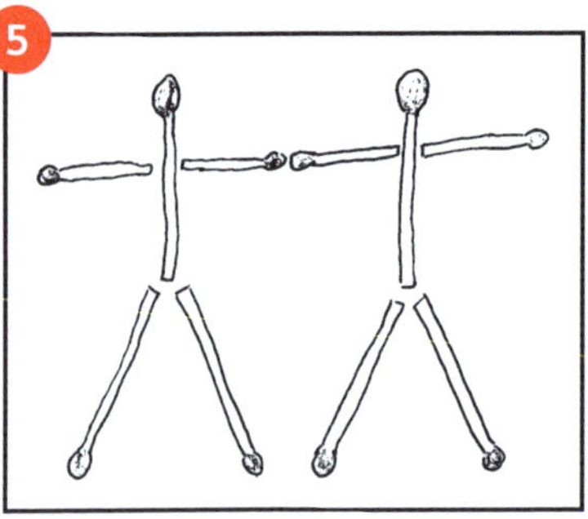

6

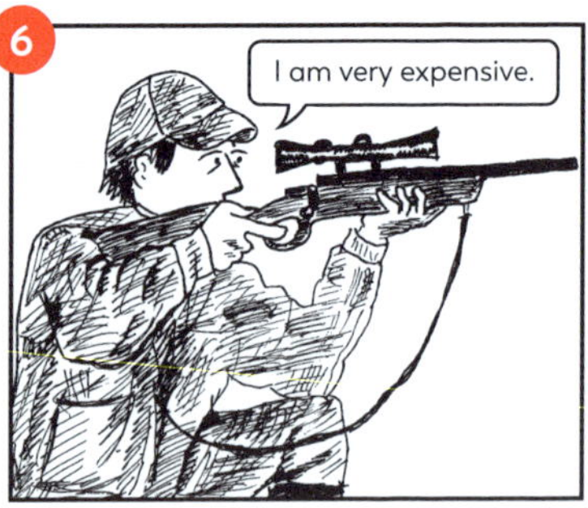

ANSWERS

ROUND 1

1. c) Julie Andrews (1935). Julie Christie was born in 1940 and Julie Walters in 1950.

2. Kristen Stewart

3. b) *To Kill a Mockingbird*

4. a) *The Eternals*

5. c) *Airplane!* by Jim Abrahams, David Zucker and Jerry Zucker.

Robert Hays, who played Ted Striker, the ex-pilot who saves the day, could actually fly a plane. He got his licence a few years before filming *Airplane!* to surprise his father, who had flown in the Marines.

6. *On the Town* and *Watership Down*.

7. a) Learning to make shoes. He trained with master shoemaker Stefano Bemer.

8. a) Michael Clayton

9. 1986

10. *Dutch in Seven Lessons* (1948), *One Wild Oat* (1951), *Laughter in Paradise* (1951), *The Lavender Hill Mob* (1951), *Young Wives' Tale* (1951), *Monte Carlo Baby* (1951), *Secret People* (1952), *Roman Holiday* (1953), *Sabrina* (1954), *War and Peace* (1956), *Funny Face* (1957), *Love in the Afternoon* (1957), *Green Mansions* (1959), *The Nun's Story* (1959), *The Unforgiven* (1960), *Breakfast at Tiffany's* (1961), *The Children's Hour* (1961), *Charade* (1963), *Paris When It Sizzles* (1964), *My Fair Lady* (1964), *How to Steal a Million* (1966),

Two for the Road (1967), *Wait Until Dark* (1967), *Robin and Marian* (1976), *Bloodline* (1979), *They All Laughed* (1981), *Always* (1989).

ROUND 2

1. a) *Black Hawk* ***Down*** *by Law*

1. b) *Somewhere in* ***Time*** *Bandits*

1. c) *Meet Joe* ***Black*** *Narcissus*

1. d) *My Blue* ***Heaven*** *Can Wait*

1. e) *Lady* ***Bird*** *on a Wire*

2. a) *House*

2. b) *Rock*

2. c) *Blues*

2. d) *Disco*

2. e) *Country*

ROUND 3

1. a) Eminem

1. b) Bjork

1. c) Roy Orbison

Orbison's character (Johnny Banner) had a guitar that turned into a rifle. At one point, he delivers the line: "I can kill you with this – and play your funeral march at the same time." Though Orbison was pleased with the film, it was a box office flop, and his MGM five-film contract was cancelled.

1. d) Chris Rea

Parting Shots, directed by Michael Winner, has often been considered one of the worst films ever made. It was Winner's last film.

1. e) Mariah Carey

2. a) Margot Robbie and Marion Ravenwood.

2. b) Katharine Ross and Kylo Ren.

2. c) Charles Bronson and Cat Ballou.

2. d) Andrew Garfield and Auric Goldfinger.

2. e) Gene Wilder and Gale Weathers.

ROUND 4

1. a) Cate Blanchett

1. b) *Stardust*

1. c) *The Silence of the Lambs* (1991) – at time of writing, these are the only three films to win all of the "Big 5" Oscars: Best Picture, Best Director, Best Actor, Best Actress and Best Screenplay, either Original or Adapted.

1. d) *Underworld* (2013–2016) – *Underworld: Evolution, Underworld: Rise of the Lycans, Underworld: Awakening, Underworld: Blood Wars.*

1. e) *Richard III*

2. a) *Practical Magic*

2. b) Quaid

2. c) Rome

2. d) Sebastian

2. e) Tina Turner

ROUND 5

1. *The Hurt Locker* (2008)
2. *The Darkest Hour* (2017)
3. *The Departed* (2006)
4. *West Side Story* (1961)
5. *Matchstick Men* (2003)
6. *The Deer Hunter* (1978)

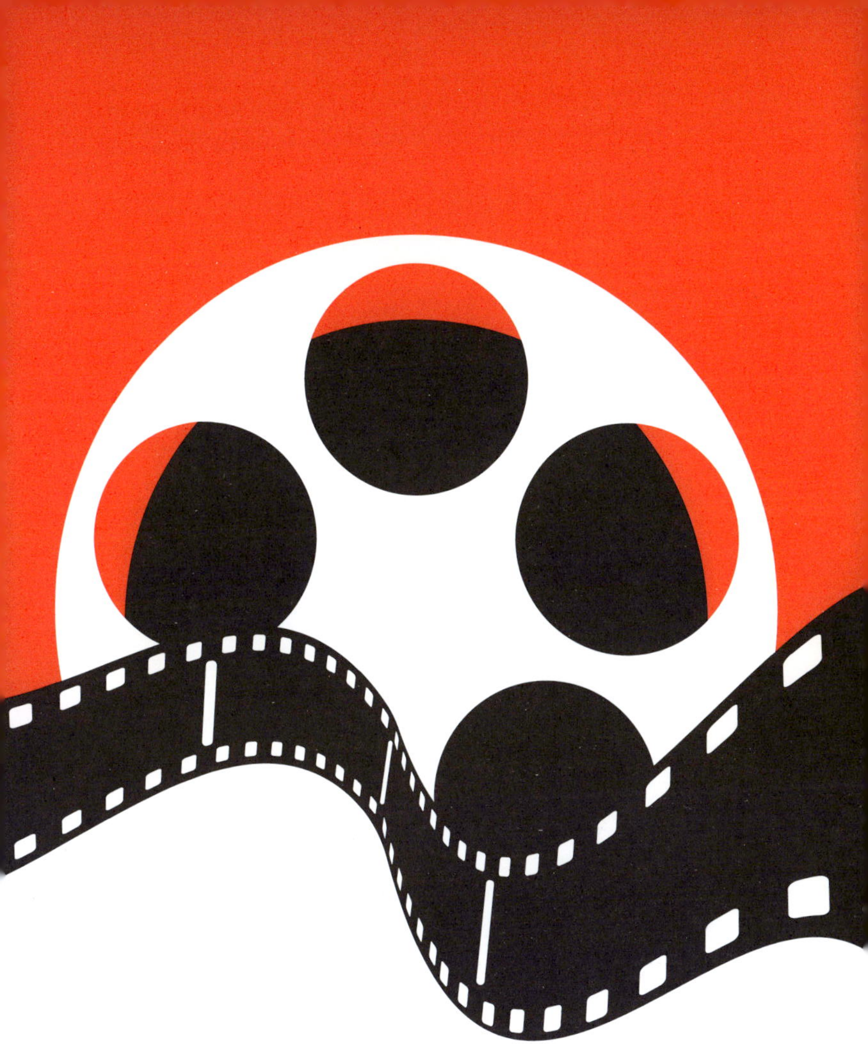

QUIZ 14

ROUND 1

STARTER FOR 10

Ten questions to begin!

1. THE FIRST QUESTION

Which of these films named after places was released first?

a) *Nebraska*

b) *Chicago*

c) *Munich*

2. THE ANAGRAM

Unscramble the actor's name: CHARITABLE SIN

3. FILM QUOTE

What film is the following quote from?

"Some people are worth melting for."

a) *The Notebook* (2004)

b) *Some Like It Hot* (1959)

c) *Frozen* (2013)

d) *Society* (1989)

4. THUMBS DOWN

What film is this the one-star review of?

"Don't let your kids watch this, some of it is very inappropriate – one scene in particular. Definitely not PG. Also, it's not that good... Maybe it was just the song that was good!"

a) *Mannequin* (1987)

b) *Big* (1988)

c) *Ghostbusters* (1984)

5. ODD ONE OUT

Which of these films was not directed by Guillermo del Toro? Bonus point if you know who it was directed by.

a) *The Neon Demon* (2016)

b) *The Devil's Backbone* (2001)

c) *Pan's Labyrinth* (2006)

6. RHYMING FILMS

I'll give you the initials of two films whose titles rhyme with each other. I'll also give you one of the stars and the years they were released, just name the films for a point each.

WTCS, Daisy Edgar-Jones (2022) and SA, John Cusack (1989).

7. CELLULOID OR CELLULIED?

Which of the following is true about Christopher Lee?

a) Christopher Lee was so taken with the location for *The Wicker Man* (1973) that he bought the island.

b) In 2013, Christopher Lee became the oldest person to have a top-20 hit single in the USA (aged 91).

c) Christopher Lee struggled to play Count Dracula as, in real life, he suffered from severe hemophobia (fear of blood).

8. WHAT MIGHT HAVE BEEN

Which of these roles did Marilyn Monroe turn down?

a) Mary Poppins (1964)

b) Norma Desmond (*Sunset Boulevard* – 1950)

c) Holly Golightly (*Breakfast at Tiffany's* – 1961)

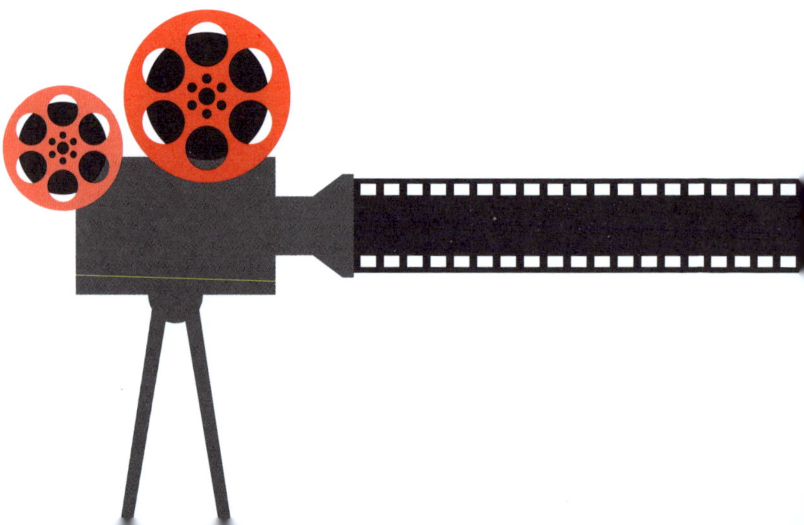

9. WHAT YEAR?

In what year did the following things happen?

Films released this year include: *The Shape of Water, Wonder Woman, Get Out, Dunkirk, Logan, Three Billboards Outside Ebbing, Missouri, Call Me by Your Name, Darkest Hour* and *Star Wars: Episode VIII – The Last Jedi*. In October, Harvey Weinstein is expelled from the Academy of Motion Picture Arts and Sciences after multiple allegations of sexual harassment are made against him. John Hurt, Bill Paxton, Roger Moore, Martin Landau, George A. Romero, Harry Dean Stanton and Jerry Lewis all pass away. Finn Wolfhard makes his movie debut in *It*. It was at this year's Academy Awards ceremony that *La La Land* was mistakenly announced as the winner of Best Picture. The actual winner was *Moonlight* by Barry Jenkins. But what was the year?

10. GIVE ME FIVE

A chance for five points! Name five titles of songs from the soundtrack album to the film *Grease* (1978). There are 24 possible answers. Or, if that's a little too easy for you, name the five tracks that feature John Travolta (Danny Zuko).

ROUND 2

1. BACKSTAGE

This round is about films that are about the making of other films. I will tell you the director, the star and the original movie that this film depicts being made – just name the film they made!

a) Tim Burton directing Johnny Depp in a film about the making of *Plan 9 From Outer Space* (1957).

b) Simon Curtis directing Michelle Williams in a film about the making of *The Prince and the Showgirl* (1957).

c) E. Elias Merhige directing Willem Dafoe in a film about the making of *Nosferatu* (1922).

d) David Fincher directing Gary Oldman in a film about the making of *Citizen Kane* (1941).

e) John Lee Hancock directing Emma Thompson in a film about the making of *Mary Poppins* (1964).

2. ONE OF OUR ______ IS MISSING!

Just fill in the missing word – there's always a theme, and this time it's... occupations.

a) *The Constant* ________ (2005)

b) *Universal* ________ (1992)

c) *The* ________ *of Panama* (2001)

d) ________ *Betty* (2000)

e) *The Lincoln* ________ (2011)

ROUND 3

1. ASK ME ANYTHING

Film titles that are questions. I will give you a star, the year of release and the initials of the title – just name these films that end with a question mark.

a) Ashton Kutcher (2000), DWMC?

b) Barbra Streisand (1972), WUD?

c) John Candy (1989), WHC?

d) Melissa McCarthy (2018), CYEFM?

e) Bette Davis (1962), WEHTBJ?

2. THE ODD COUPLE

I'll describe an actor and a film character that share the same initials. A point for each you can name.

a) **Actor:** American actor born in 1982. First found fame in *The Princess Diaries* movies (2001–2004) playing Mia Thermopolis. Moving to adult roles, she starred as Andrea "Andy" Sachs in *The Devil Wears Prada* (2006), Maggie Murdock in *Love & Other Drugs* (2010) and portrayed Selina Kyle/Catwoman in *The Dark Knight Rises* (2012).
Character: The corrupt LAPD narcotics detective that Jake Hoyt (Ethan Hawke) is assigned to shadow in *Training Day* (2001). Denzel Washington's portrayal earned him the Best Actor Academy Award (among others).

b) **Actor:** American actor born in 1967. Born to acting parents, she first found fame in two David Lynch movies: *Blue Velvet* (1986) and *Wild at Heart* (1990) before moving on to mainstream success playing Ellie Sattler in the *Jurassic Park* series of films (1993–2022). **Character:** The titular character in the 2013 Coen Brothers film about a struggling folk musician in 1960s New York City. Portrayed by Oscar Isaac.

c) **Actor:** English actor born in 1988. Best known for playing Ron Weasley in the *Harry Potter* film series (2001–2011), he has also starred in films such as *Driving Lessons* (2006), *CBGB* (2013) and *Knock at the Cabin* (2023). **Character:** The main antagonist from the 2004 movie *Mean Girls* (and the musical version), portrayed by Rachel McAdams in 2004 and Reneé Rapp in the 2024 musical adaptation. In 2019, *The Independent* named her the "meanest high school film character of all time".

d) **Actor:** American actor born in 1990. Although best known for portraying *The Marvelous Mrs. Maisel* (2017–2023) on TV, she has appeared in movies including *Beautiful Creatures* (2013), *Patriots Day* (2016) and *The Courier* (2020) and appears as Lois Lane in the 2025 James Gunn version of *Superman*. **Character:** The anchorman portrayed by Will Ferrell in two movies (2004 and 2013). In the first film, he is the top-rated newsman in 1970s San Diego (and also plays amazing jazz flute) until his male-dominated world is disturbed by the hire of a new anchorwoman (Christina Applegate).

e) **Actor:** English actor born in 1970. Starred in (and co-wrote) three films with Edgar Wright (*Shaun of the Dead* – 2004, *Hot Fuzz* – 2007, and *The World's End* – 2013). He has also found fame playing Benji Dunn in the *Mission Impossible* movies (2006–present) and Montgomery "Scotty" Scott in the 2009–2016 reboots of *Star Trek*. **Character:** The anti-hero from two John Carpenter movies: *Escape from New York* (1981) and *Escape from LA* (1996), played both times by Kurt Russell. He is a former US Green Beret asked by the government to perform dangerous rescue missions in exchange for a pardon.

ROUND 4

1. BRAINSTORM

Complete the lists and spot the links – a point for each correct answer.

a) Which American city appears in the title of a 1993 film starring Tom Hanks and Denzel Washington, a 1940 film starring Cary Grant and Katharine Hepburn and a 1984 film starring Michael Paré and Nancy Allen?

b) Russell Crowe, Karl Urban, Anna Paquin and Sam Neill were all born in which country?

c) Matt Damon, Alain Delon and John Malkovich have all played which character created by the author Patricia Highsmith?

d) What was Jonesy in 1979, Goose in 2019, Thackery Binx in 1993 and Mr Bigglesworth in 1997?

e) Which musician played Pontius Pilate in 1988, Andy Warhol in 1996 and Nikola Tesla in 2006?

2. IT FOLLOWS

The first letter of each answer follows the first letter of the last. So, if the answer to c) is "Apple", the answer to d) will begin with "B". If you get to Z, go to A. Each question is worth one point.

a) What word goes before ________ *of the Sun* for a 1987 Steven Spielberg film, before ________ *Records* for a 1995 film starring Liv Tyler and before ________ *State* in the title of a 2013 Dwayne Johnson film?

b) Name the 1982 Werner Herzog film, starring Klaus Kinski, in which the plot centres around an attempt to transport a steamship over the Andes mountains (which Herzog attempted to actually achieve).

c) What is the name of the lead character in the *Despicable Me* film series (2010–2022), voiced by Steve Carell?

d) It was announced in 2024 that a sequel is in development to which 1996 Adam Sandler sports comedy film?

e) Which song, sung by Ryan Gosling, from *Barbie* (2023) was nominated for an Academy Award?

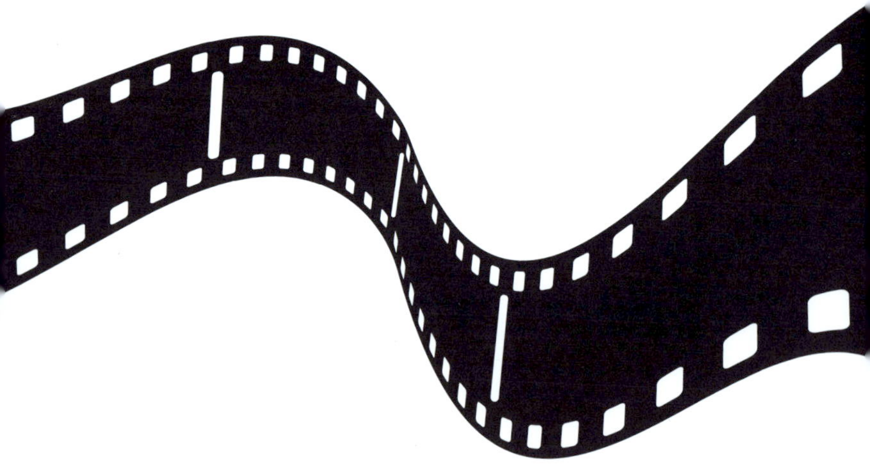

ROUND 5

THE LAST PICTURE SHOW

Say what you see! Can you identify the films from these picture clues? Each picture is worth a point.

1

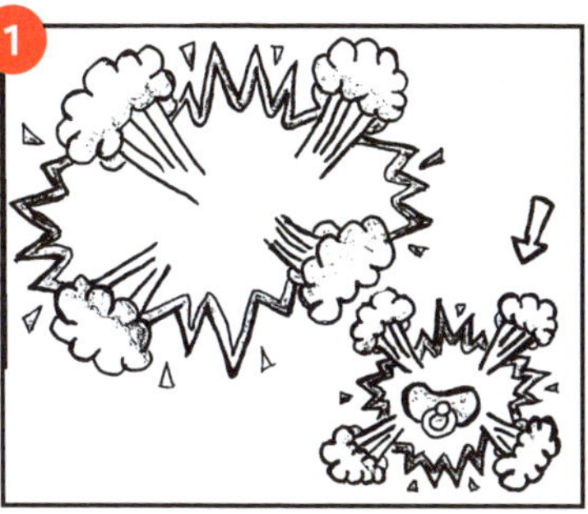

2

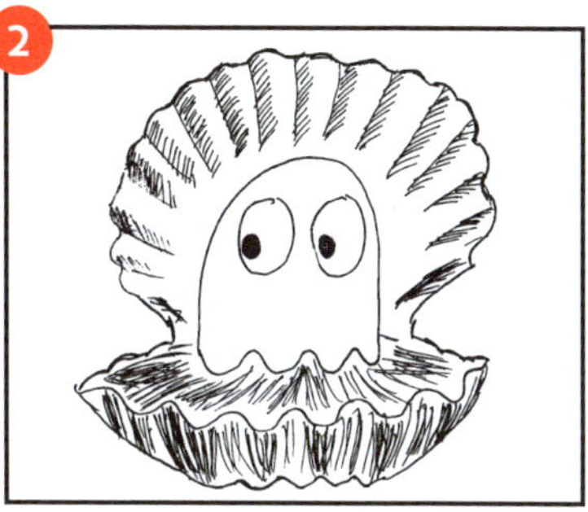

3

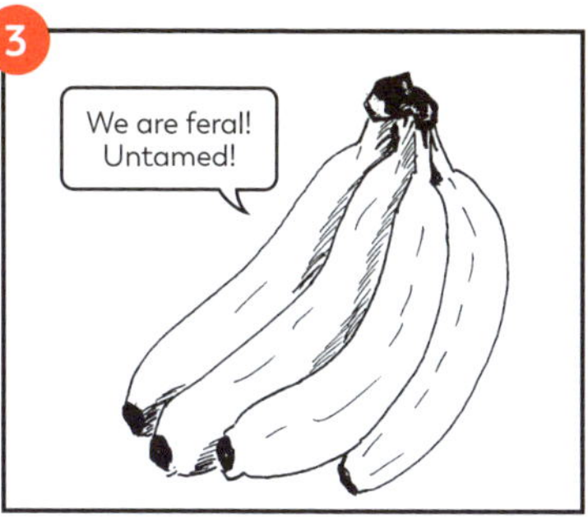

4

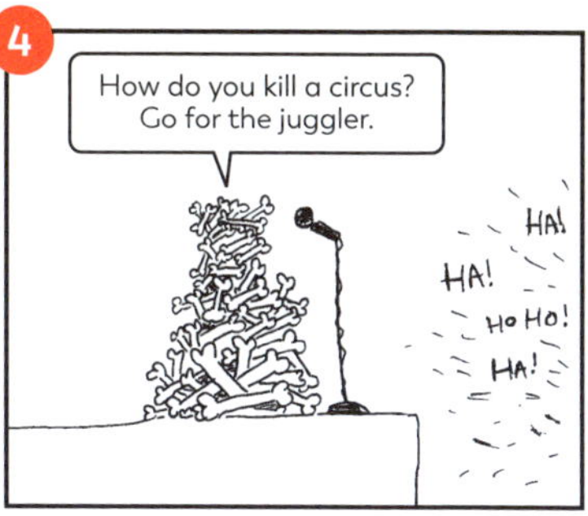

5

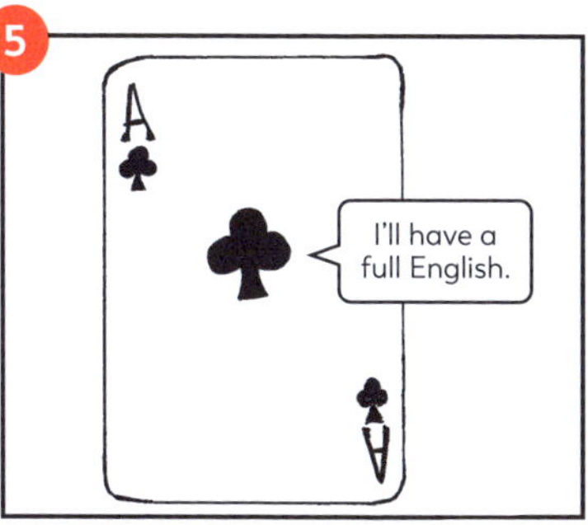

6

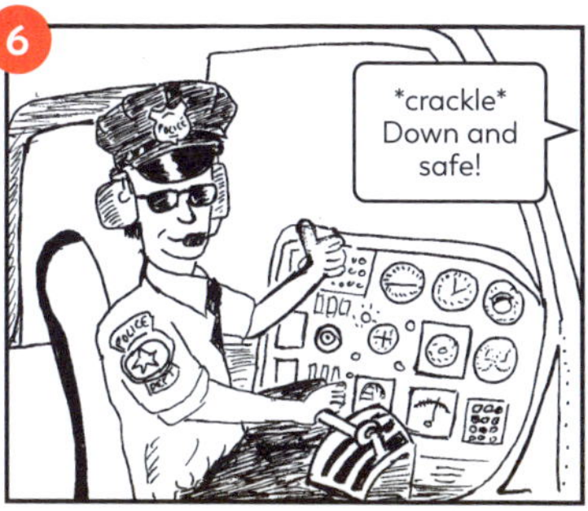

ANSWERS

ROUND 1

1. b) *Chicago* (2002). *Munich* was 2005 and *Nebraska* was 2013.

2. Christian Bale

3. c) *Frozen*

4. c) *Ghostbusters*

5. a) *The Neon Demon* by Nicolas Winding Refn.

6. *Where the Crawdads Sing* and *Say Anything...*

7. b) In 2013, Christopher Lee became the oldest person to have a top-20 hit single in the USA (aged 91).

It was a heavy-metal Christmas single called "Jingle Hell". He had an entire recording career, including two heavy-metal albums he recorded in 2010 and 2013.

8. c) Holly Golightly (*Breakfast at Tiffany's*)

Monroe was Truman Capote's (author of the novella the film is based on) first choice. He said, "Paramount double-crossed me in every way and cast Audrey."

9. 2017

10. "Grease", **"Summer Nights"**, "Hopelessly Devoted to You", **"You're the One That I Want"**, **"Sandy"**, "Beauty School Dropout", "Look at Me, I'm Sandra Dee", **"Greased Lightnin'"**, "It's Raining on Prom Night", "Alone at a Drive-In Movie", "Blue Moon", "Rock

and Roll Is Here to Stay", "Those Magic Changes", "Hound Dog", "Born to Hand Jive", "Tears on My Pillow", "Mooning", "Freddy, My Love" , "Rock 'n' Roll Party Queen", "There Are Worse Things I Could Do", "Look at Me, I'm Sandra Dee (reprise)", **"We Go Together"**, "Love Is a Many-Splendored Thing", "Grease (reprise)".

Originally the song "Greased Lightnin'" was to be performed by the character Kenickie (played by Jeff Conaway), but John Travolta insisted it should be sung by his character, Danny Zuko.

ROUND 2

1. a) *Ed Wood* (1994)

Weirdly, there is a film from 1995 starring Karen Black called *Plan 10 from Outer Space* that has no connection at all to Ed Wood's films (other than featuring aliens).

1. b) *My Week with Marilyn* (2011)

1. c) *Shadow of the Vampire* (2000)

1. d) *Mank* (2020)

1. e) *Saving Mr. Banks* (2013)

2. a) *Gardener*

2. b) *Soldier*

2. c) *Tailor*

2. d) *Nurse*

2. e) *Lawyer*

ROUND 3

1. a) *Dude, Where's My Car?*

1. b) *What's Up Doc?*

1. c) *Who's Harry Crumb?*

1. d) *Can You Ever Forgive Me?*

1. e) *What Ever Happened to Baby Jane?*

2. a) Anne Hathaway and Alonzo Harris.

2. b) Laura Dern and Llewyn Davis.

2. c) Rupert Grint and Regina George.

2. d) Rachel Brosnahan and Ron Burgundy.

2. e) Simon Pegg and Snake Plissken.

ROUND 4

1. a) Philadelphia. *Philadelphia*, *The Philadelphia Story* and *The Philadelphia Experiment*.

1. b) New Zealand

1. c) Tom Ripley. Matt Damon in *The Talented Mr Ripley* (1999), Alain Delon in *Purple Noon* (*Plein Soleil*) (1960) and John Malkovich in *Ripley's Game* (2002).

1. d) A cat. Jonesy was in *Alien*, Goose was in *Captain Marvel*, Thackery Binx was (the boy transformed into a cat) in *Hocus Pocus* and Mr Bigglesworth is Dr Evil's cat in *Austin Powers: International Man of Mystery*.

1. e) David Bowie. *The Last Temptation of Christ*, *Basquiat* and *The Prestige*.

2. a) Empire – *Empire of the Sun*, *Empire Records* and *Empire State*.

2. b) *Fitzcarraldo*

2. c) Gru

2. d) *Happy Gilmore*

2. e) "I'm Just Ken" sung by Ryan Gosling. It lost to "What Was I Made For?" by Billie Eilish, which is also from *Barbie*.

ROUND 5

1. *Baby Boom* (1987)
2. *Ghost in the Shell* (1995/2017)
3. *The Wild Bunch* (1969)
4. *Funny Bones* (1995)
5. *The Breakfast Club* (1985)
6. *Cop Land* (1997)

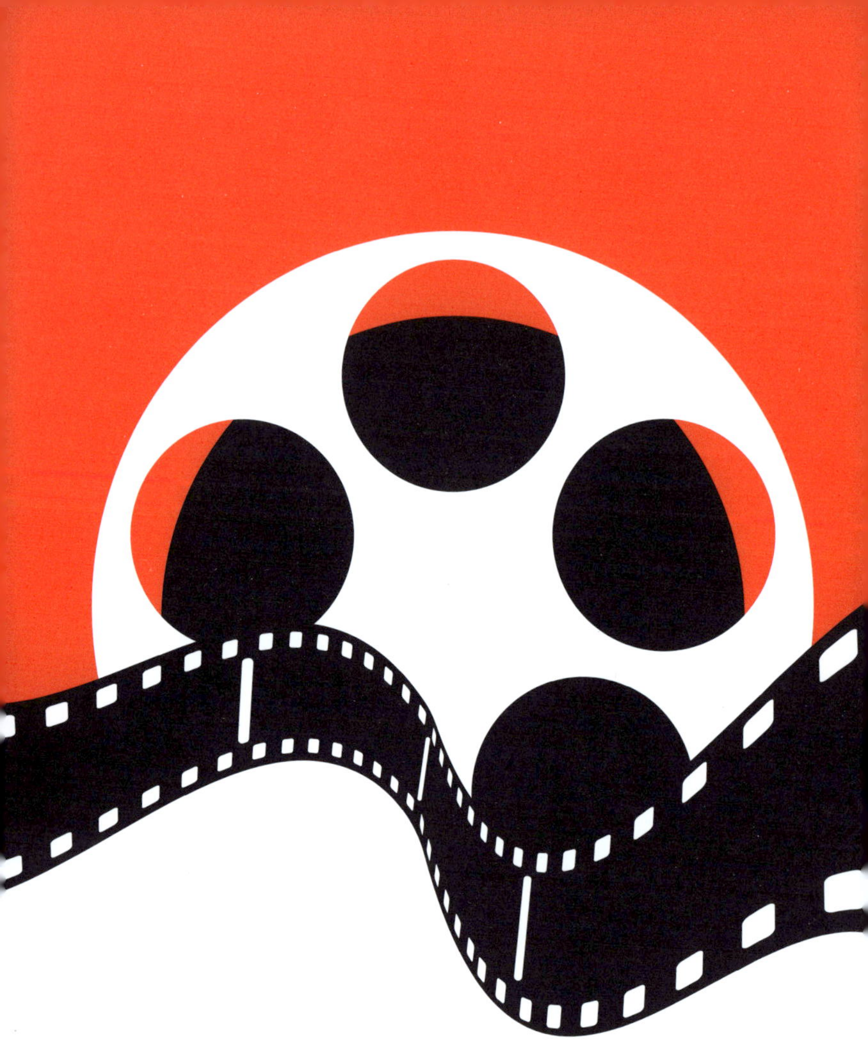

QUIZ 15

ROUND 1

STARTER FOR 10

Ten questions to begin!

1. THE FIRST QUESTION

Which of these films was first to win the Best International Feature Film Oscar?

a) *Life Is Beautiful*

b) *Cinema Paradiso*

c) *The Lives of Others*

2. THE ANAGRAM

Unscramble the actor's name: RASHLY WON RODEO

3. FILM QUOTE

What film is the following quote from?

"I find your lack of faith disturbing."

a) *Star Wars: Episode IV – A New Hope* (1977)

b) *The Godfather* (1972)

c) *The Italian Job* (1969)

d) *The Exorcist* (1973)

4. THUMBS DOWN

What film is this the one-star review of?

"The only scene I found funny was when they put the chicken in the oven sitting up on its legs."

a) *The Hangover* (2009)

b) *Withnail and I* (1987)

c) *Chicken Run* (2000)

5. ODD ONE OUT

Which of these films was not directed by Clint Eastwood? Bonus point if you know who it was directed by.

a) *Bronco Billy* (1980)

b) *All the Pretty Horses* (2000)

c) *Pale Rider* (1985)

6. RHYMING FILMS

I'll give you the initials of two films whose titles rhyme with each other. I'll also give you one of the stars and the years they were released, just name the films for a point each.

ESOTSM, Jim Carrey (2004) and CEOTTK, Richard Dreyfuss (1977).

7. CELLULOID OR CELLULIED?

Which of the following is true about Christopher Walken?

a) Walken is a trained ski-jumper and was able to advise (as well as appear in) *Eddie the Eagle* (2015).

b) Walken is a trained plumber and was able to fix a broken tap on the set of *Mouse Hunt* (1997).

c) Walken is a trained dancer and in 2001 he appeared in Fatboy Slim's "Weapon of Choice" music video.

8. WHAT MIGHT HAVE BEEN

Which of these roles did Oscar Isaac turn down?

a) Sebastian "Seb" Wilder (*La La Land* – 2016)

b) Freddie Mercury (*Bohemian Rhapsody* – 2018)

c) "Mad Max" Rockatansky (*Mad Max: Fury Road* – 2015)

9. WHAT YEAR?

In what year did the following things happen?

Films released this year include: *Batman Begins, Harry Potter and the Goblet of Fire, Kinky Boots, Sin City, The Hitchhiker's Guide to the Galaxy, Star Wars: Episode III – Revenge of the Sith, Madagascar, Capote* and *Brokeback Mountain*. The American Film Institute chooses its 100 most memorable film quotes; the winner is "Frankly, my dear, I don't give a damn" from *Gone with the Wind* (1939). Sir John Mills, Ismail Merchant, Richard Pryor and Anne Bancroft pass away. Daniel Craig is announced as the next James Bond; *Casino Royale* will arrive the next year. But what was the year?

10. GIVE ME FIVE

A chance for five points! Name five films with one- or two-word titles that star John Candy. There are 19 possible answers.

ROUND 2

1. RHYME AND REASON

All these films have titles that rhyme. I'll give you the year of release, one of the stars and the initials of the titles.

a) 1992, Russell Crowe, RS.

b) 2003, Mike Myers, TCITH.

c) 2013, Emma Watson, TBR.

d) 1999, Rob Schneider, DBMG.

e) 2011, Hugh Jackman, RS.

2. ONE OF OUR ______ IS MISSING!

Just fill in the missing word – there's always a theme, and this time it's... flowers and shrubs.

a) *The* ________ *Hill Mob* (1951)

b) *Stanley and* ________ (1990)

c) *Blue* ________ (2013)

d) ________ *Miller* (1974)

e) *The Name of the* ________ (1986)

ROUND 3

1. WHAT DREAMS MAY COME

The following films are adaptations of Shakespeare plots. I will give you the play, two stars, the director and the year of the film. Just name the film.

a) *Romeo and Juliet*. Starring Natalie Wood and George Chakiris, directed by Jerome Robbins and Robert Wise, 1961.

b) *The Taming of the Shrew*. Starring Julia Stiles and Heath Ledger, directed by Gil Junger, 1999.

c) *King Lear*. Starring Tatsuya Nakadai and Akira Terao, directed by Akira Kurosawa, 1985.

d) *The Tempest*. Starring Alicia Vikander and Domhnall Gleeson, directed by Alex Garland, 2014.

e) *Hamlet*. Starring Matthew Broderick (voice) and James Earl Jones (voice), directed by Roger Allers and Rob Minkoff, 1994.

2. THE ODD COUPLE

I'll describe an actor and a film character that share the same initials. A point for each you can name.

a) **Actor:** American actor born in 1966. Her breakthrough role was alongside Eddie Murphy in *Boomerang* (1992). Later she became the first African American to win the Academy Award for Best Actress for her performance in *Monster's Ball* (2001). Other roles include Storm in the *X-Men* series of films (2000–2014) and Jinx in *Die Another Day* (2002).

Character: The anchorman for UBS Evening News in the film *Network* (1976), Peter Finch won a posthumous Oscar for his performance. The character is given his own show after his ranting on air that "I'm as mad as hell, and I'm not going to take this anymore!" proves a ratings hit.

b) **Actor:** American actor born in 1998. Her first big role was in *Pacific Rim: Uprising* (2018). She has also appeared in *Bad Times at the El Royale* (2018), *Civil War* (2024) and *Alien: Romulus* (2024). In 2023, she portrayed Priscilla Presley in Sofia Coppola's *Priscilla*. **Character:** The FBI agent on the hunt for serial killer "Buffalo Bill" who attempts to gain information from the imprisoned cannibal Hannibal Lecter (Anthony Hopkins) in the film *The Silence of the Lambs* (1991), played by Jodie Foster. The character also appears in the sequel *Hannibal* (2001), played by Julianne Moore.

c) **Actor:** American actor born in 1922. A character actor, he won two consecutive Best Supporting Actor Academy Awards for his performances as Ben Bradlee in *All the President's Men* (1976) and as Dashiell Hammett in *Julia* (1977). He was nominated again for playing Howard Hughes in *Melvin and Howard* (1980). Other notable performances came in *Tora! Tora! Tora!* (1970) and *Magnolia* (1999) – his final screen appearance. **Character:** An animated femme fatale from the 1988 movie *Who Framed Roger Rabbit*. The wife of Roger, she is best remembered for the line "I'm not bad, I'm just drawn that way". Voiced by Kathleen Turner (speaking) and Amy Irving (singing).

d) **Actor:** Irish actor and singer born in 1989. Her first film role was in *Beast* (2017), and she then starred in *Wild Rose* (2018), which earned her a BAFTA nomination for Best Actress. Since then, she has starred in *I'm Thinking of Ending Things* (2020), *Men* (2022) and *Women Talking* (2022). In 2024, she filmed the role of Agnes Shakespeare in *Hamnet* (2025), directed by Chloe Zhao. **Character:** A Scottish school mistress in a film that features the character's name from 1969. This teacher is seen as eccentric by the rest of the staff as she tries to teach her pupils the ways of life. Maggie Smith won the Best Actress Oscar for her performance.

e) **Actor:** Australian actor born in 1972. She found international fame as Muriel Heslop in *Muriel's Wedding* (1994). She went on to star in *The Sixth Sense* (1999), *Little Miss Sunshine* (2006), *Krampus* (2015) and *Knives Out* (2019). **Character:** A millionaire businessman, handsome and cultured who, out of boredom, attempts to mastermind a perfect crime. He was portrayed by Steve McQueen in 1968 and by Pierce Brosnan in the 1999 remake.

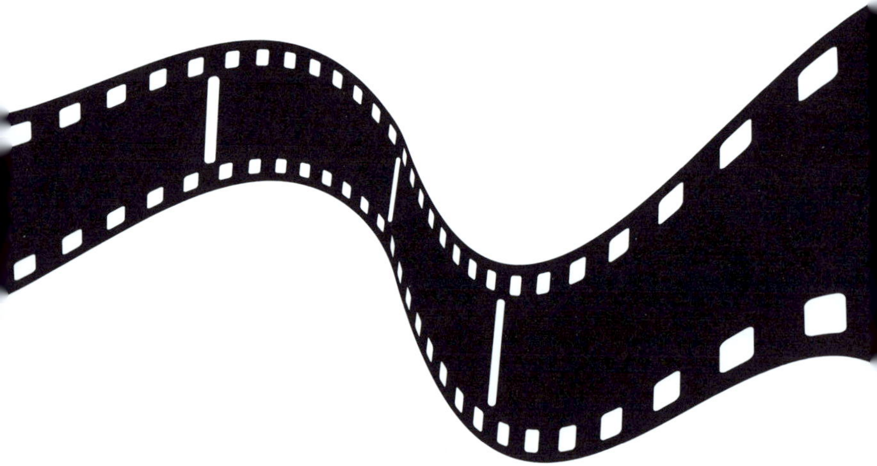

ROUND 4

1. BRAINSTORM

Complete the lists and spot the links – a point for each correct answer.

a) Which pair of actors appeared together in *Silver Streak* (1976), *Stir Crazy* (1980), *See No Evil, Hear No Evil* (1989) and *Another You* (1991)?

b) Which character was portrayed by Harvey Spencer Stephens in 1976, Jonathan Scott-Taylor in 1978 and Sam Neill in 1981?

c) Which profession connects Steve Martin in a 1986 film, Laurence Olivier in a 1976 film and Jennifer Aniston in a film from 2011?

d) What comes next in this list? *Snow White* (2025), *Barbie* (2023), *Little Women* (2019)...?

e) Which city appears in the title of a 1984 film by Wim Wenders, a 1951 film by Vincente Minnelli and a 1972 film by Bernardo Bertolucci?

2. IT FOLLOWS

The first letter of each answer follows the first letter of the last. So, if the answer to c) is "Apple", the answer to d) will begin with "B". If you get to Z, go to A. Each question is worth one point.

a) Which legendary figure has been portrayed by Douglas Fairbanks, Kevin Costner, Russell Crowe, Sean Connery and Taron Egerton?

b) Daniel Craig's final three *James Bond* films all won Oscars for best what?

c) What word goes before ________ *Lies*, ________ *Crime* and ________ *Romance* to complete the titles of three films?

d) James Spader provides the voice for which Marvel Cinematic Universe villain?

e) Complete the trio of gargoyles from Disney's *The Hunchback of Notre Dame* (1996), Laverne, Hugo and...?

ROUND 5

THE LAST PICTURE SHOW

Say what you see! Can you identify the films from these picture clues? Each picture is worth a point.

1

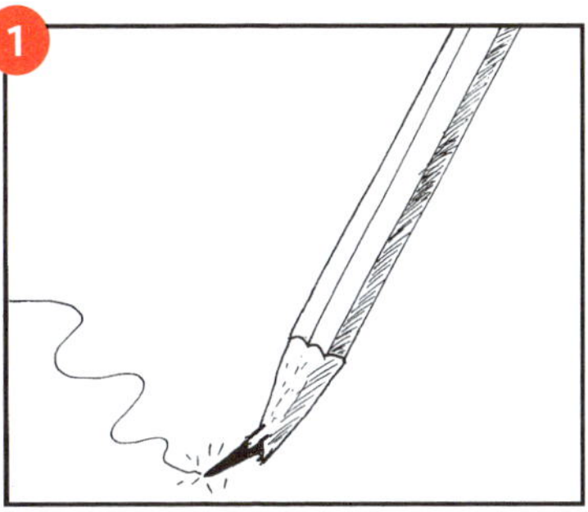

2

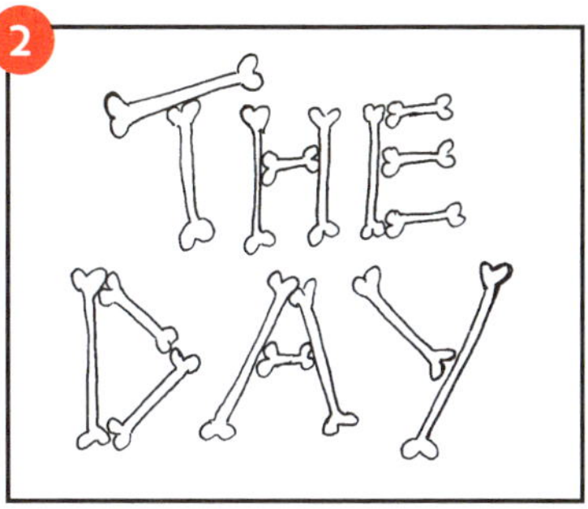

3

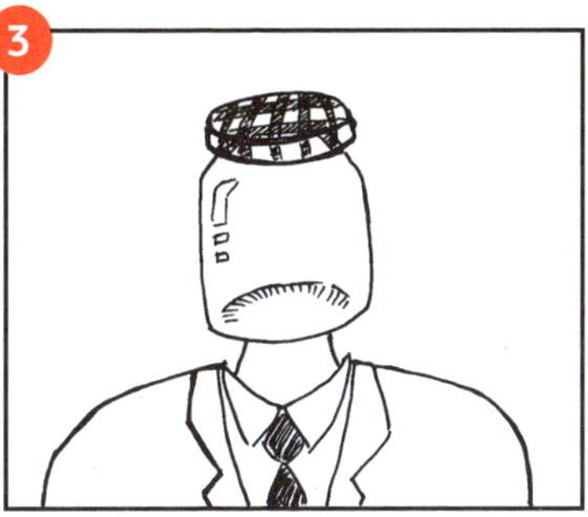

4

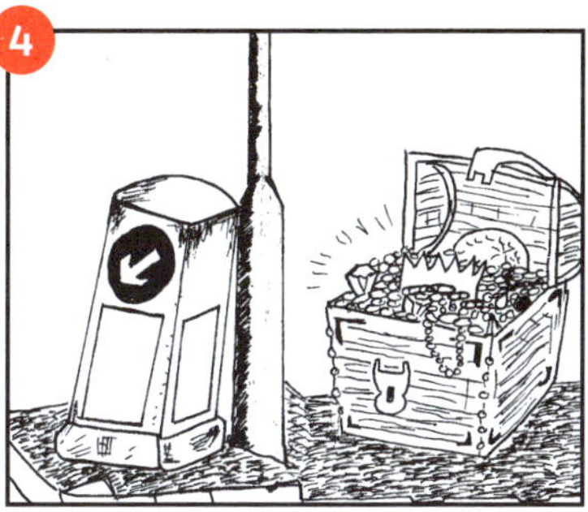

5

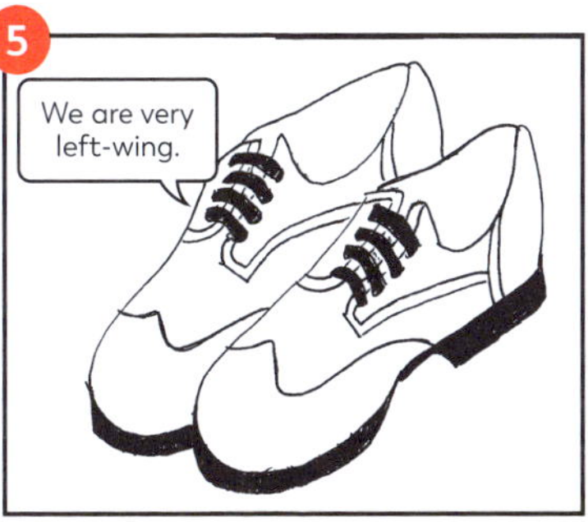

6

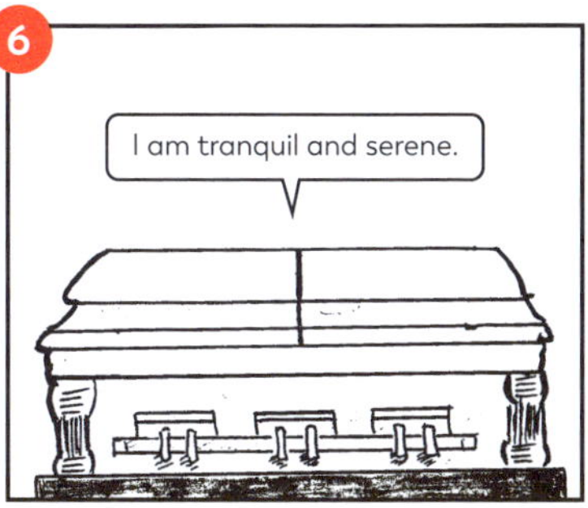

ANSWERS

ROUND 1

1. b) *Cinema Paradiso* (won in 1990). *Life Is Beautiful* was 1999 and *The Lives of Others* was 2007.

2. Woody Harrelson

3. a) *Star Wars: Episode IV – A New Hope*

4. b) *Withnail and I*

5. b) *All the Pretty Horses* by Billy Bob Thornton.

6. *Eternal Sunshine of the Spotless Mind* and *Close Encounters of the Third Kind.*

7. c) Walken is a trained dancer and in 2001 he appeared in Fatboy Slim's "Weapon of Choice" music video.

8. b) Freddie Mercury (*Bohemian Rhapsody*)

9. 2005

10. *Tunnel Vision* (1976), *1941* (1979), *Deadly Companion* (1980), *Stripes* (1981), *Heavy Metal* (1981 – voice), *Going Berserk* (1983), *Splash* (1984), *Brewster's Millions* (1985), *Summer Rental* (1985), *Volunteers* (1985), *Spaceballs* (1987), *Speed Zone* (1989), *Uncle Buck* (1989), *Home Alone* (1990), *Delirious* (1991), *JFK* (1991), *Cool Runnings* (1993), *Wagons East* (1994), *Canadian Bacon* (1995).

ROUND 2

1. a) *Romper Stomper*

1. b) *The Cat in the Hat*

1. c) *The Bling Ring*

1. d) *Deuce Bigalow: Male Gigolo*

1. e) *Real Steel*

2. a) *Lavender*

2. b) *Iris*

2. c) *Jasmine*

2. d) *Daisy*

2. e) *Rose*

ROUND 3

1. a) *West Side Story*

1. b) *10 Things I Hate About You*

1. c) *Ran*

1. d) *Ex Machina*

1. e) *The Lion King*

2. a) Halle Berry and Howard Beale.

2. b) Cailee Spaeny and Clarice Starling.

2. c) Jason Robards and Jessica Rabbit.

2. d) Jessie Buckley and Jean Brodie.

2. e) Toni Collette and Thomas Crown.

ROUND 4

1. a) Gene Wilder and Richard Pryor.

1. b) Damien (Thorn). Harvey Spencer Stephens: *The Omen*, Jonathan Scott-Taylor: *Damien: Omen II*, Sam Neill: *Omen III: The Final Conflict*.

1. c) Dentist. *Little Shop of Horrors* – Steve Martin plays Orin Scrivello, *Marathon Man* – Laurence Olivier plays Dr Christian Szell, and *Horrible Bosses* – Jennifer Anniston plays Dr Julia Harris.

1. d) *Lady Bird* (2017). These are films directed by Greta Gerwig going back in reverse order from her most recent (at time of writing). She also co-directed a film in 2008 called *Nights and Weekends.*

1. e) Paris. *Paris, Texas, An American in Paris* and *Last Tango in Paris.*

2. a) Robin Hood. *Robin Hood* (1922) Douglas Fairbanks, (2010) Russell Crowe, (2018) Taron Egerton, *Robin Hood: Prince of Thieves* (1991) Kevin Costner, *Robin and Marion* (1976) Sean Connery.

2. b) Song. "Skyfall" – Adele, "Writings on the Wall" – Sam Smith (*Spectre*) and "No Time to Die" – Billie Eilish.

2. c) True. *True Lies* (1994), *True Crime* (1999) and *True Romance* (1993).

2. d) Ultron. *Avengers: Age of Ultron* (2015).

2. e) Victor

Victor and Hugo were a nod to the author of the source novel. Laverne was named after one of The Andrews Sisters who had previously provided vocals for some Disney short films.

ROUND 5

1. *Point Break* (1991)
2. *The Remains of the Day* (1993)
3. *Jarhead* (2005)
4. *Treasure Island* (1950)
5. *The Red Shoes* (1948)
6. *Dead Calm* (1989)

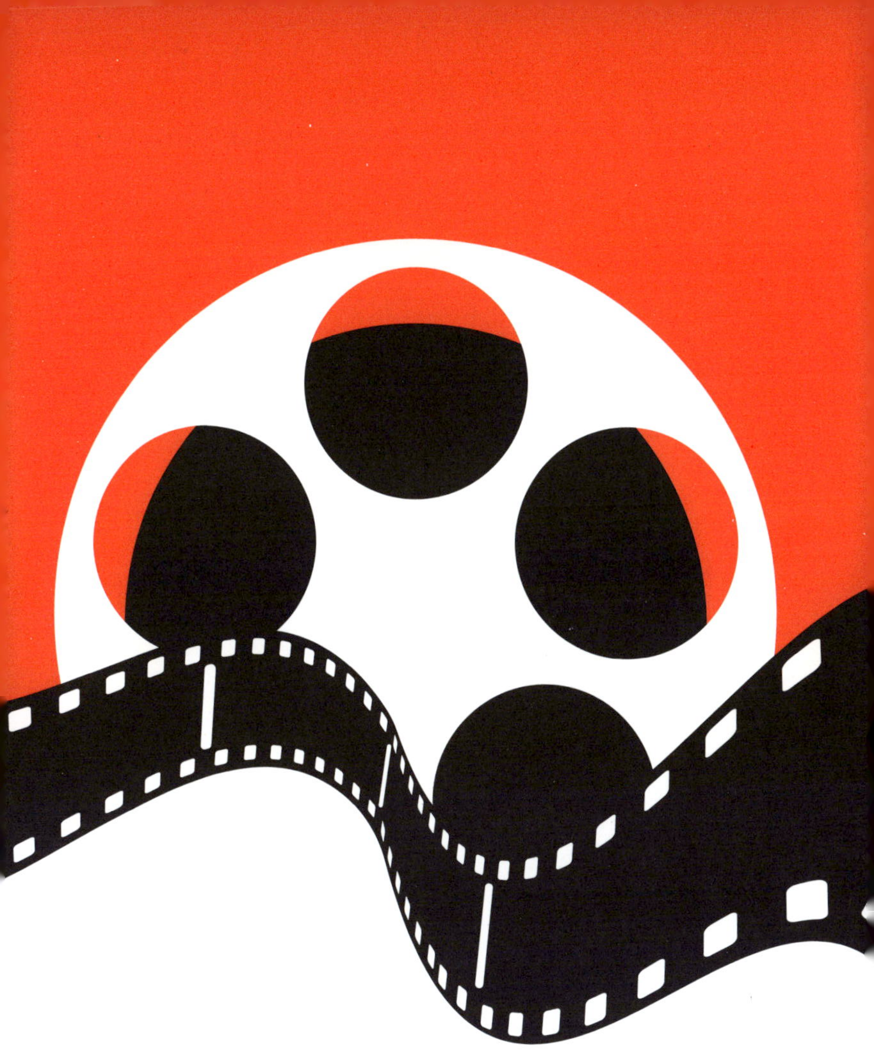

QUIZ 16

ROUND 1

STARTER FOR 10

Ten questions to begin!

1. THE FIRST QUESTION

Which of the following delicious films was released first?

a) *Cloudy with a Chance of Meatballs*

b) *Chocolat*

c) *Fried Green Tomatoes at the Whistle Stop Café*

2. THE ANAGRAM

Unscramble the actor's name: BROKEN STATUE

3. FILM QUOTE

What film is the following quote from?

"He's not the Messiah. He's a very naughty boy!"

a) *South Park: Bigger, Longer and Uncut* (1999)

b) *Monty Python's Life of Brian* (1979)

c) *Bruce Almighty* (2003)

d) *The Last Temptation of Christ* (1988)

4. THUMBS DOWN

What film is this the one-star review of?

"The combat scenes were alright, but completely unrealistic. The music was out of place, perhaps it's a little more interesting if you're as high as the producers of it. The plot was clearly written by someone high as a kite. The characters are completely unrelatable."

a) *Apocalypse Now* (1979)

b) *Dunkirk* (2017)

c) *Tropic Thunder* (2008)

5. ODD ONE OUT

Which of these films was not directed by John Schlesinger? Bonus point if you know who it was directed by.

a) *Billy Liar* (1963)

b) *A Kind of Loving* (1962)

c) *A Taste of Honey* (1961)

6. RHYMING FILMS

I'll give you the initials of two films whose titles rhyme with each other. I'll also give you one of the stars and the years they were released, just name the films for a point each.

KL, Humphrey Bogart (1948) and F, Frances McDormand (1996).

7. CELLULOID OR CELLULIED?

Which of the following is true about Brian Dennehy?

a) For years Brian Dennehy lied about serving and being wounded in Vietnam.

b) For years Brian Dennehy falsely claimed to be Ernest Hemingway's nephew.

c) Brian Dennehy pretended he could speak Russian to get a part in *Gorky Park* (1983).

8. WHAT MIGHT HAVE BEEN

Which of these roles did Hugh Jackman turn down?

a) James Bond (*Casino Royale* – 2006)

b) Ethan Hunt (*Mission: Impossible* – 1996)

c) Anton Chigurh (*No Country for Old Men* – 2007)

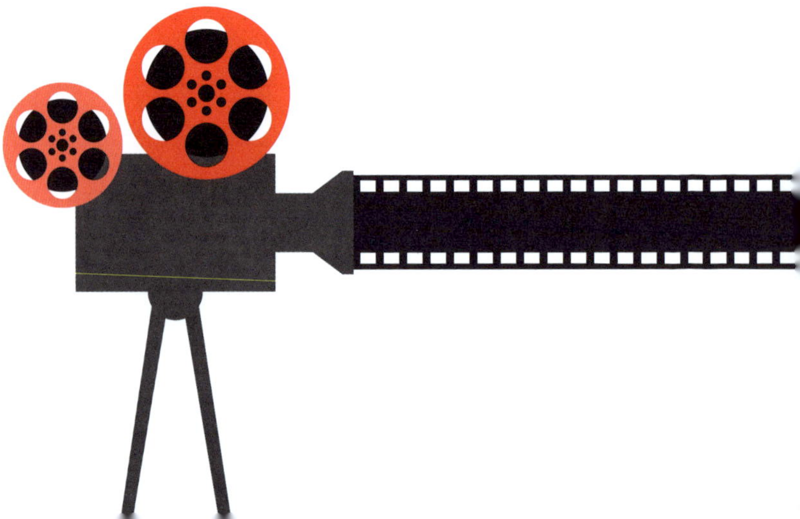

9. WHAT YEAR?

In what year did the following things happen?

Films released this year include: *Twins, Cinema Paradiso, Who Framed Roger Rabbit, Beetlejuice, My Neighbor Totoro, Akira, The Accused, A Fish Called Wanda* and *Big*. *Rain Man* is a huge success and will win the Oscar for Best Picture (the following year) – MGM will not have another Best Picture nomination until *Licorice Pizza*. Vanessa Kirby, Ana de Armas, Nicholas Braun, Awkwafina, Michael Cera, Rupert Grint, Glen Powell and Emma Stone are born. Emeric Pressburger, Kenneth Williams, Roy Kinnear and Hal Ashby pass away. *Die Hard* is released in July, despite being set at Christmas. But what was the year?

10. GIVE ME FIVE

A chance for five points! Name five films (up to 2024) that saw Meryl Streep receive an Oscar nomination. There are 21 possible answers.

ROUND 2

1. NEXT

A round about sequels. I'll give you a film, you tell me the name of the sequel.

a) *Zombieland* (2009)

   i) *Zombieland: Brunch of the Dead*
   ii) *Zombieland: Dead White and Blue*
   iii) *Zombieland: Double Tap*

b) *Alfie* (1966)

   i) *Alfie Ties the Knot*
   ii) *Alfie Darling*
   iii) *It's All About Alfie*

c) *Friday* (1995)

   i) *Saturday*
   ii) *Next Friday*
   iii) *It's Friday Again*

d) *The Whole Nine Yards* (2000)

   i) *The Whole Ten Yards*
   ii) *Tell Me When It Hurts*
   iii) *The Whole Nine Yards and Then Some*

e) *I Know What You Did Last Summer* (1997)

   i) *I Know What You Did Last Fall*
   ii) *You Can Run but You Can't Hide*
   iii) *I Still Know What You Did Last Summer*

2. ONE OF OUR _____ IS MISSING!

Just fill in the missing word – there's always a theme, and this time it's… parts of a clock.

a) _______ *M for Murder* (1954)

b) *The Curious _______ of Benjamin Button* (2008)

c) *The Pit and the _______* (1961)

d) *Eyes Without a _______* (1960)

e) *The _______ That Rocks the Cradle* (1992)

ROUND 3

1. HEAR MY SONG

I will give you the titles of three songs from famous musicals – just tell me the name of the film they are taken from for a point.

a) "Maria", "America", "Somewhere".

b) "Grow for Me", "Somewhere That's Green", "Suddenly, Seymour".

c) "Another Day of Sun", "City of Stars", "Audition (the Fools Who Dream)".

d) "A Million Dreams", "Never Enough", "Rewrite the Stars".

e) "Wouldn't It Be Loverly?", "The Rain in Spain", "I've Grown Accustomed to Her Face".

2. THE ODD COUPLE

I'll describe an actor and a film character that share the same initials. A point for each you can name.

a) **Actor:** American actor born in 1938. Found fame playing Joe Buck in *Midnight Cowboy* (1969) and Ed Gentry in *Deliverance* (1972). He won the Best Actor Oscar for his performance of Luke Martin the Vietnam veteran in *Coming Home* (1978). He is the father of Angelina Jolie.
Character: The central protagonist in the *Friday the 13th* series of films. He made his debut appearance in 1980, though he was not the main character until the first sequel onwards. His trademark hockey-mask look did not appear until the third film *Friday the 13th Part III*.

b) **Actor:** American actor born in 1980. Her breakthrough role was Alma Del Mar in the 2005 movie *Brokeback Mountain*, for which she was Oscar nominated. Her next major role was portraying Marilyn Monroe in *My Week with Marilyn* (2011) and again she was Oscar nominated. Her other films include *Manchester by the Sea* (2016), *Venom* (2018) and *The Fabelmans* (2022). **Character:** Alongside James P. Sullivan, he is a central character in the films *Monsters, Inc* (2001) and *Monsters University* (2013). He is a small, green, one-eyed monster voiced by Billy Crystal.

c) **Actor:** American actor born in 1924. Known for playing mostly tough-guy roles in films such as *The Big Heat* (1953), *The Man Who Shot Liberty Valance* (1962) *The Dirty Dozen* and *Point Blank* (both 1967) and *The Big Red One* (1980). He could also play comedy roles (in *Cat Ballou* – 1965, and *Paint Your Wagon* – 1969, for example). Before acting, he served in the Second World War, and his decorations include the Purple Heart. **Character:** From the *Harry Potter* series of films (2001–2011), this character debuts in *Harry Potter and the Chamber of Secrets* (2002). He is the head of a wizarding family, his wife is Narcissa, and their son is called Draco. He was portrayed in the films by Jason Isaacs.

d) **Actor:** American actor born in 1983. Also a singer who records under the name Childish Gambino, this actor played Aaron Davis in *Spider-Man: Homecoming* (2017), Lando Calrissian in *Solo: A Star Wars Story* (2018) and was the voice of Simba in *The Lion King* (2019) and *Mufasa: The Lion King* (2024). **Character:** The well-meaning but annoying shower-curtain-ring salesman portrayed by John Candy in the 1987 film *Planes, Trains and Automobiles*. Neal Page (Steve Martin) gets stuck with Candy's character as they both attempt to make it home for Christmas.

e) **Actor:** Irish actor born in 1930. An actor and singer who is almost as well known for his "hellraiser" lifestyle as his movies. He was nominated for two Best Actor Oscars, firstly for *This Sporting Life* (1963), then 27 years later for *The Field* (1990). Other performances include *A Man Called Horse* (1970) and its sequels, King Arthur in *Camelot* (1967), *The Wild Geese* (1978) and the first two *Harry Potter* movies (2001–2002) in which he portrayed Albus Dumbledore.
Character: The character that Eddie Murphy made his film debut with in *48 Hours* (1982), playing opposite Nick Nolte in that action comedy. He then reprised the role for the sequel *Another 48 Hours* (1990). Murphy played the fast-talking convict to Nolte's taciturn cop.

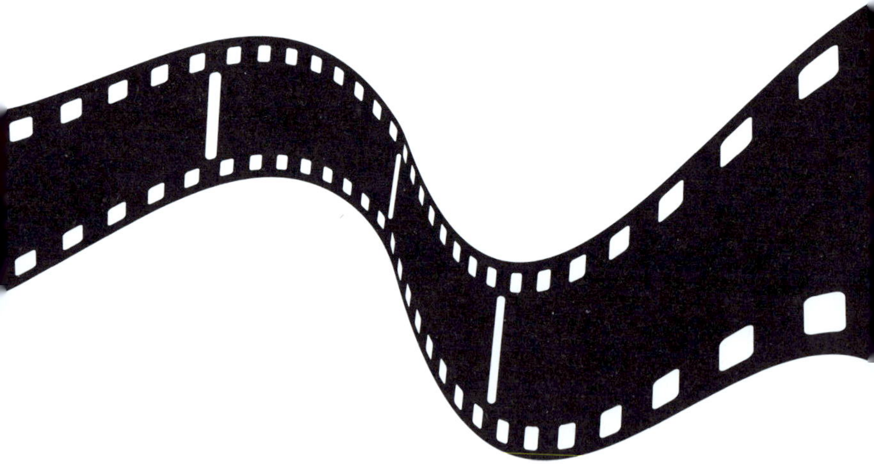

ROUND 4

1. BRAINSTORM

Complete the lists and spot the links – a point for each correct answer.

a) What connects Jay and Mark, Peter and Bobby, Anthony and Joseph, and Joel and Ethan?

b) The title of which 1994 film starring Jack Nicholson and Michelle Pfeiffer is pluralized (though incorrectly spelled) in a 2024 film title starring Brad Pitt and George Clooney?

c) Which historical figure was portrayed by Ingrid Bergman in 1948, Milla Jovovich in 1999 and Jane Wiedlin in 1989?

d) What connects Val Kilmer in 1991, Sam Riley in 2007, Rami Malek in 2018 and Kristen Stewart in 2010?

e) Which American journalist and author has been portrayed by Bill Murray and Johnny Depp?

2. IT FOLLOWS

The first letter of each answer follows the first letter of the last. So, if the answer to c) is "Apple", the answer to d) will begin with "B". If you get to Z, go to A. Each question is worth one point.

a) What is the name of the 2021 film by Edgar Wright, starring Anya Taylor-Joy, that marked the final screen appearance of Diana Rigg?

b) What word goes after *Hit* ________ (2023), *Monkey* ________ (2024), *First* ________ (2018) and *Demolition* ________ (1993) to make titles of films from those years?

c) Can you name the American filmmaker who co-wrote *Barbie* (2023), co-wrote *The Life Aquatic with Steve Zissou* (2004) and wrote and directed *White Noise* (2022) and *Marriage Story* (2019)?

d) What is the surname of Frank, the puppeteer, filmmaker and actor, best known for his work with the Muppets and his portrayal (puppeteer and voice) of Yoda from the *Star Wars* films?

e) What is the name of the actor probably best known for the two characters *Foxy Brown* (1974) and *Jackie Brown* (1997)?

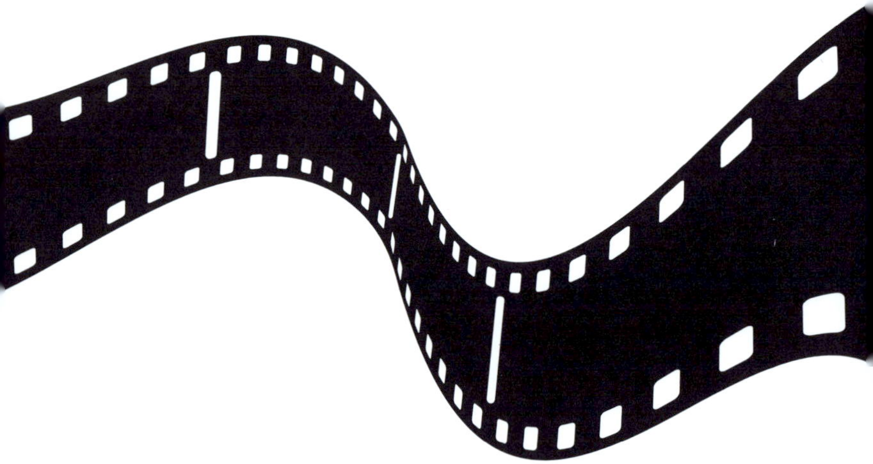

ROUND 5

THE LAST PICTURE SHOW

Say what you see! Can you identify the films from these picture clues? Each picture is worth a point.

1

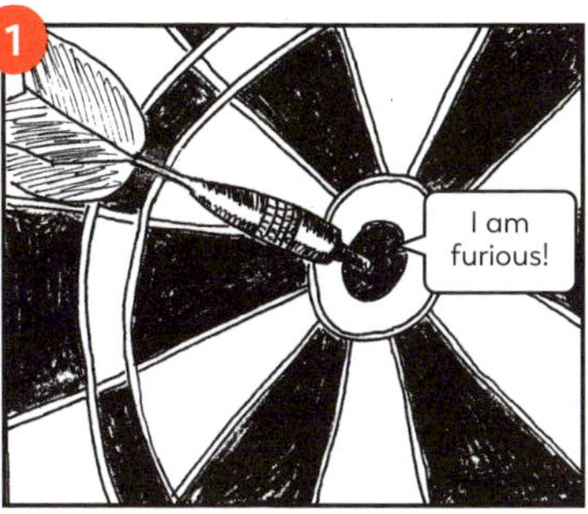

2

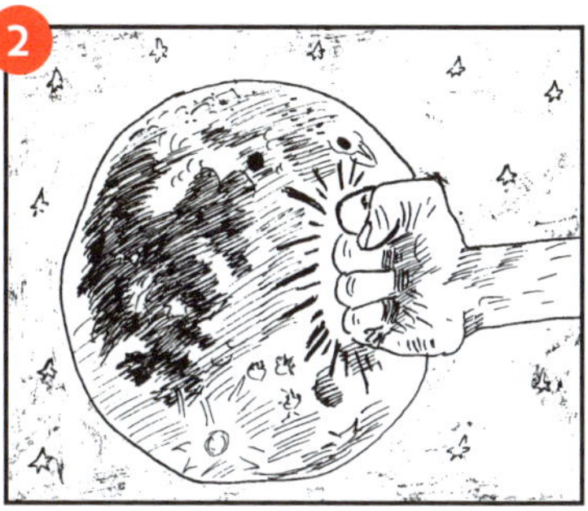

3

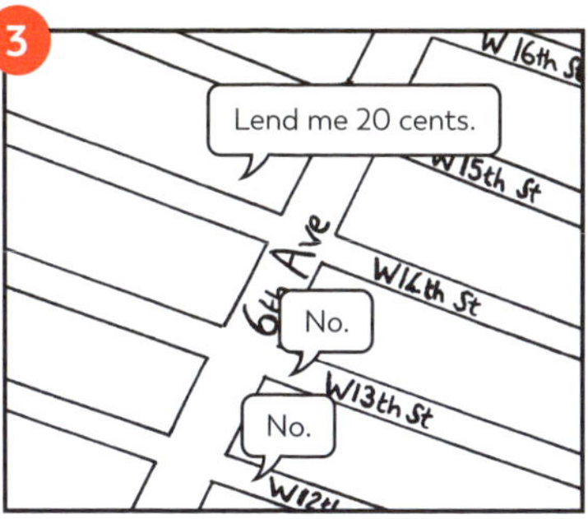

4

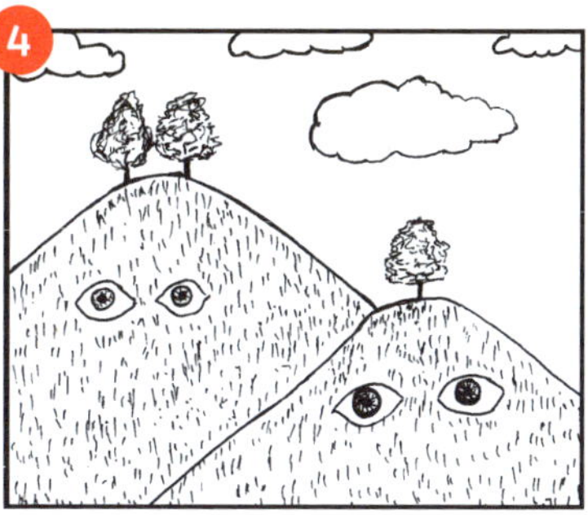

5

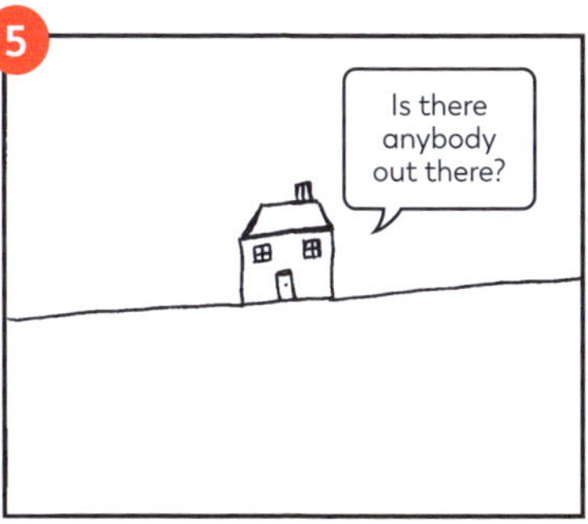

6

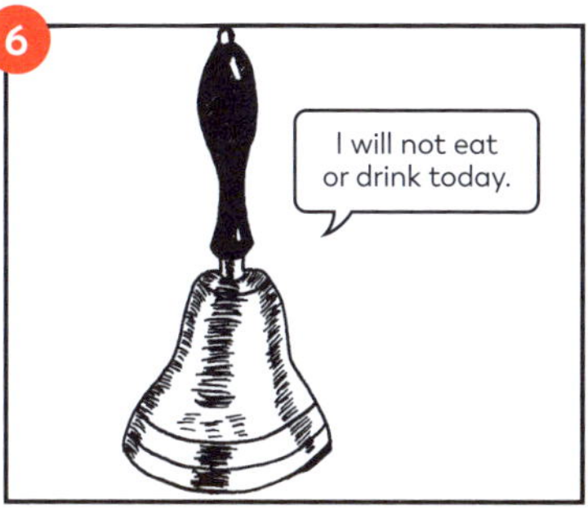

ANSWERS

ROUND 1

1. c) *Fried Green Tomatoes at the Whistle Stop Café* (1991). *Chocolat* was 2000, *Cloudy with a Chance of Meatballs* was 2009.

2. Buster Keaton

Buster Keaton claimed Harry Houdini inspired the nickname "Buster" after witnessing him tumble unhurt down a flight of stairs as an infant.

3. b) *Monty Python's Life of Brian*

4. a) *Apocalypse Now*

5. c) *A Taste of Honey* by Tony Richardson.

6. *Key Largo* and *Fargo*.

7. a) For years Brian Dennehy lied about serving in and being wounded in Vietnam (he stated that he began "shooting his mouth off in bars" then, later, didn't know how to set the record straight).

8. a) James Bond (*Casino Royale*)

9. 1988

10. *The Deer Hunter* (1978), ***Kramer vs. Kramer* (1979 – win)**, *The French Lieutenant's Woman* (1981), ***Sophie's Choice* (1982 – win)**, *Silkwood* (1983), *Out of Africa* (1985), *Ironweed* (1987), *A Cry in the Dark* (1988), *Postcards from the Edge* (1990), *The Bridges of Madison County* (1995), *One True Thing* (1998), *Music of the Heart* (1999), *Adaptation* (2002), *The Devil Wears Prada* (2006), *Doubt* (2008), *Julie & Julia* (2009), ***The Iron Lady* (2011 – win)**, *August:*

Osage County (2013), *Into the Woods* (2014), *Florence Foster Jenkins* (2016), *The Post* (2017).

ROUND 2

1. a) iii) *Zombieland: Double Tap* (2019)

1. b) ii) *Alfie Darling* (1975)

It was based on a novel by Bill Naughton who wrote the play the original *Alfie* was based on. Michael Caine did not return; instead, Alan Price (the musician) took the part. It was not a success, with *Time Out* calling it "... an advert with no product to sell".

1. c) ii) *Next Friday* (2000)

The next film is called *Friday After Next* (2002).

1. d) i) *The Whole Ten Yards* (2004)

1. e) iii) *I Still Know What You Did Last Summer* (1998)

There was also a third film, straight to video, with no original cast members, called *I'll Always Know What You Did Last Summer* (2006). Sadly, that was the last one, but I'd have liked to have heard the next title.

2. a) *Dial*

2. b) *Case*

2. c) *Pendulum*

2. d) *Face*

2. e) *Hand*

ROUND 3

1. a) *West Side Story* (1961)

1. b) *Little Shop of Horrors* (1986)

1. c) *La La Land* (2016)

1. d) *The Greatest Showman* (2017)

1. e) *My Fair Lady* (1964)

2. a) Jon Voight and Jason Voorhees.

2. b) Michelle Williams and Mike Wazowski.

2. c) Lee Marvin and Lucius Malfoy.

2. d) Donald Glover and Del Griffith.

2. e) Richard Harris and Reggie Hammond.

ROUND 4

1. a) They are brothers who make/have made films together. Jay and Mark Duplass, Peter and Bobby Farrelly, Anthony and Joseph Russo, and Joel and Ethan Coen.

1. b) *Wolf* (*Wolfs*)

1. c) Joan of Arc. Ingrid Bergman: *Joan of Arc*, Milla Jovovich: *The Messenger: The Story of Joan of Arc*, Jane Wiedlin: *Bill and Ted's Excellent Adventure*.

1. d) In those years, they portrayed lead singers in bands. Val Kilmer played Jim Morrison in *The Doors*, Sam Riley played Ian Curtis in *Control*, Rami Malek played Freddie Mercury in *Bohemian Rhapsody* and Kristen Stewart played Joan Jett in *The Runaways*.

1. e) Hunter S. Thompson. Johnny Depp played him in *Fear and Loathing in Las Vegas* (1998) and Bill Murray played him in *Where the Buffalo Roam* (1980).

2. a) *Last Night in Soho*

2. b) "Man". *Hit Man, Monkey Man, First Man* and *Demolition Man.*

2. c) Noah Baumbach

2. d) Oz

2. e) Pam Grier

ROUND 5

1. *Raging Bull* (1980)
2. *Moonstruck* (1987)
3. *Mean Streets* (1973)
4. *The Hills Have Eyes* (1977)
5. *Home Alone* (1990)
6. *Belfast* (2021)

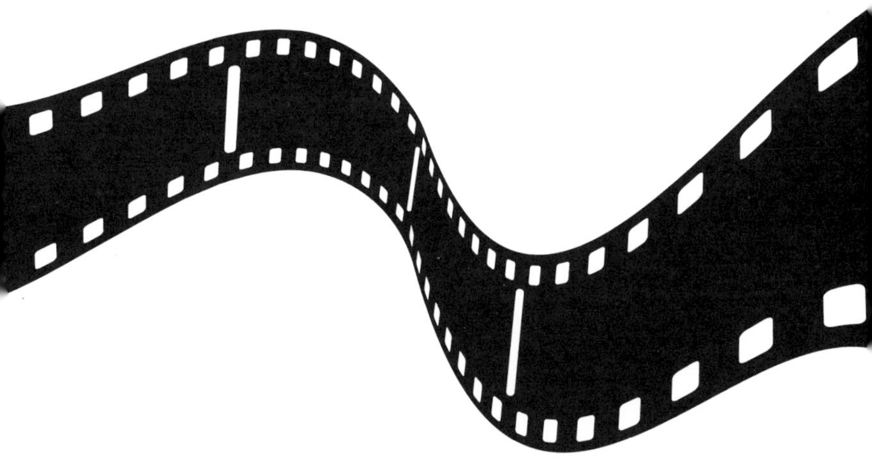

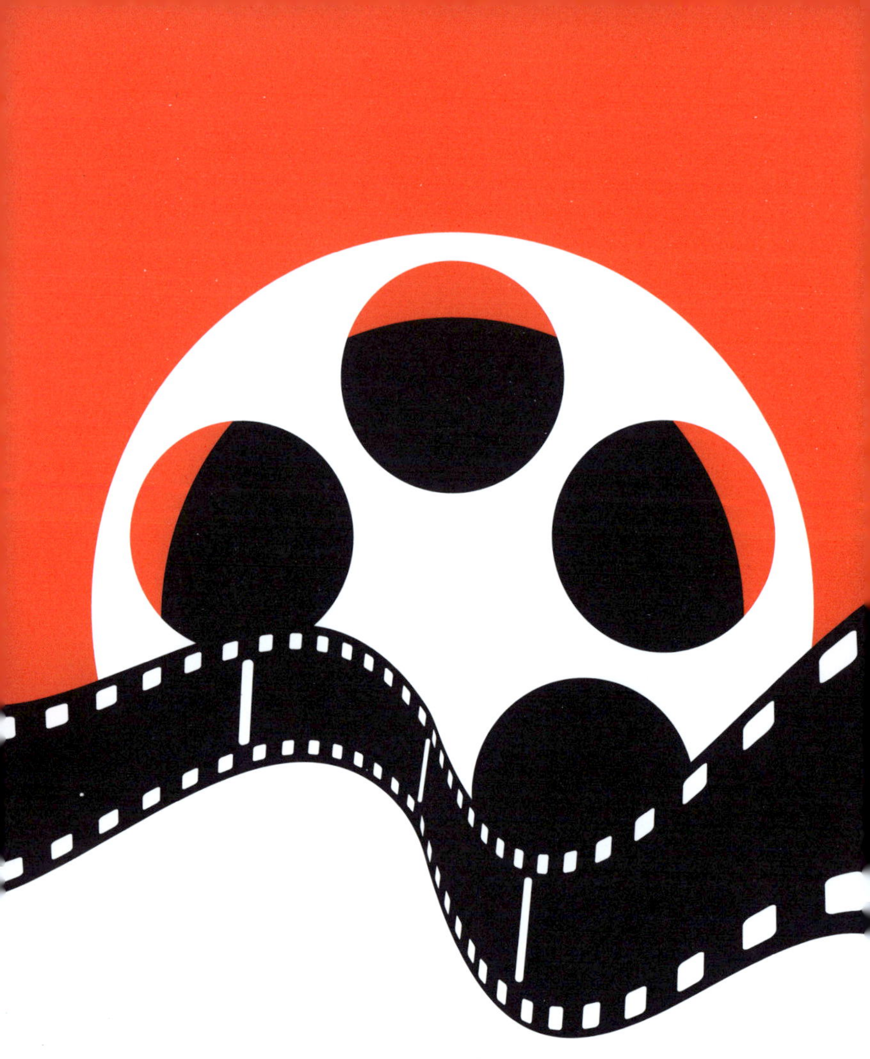

QUIZ 17

ROUND 1

STARTER FOR 10

Ten questions to begin!

1. THE FIRST QUESTION

Which of these "First" films was released first?

a) *The First Wives Club*

b) *First Blood*

c) *First Knight*

2. THE ANAGRAM

Unscramble the actor's name: AIM GUN CLEARLY

3. FILM QUOTE

What film is the following quote from?

"Roads? Where we're going, we don't need roads!"

a) *WALL-E* (2008)

b) *Labyrinth* (1986)

c) *Back to the Future* (1985)

d) *Waterworld* (1995)

4. THUMBS DOWN

What film is this the one-star review of?

"Just back and forth shots of [REDACTED] and [REDACTED] just wandering around and doing nothing, or being together and doing nothing. Also, it's tagged as a 'comedy'... WHAT COMEDY??? Comedy means funny stuff, nothing funny happens at any point!"

a) *Eternal Sunshine of the Spotless Mind* (2004)

b) *Lost in Translation* (2003)

c) *Being John Malkovich* (1999)

5. ODD ONE OUT

Which of these films was not directed by Richard Attenborough? Bonus point if you know who it was directed by.

a) *Amadeus* (1984)

b) *Gandhi* (1982)

c) *Chaplin* (1992)

6. RHYMING FILMS

I'll give you the initials of two films whose titles rhyme with each other. I'll also give you one of the stars and the years they were released, just name the films for a point each.

TWB, William Holden (1969) and NL, Peter Weller (1991).

7. CELLULOID OR CELLULIED?

Which of the following is true about *Nosferatu* (1922) director F. W. Murnau?

a) There are no known photographs of F. W. Murnau.

b) F. W. Murnau's skull was stolen by grave robbers.

c) F. W. Murnau was terrified of bats.

8. WHAT MIGHT HAVE BEEN

Which of these roles did Madonna turn down?

a) Madison (*Splash* – 1984)

b) Elle Woods (*Legally Blonde* – 2001)

c) Catwoman (*Batman Returns* – 1992)

9. WHAT YEAR?

In what year did the following things happen?

Films released this year include: *Jaws, One Flew Over the Cuckoo's Nest, The Rocky Horror Picture Show, Tommy, Dog Day Afternoon, Monty Python and the Holy Grail* and *Barry Lyndon*. Bradley Cooper, Drew Barrymore, Pedro Pascal, Angelina Jolie, Marion Cotillard and Milla Jovovich are born. Director Pier Paolo Pasolini is brutally murdered at a beach in Ostia, Italy. Gene Siskel and Roger Ebert team up to review films for the first time; they will co-host various shows for the next 24 years. But what was the year?

10. GIVE ME FIVE

A chance for five points! You have a choice here: Name five of the actors that make up the "11" in either *Oceans 11* from 1960 *or* from the remake in 2001. There are, of course, 11 possible answers for each.

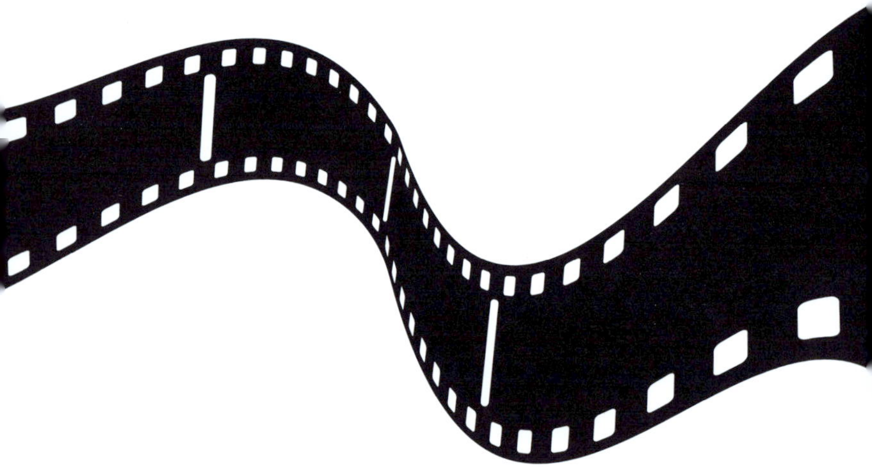

ROUND 2

1. ENCORE

Here are five film titles with alliterative missing words – can you fill the words in? A point for each title completed.

a) *The Fabulous* _ _ _ _ _/_ _ _ _ (1999)

b) *The* _ _ _ _ _/_ _ _ _ _/ *of Success* (1957)

c) *Charlie* _ _ _ _ _ _ _ _/_ _ _ (2007)

d) *McCabe &* _ _ _/_ _ _ _ _ _ _ (1971)

e) _ _ _ _ _ _ _ _/_ _ _/ *Odds* (1984)

2. ONE OF OUR ______ IS MISSING!

Just fill in the missing word – there's always a theme, and this time it's... games (board and card).

a) ________ *of Spies* (2015)

b) ________ *in Atlantis* (2001)

c) ________ *Petticoat* (1959)

d) *Never Let Me* ________ (2010)

e) *Flight* ________ (2024)

ROUND 3

1. YOU DON'T KNOW JACK

(Or do you?) These films starred either Jack Nicholson, Jack Black or Jack Lemmon. A point for each you can identify.

a) *Mister Roberts*

b) *Shallow Hal*

c) *The China Syndrome*

d) *Blood and Wine*

e) *The Two Jakes*

2. THE ODD COUPLE

I'll describe an actor and a film character that share the same initials. A point for each you can name.

a) **Actor:** American actor born in 1966. One of the most successful comedy actors of the modern age, his starring roles include *Billy Madison* (1995), *Happy Gilmore* (1996), *The Wedding Singer* (1998), *50 First Dates* (2004) and *Murder Mystery* (2019). He has also received critical acclaim for serious parts in *Punch-Drunk Love* (2002) and *Uncut Gems* (2019). **Character:** The original name of the character that later becomes Darth Vader in the *Star Wars* universe. Played by Jake Lloyd and Hayden Christensen in the *Star Wars* prequels (1995–2005).

b) **Actor:** American actor born in 1957. Made her debut in *Reuben, Reuben* (1983) but her breakout role was Rachel Lapp in *Witness* (1985). She cemented her star status with *Top Gun* (1986) the following year. **Character:** The young boy left home alone in the film series of the same name. Played in the first two films (*Home Alone* – 1990, and *Home Alone 2: Lost in New York* – 1992) by Macaulay Culkin.

c) **Actor:** American actor born in 1924. Widely regarded as one of the greatest actors of the twentieth century, he is often credited with changing the nature of screen acting. Key performances include Stanley Kowalski in *A Streetcar Named Desire* (1951), Johnny Strabler in *The Wild One* (1953), Terry Malloy in *On the Waterfront* (1954), Don Vito Corleone in *The Godfather* (1972), Paul in *Last Tango in Paris* (1972) and Colonel Walter E. Kurtz in *Apocalypse Now* (1979). **Character:** From Peter Jackson's *The Lord of the Rings* trilogy (2001–2003), this hobbit and his cousin Pippin join forces with Frodo in the "fellowship of the ring", though Frodo and Pippin are separated from the rest of the group for much of the adventure. He was portrayed in these films by Dominic Monaghan.

d) **Actor:** American actor born in 1943. This actor's first major role was Nikanor "Nick" Chevotarevich in *The Deer Hunter* (1978), for which he won the Best Supporting Actor Oscar. He often plays villainous parts, including antagonists in *A View to a Kill* (1985), *King of New York* (1990), *Batman Returns* (1992) and *The Prophecy* (1995). He is also well known for memorable small roles in *True Romance* (1993), *Pulp Fiction* (1994) and *Sleepy Hollow* (1999). **Character:** The protagonist of the 1976 horror film by Brian De Palma based on the 1974 novel by Stephen King. This shy teenager is mocked and bullied at school until she uses her telekinetic powers to wreak her revenge.

e) **Actor:** Canadian actor born in 1963. Best known for three creations – his spoof of James Bond, *Austin Powers* (1997–2002); the teenage rock fan Wayne Campbell; and for his voice work as *Shrek* (2001). **Character:** The time-travelling teenage star of the *Back to the Future* trilogy (1985–1990) portrayed by Michael J. Fox.

ROUND 4

1. BRAINSTORM

Complete the lists and spot the links – a point for each correct answer.

a) What first name is shared by the actors Cagney, Coburn, Cromwell and Caan?

b) Which American city was the location for the following films: *Bullitt* (1968), *Dirty Harry* (1971), *Ant-Man* (2015) and *Mrs. Doubtfire* (1993)?

c) What is the *Milano* in a film from 2014, the *Gunstar* in a 1984 film, the *Endurance* from 2014 and *Discovery One* from 1968?

d) Rose Byrne, Jacob Elordi, Eric Bana and Chris Hemsworth were all born in which country?

e) Which character has been portrayed by Alec Baldwin, Harrison Ford, Ben Affleck and Chris Pine?

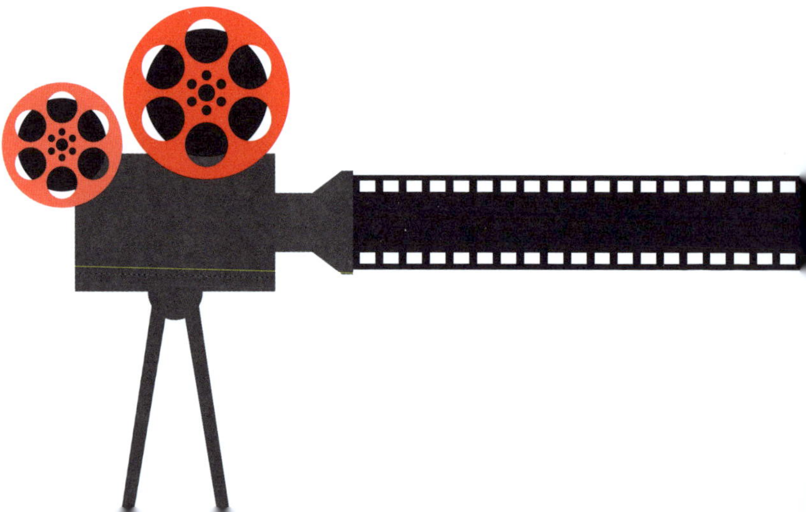

2. IT FOLLOWS

The first letter of each answer follows the first letter of the last. So, if the answer to c) is "Apple", the answer to d) will begin with "B". If you get to Z, go to A. Each question is worth one point.

a) In 1982, John Huston directed the only musical of his career. What was it called?

b) What word connects the title of the debut film by Rian Johnson (2005), the character played by Paul Newman in *Cat on a Hot Tin Roof* (1958) and the character played by Steve Carell in *Anchorman: The Legend of Ron Burgundy* (2004)?

c) What is the surname of Billy, the central character in the 1969 Ken Loach film *Kes*, and the name of a friendly ghost in a 1995 film starring Christina Ricci?

d) What is the name of the character played by Dave Bautista in *The Guardians of the Galaxy* films (2014–2023)?

e) What is the first name of the boy that discovers and befriends E.T. in *E.T. the Extra-Terrestrial* (1982), the name of *Pete's Dragon* (1977) and the antagonist of *Tomorrow Never Dies* (1997) played by Jonathan Pryce?

ROUND 5

THE LAST PICTURE SHOW

Say what you see! Can you identify the films from these picture clues? Each picture is worth a point.

1
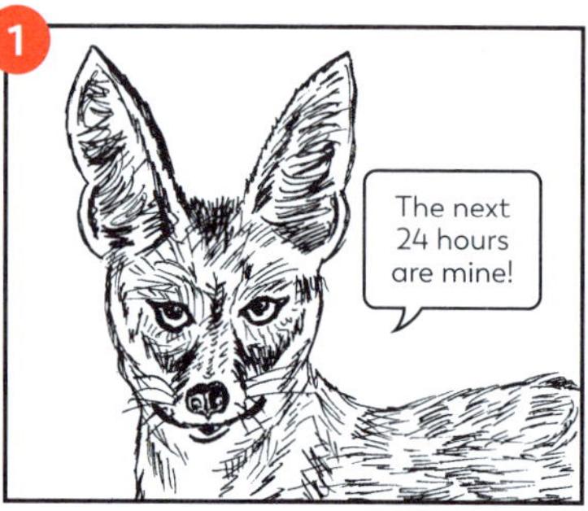

2
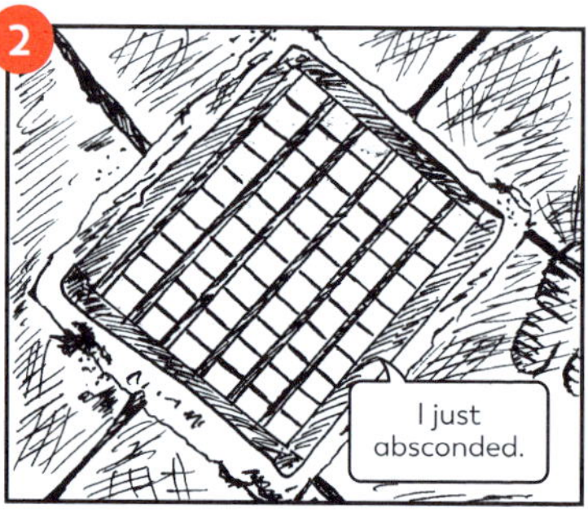

3
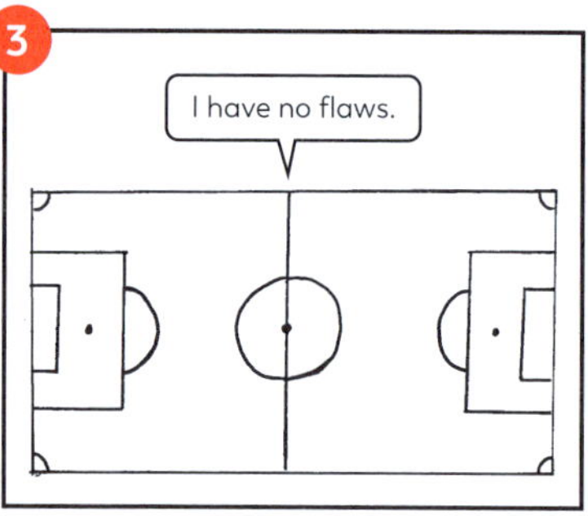

4
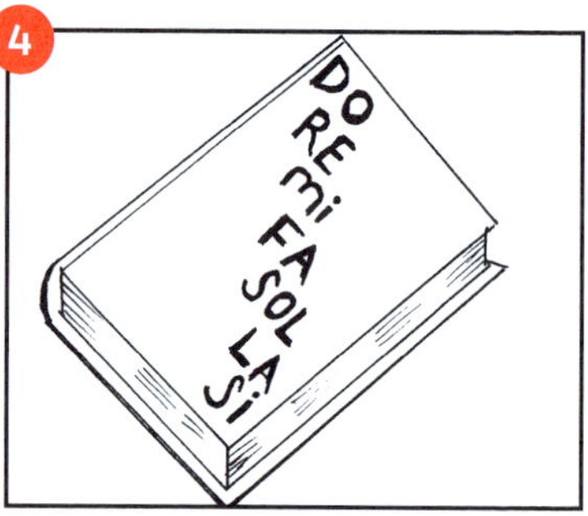

5
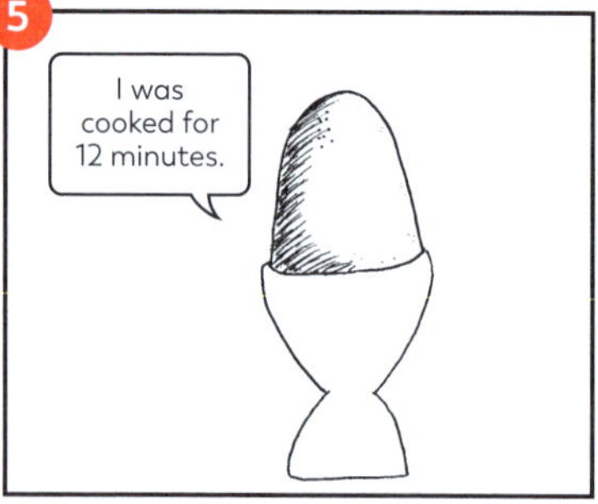

6
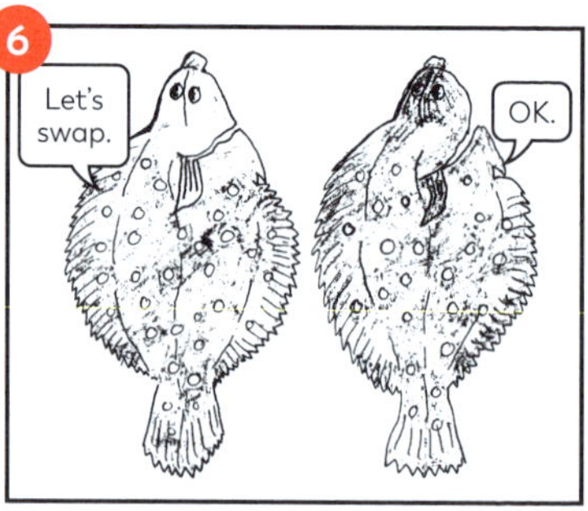

ANSWERS

ROUND 1

1. b) *First Blood* (1982). *The First Wives Club* was 1996, *First Knight* 1995.

2. Carey Mulligan

3. c) *Back to the Future*

4. b) *Lost in Translation*

5. a) *Amadeus* by Miloš Forman.

In *Amadeus*, Tom Hulce reportedly modelled Mozart's mood swings on tennis champion John McEnroe's famous on-court temper tantrums.

6. *The Wild Bunch* and *Naked Lunch*.

7. b) F. W. Murnau's skull was stolen by grave robbers. It was taken from the Stahnsdorf Cemetery outside Berlin in 2015 and is still missing (at time of writing).

8. c) Catwoman (*Batman Returns*)

9. 1975

10. 1960: Frank Sinatra, Dean Martin, Sammy Davis Jr, Peter Lawford, Richard Conte, Joey Bishop, Henry Silva, Buddy Lester, Richard Benedict, Norman Fell, Clem Harvey.

2001: George Clooney, Bernie Mac, Brad Pitt, Elliott Gould, Casey Affleck, Scott Caan, Eddie Jemison, Don Cheadle, Qin Shaobo, Carl Reiner, Matt Damon.

Don Cheadle was not credited on the film due to a dispute over billing, though he did return for the sequels.

ROUND 2

1. a) *The Fabulous Baker Boys*

1. b) *The Sweet Smell of Success*

1. c) *Charlie Wilson's War*

1. d) *McCabe & Mrs. Miller*

1. e) *Against All Odds*

2. a) *Bridge*

2. b) *Hearts*

2. c) *Operation*

2. d) *Go*

2. e) *Risk*

ROUND 3

1. a) Jack Lemmon

1. b) Jack Black

1. c) Jack Lemmon

1. d) Jack Nicholson

1. e) Jack Nicholson

2. a) Adam Sandler and Anakin Skywalker.

2. b) Kelly McGillis and Kevin McCallister.

2. c) Marlon Brando and Meriadoc "Merry" Brandybuck.

2. d) Christopher Walken and Carrie White.

2. e) Mike Myers and Marty McFly.

ROUND 4

1. a) James

1. b) San Francisco

1. c) They are all spaceships. The *Milano* from *Guardians of the Galaxy*, *Gunstar* from *The Last Starfighter*, the *Endurance* from *Interstellar* and *Discovery One* from *2001: A Space Odyssey*.

1. d) Australia

1. e) Jack Ryan. Alec Baldwin in *The Hunt for Red October* (1990), Harrison Ford in *Patriot Games* (1992), Ben Affleck in *The Sum of All Fears* (2002) and Chris Pine in *Jack Ryan: Shadow Recruit* (2014).

2. a) *Annie*

Huston picked up a nomination for Worst Director at the Razzie Awards for *Annie*.

2. b) Brick. Paul Newman plays "Brick" Pollitt and Steve Carell plays Brick Tamland.

2. c) Casper

In 2021, a statue of Billy Casper and his kestrel was unveiled in Barnsley. The statue is a tribute to the author of the source novel (*A Kestrel for a Knave*), Barry Hines.

2. d) Drax (the Destroyer)

2. e) Elliot(t). (Elliott Taylor in *E.T.*, Elliott the Dragon in *Pete's Dragon*, Elliot Carver in *Tomorrow Never Dies*).

ROUND 5

1. *The Day of the Jackal* (1973)
2. *The Great Escape* (1963)
3. *Pitch Perfect* (2012)
4. *The Notebook* (2004)
5. *Hard Boiled* (1992)
6. *Trading Places* (1983)

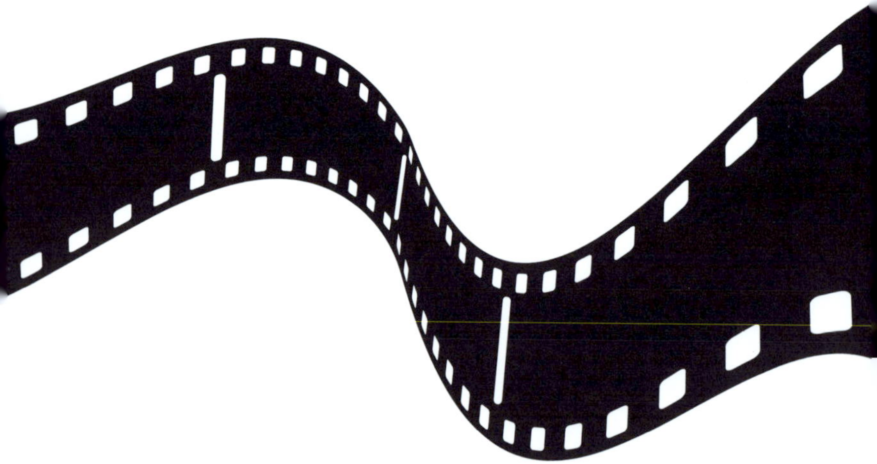

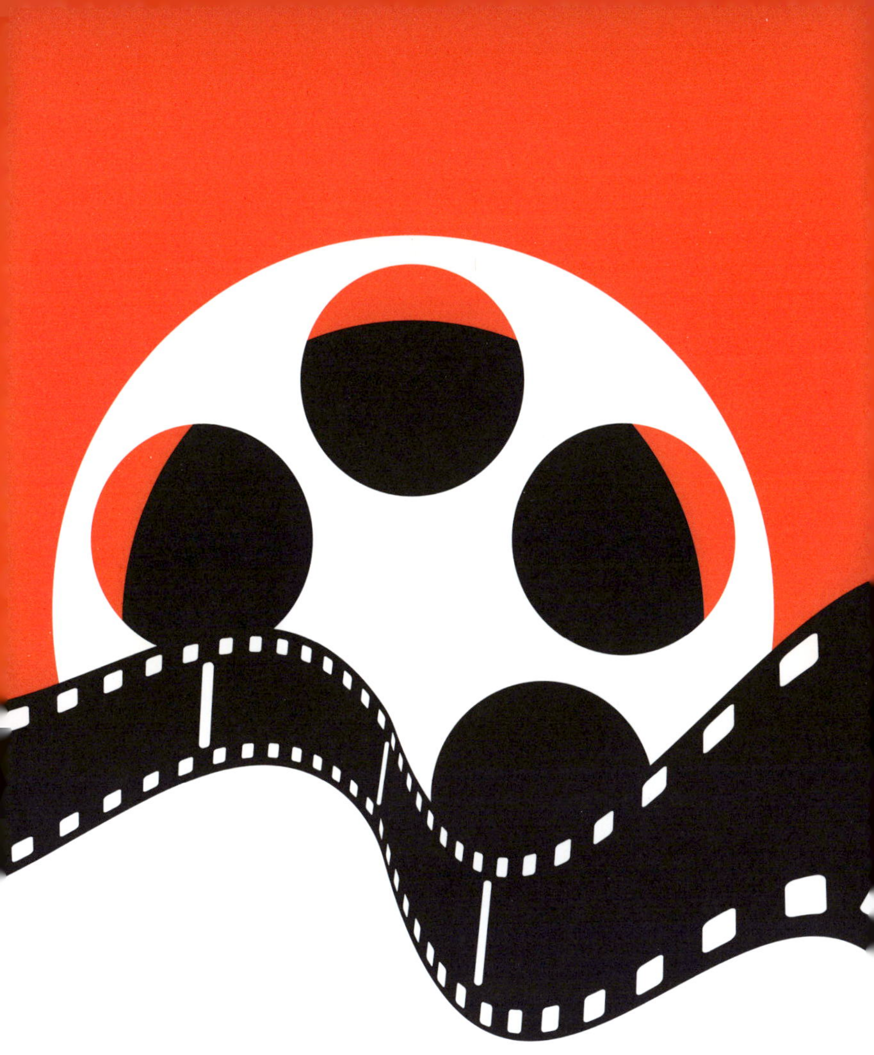

QUIZ 18

ROUND 1

STARTER FOR 10

Ten questions to begin!

1. THE FIRST QUESTION

Which of these actors named Paul was born first?

a) Paul Rudd

b) Paul Bettany

c) Paul Giamatti

2. THE ANAGRAM

Unscramble the actor's name: POETRY INSIDE I

3. FILM QUOTE

What film is the following quote from?

"No matter what anybody tells you, words and ideas can change the world."

a) *Gandhi* (1982)

b) *Dead Poets Society* (1989)

c) *The Pianist* (2002)

d) *Sex Lives of the Potato Men* (2004)

4. THUMBS DOWN

What film is this the one-star review of?

"The film literally has no redeeming qualities. It is littered with stupid, slapstick humour for four-year-olds and a lot of the effects actually look pretty rubbish if you ask me. Parts looked great, but some of it looked so computer generated you could clearly see it was nothing but a cut and paste job, with actors dropped in on backgrounds. I've seen better stuff done on YouTube."

a) *Harry Potter and the Philosopher's Stone* (*Sorcerer's Stone* in the US – 2001)

b) *Sonic the Hedgehog* (2020)

c) *Star Wars: Episode I – The Phantom Menace* (1999)

5. ODD ONE OUT

Which of these films was not directed by Oliver Stone? Bonus point if you know who it was directed by.

a) *Nixon* (1995)

b) *Lincoln* (2012)

c) *JFK* (1991)

6. RHYMING FILMS

I'll give you the initials of two films whose titles rhyme with each other. I'll also give you one of the stars and the years they were released, just name the films for a point each.

OUATITW, Henry Ford (1968) and OFOTCN, Jack Nicholson (1975).

7. CELLULOID OR CELLULIED?

Which of the following is true about Christopher Nolan?

a) Christopher Nolan doesn't use a smartphone.

b) Christopher Nolan refuses to fly anywhere.

c) Christopher Nolan will not use Sellotape.

8. WHAT MIGHT HAVE BEEN

Which of these roles did Al Pacino turn down?

a) Agent K (*Men in Black* – 1997)

b) Han Solo (*Star Wars: Episode IV – A New Hope – 1977*)

c) Lord Voldemort (*Harry Potter and the Philosopher's Stone* – *Sorcerer's Stone* in the US – 2001)

9. WHAT YEAR?

In what year did the following things happen?

Films released this year include: *The Exorcist, Papillon, The Sting, Live and Let Die, Serpico, American Graffiti, Badlands, Mean Streets, The Day of the Jackal, Westworld, Don't Look Now, The Wicker Man, Sleeper* and *Theatre of Blood*. Bruce Lee, on the cusp of international success, dies at the age of 32. Edward G. Robinson, John Ford and Veronica Lake also pass away. Adrien Brody, Kate Beckinsale, Kristen Wiig and Rian Johnson are born. But what was the year?

10. GIVE ME FIVE

A chance for five points! Name five films directed by Alan Parker. There are 15 possible answers.

ROUND 2

1. DEATH WATCH

In each question, I'm going to describe three death scenes. I will only use actor names, not characters – one actor links all three. Name the actor for one point, name each film for bonuses. Four points available per question. SPOILER ALERT!

a) ________

i) Falls from the Nakatomi Tower on Christmas Eve (1988).

ii) Killed in a duel (using swords) with Kevin Costner (1991).

iii) Bitten by a large snake owned by Ralph Fiennes (2011).

b) ________

i) Shot by Kyle MacLachlan using Fred Pickler's gun (1986).

ii) Decapitated on the roof of a train by a railway signal (1994).

iii) Shot by Christopher Walken after smoking a final Chesterfield cigarette (1993).

c) ________

i) Has two knives thrown at him by Danny Trejo while he is talking to Antonio Banderas (1995).

ii) Killed by Peter Stormare, dismembered (offscreen) and fed into a woodchipper (1996).

iii) Suffers a heart attack in a car park brawl alongside his friends Jeff Bridges and John Goodman (1998).

d) _______

- **i)** Murdered by Robert Mitchum (off camera) who then ties her body to a Model-T Ford and submerges it (1955).
- **ii)** Accidently hit by a car driven by Betty Field (1949).
- **iii)** Has a heart attack after rescuing Gene Hackman who was trapped underwater (1972).

e) _______

- **i)** Pushed off a cliff by a herd of cattle (1990).
- **ii)** Falls off a satellite dish after a fight with Pierce Brosnan, the dish then lands on him (1995).
- **iii)** Pierced by three arrows shot by Lawrence Makoare (2001).

2. ONE OF OUR _______ IS MISSING!

Just fill in the missing word – there's always a theme, and this time it's... vehicles.

a) *Bullet* _______ (2022)

b) _______ *Thieves* (1948)

c) *The* _______ *That Ate Paris* (1974)

d) *The* _______ *Diaries* (2004)

e) *Show* _______ (1936)

ROUND 3

1. THE LAST WORD

Here are five pairs of films where the title ends with the same word. I will give you that word, one actor from the film and the years they were released. Name both films – a point for each.

a) The word is "Club". Film one was released in 2013 starring Matthew McConaughey. Film two was released in 1996 starring Goldie Hawn.

b) The word is "Love". Film one was released in 2011 starring Steve Carell. Film two was released in 2000 starring Tony Leung Chiu-wai.

c) The word is "Train". Film one was released in 2016 starring Emily Blunt. Film two was released in 1995 starring Wesley Snipes.

d) The word is "Sea". Film one was released in 2016 starring Casey Affleck. Film two was released in 2011 starring Rachel Weisz.

e) The word is "World". Film one was released in 2017 starring Michelle Williams. Film two was released in 2001 starring Thora Birch.

2. THE ODD COUPLE II

This time I'll describe a film character and a director that share the same initials. A point for each you can name.

a) **Character:** The central protagonist of the initial *Alien* series of films (1979–1997), portrayed by Sigourney Weaver. In the first film the character, a warrant officer, is awakened from stasis as the ship (the *Nostromo*) has received a transmission from a nearby planetoid. **Director:** American director, actor, screenwriter and producer born in 1972. Best known as a horror director, his films include *Cabin Fever* (2002) and *Hostel* (2005). He has also acted in many films, including the part of Donny "The Bear Jew" Donowitz in *Inglourious Basterds* (2009). In 2024, he directed his eleventh film *Borderlands* starring Cate Blanchett.

b) **Character:** The female protagonist from *The African Queen* (1951), portrayed by Katharine Hepburn. The character is a missionary in East Africa with her brother Samuel. The war and the captain of the *African Queen* (a small steamboat), played by Humphrey Bogart, will change her life forever. **Director:** English director born in 1937. Hugely successful and eclectic director. Best known for films such as *Alien* (1979), *Blade Runner* (1982), *Thelma and Louise* (1991), *Gladiator* (2000) and *Napoleon* (2023). Nominated for three Best Director Academy Awards, he was awarded the BAFTA Fellowship in 2018.

c) **Character:** Bruce Wayne/Batman's butler. This father figure to the Caped Crusader has been played by several actors including Alan Napier in *Batman: The Movie* (1966), Michael Gough in *Batman* (1989) and the three subsequent films in that series, Michael Caine in Christopher Nolan's trilogy (2005–2012) and Andy Serkis in *The Batman* (2022). **Director:** American director born in 1961. Rose to prominence with his sophomore film *Election* (1999), which he also wrote and received an Academy Award nomination for Best Adapted Screenplay for – he won that award for his *Sideways* (2004) and *The Descendants* (2011). His 2023 film *The Holdovers* was nominated for five Academy Awards (and had one win for Best Supporting Actress).

d) **Character:** The main antagonist in the MCU movie *Black Panther* (2018). Played by Michael B. Jordan, he is a Navy SEAL who seeks revenge for the death of his father and to claim the throne of Wakanda. **Director:** American director born in 1909 in Constantinople (now Istanbul). In a career that spanned over 30 years, he was nominated for four Best Director Oscars; he won twice for *Gentleman's Agreement* (1947) and *On the Waterfront* (1954) but failed to win for *A Streetcar Named Desire* (1951) and *East of Eden* (1955). Kubrick called him "the best director we have in America".

e) **Character:** Portrayed by Carl Weathers in the first four *Rocky* films (1976–1985). In the first two films he fights Rocky (Sylvester Stallone), but in the latter he becomes his ally. The character's son went on to head up another franchise starring Michael B. Jordan. **Director:** Mexican director born in 1961. His breakthrough movie was *Y tu mamá también* (2001) and followed that by directing the third *Harry Potter* film (*The Prisoner of Azkaban* – 2004), which is widely regarded as the best entry in the series. His next film was the P. D. James adaptation *Children of Men* (2006). He won the Best Director Academy Award for his films *Gravity* (2013) and *Roma* (2018).

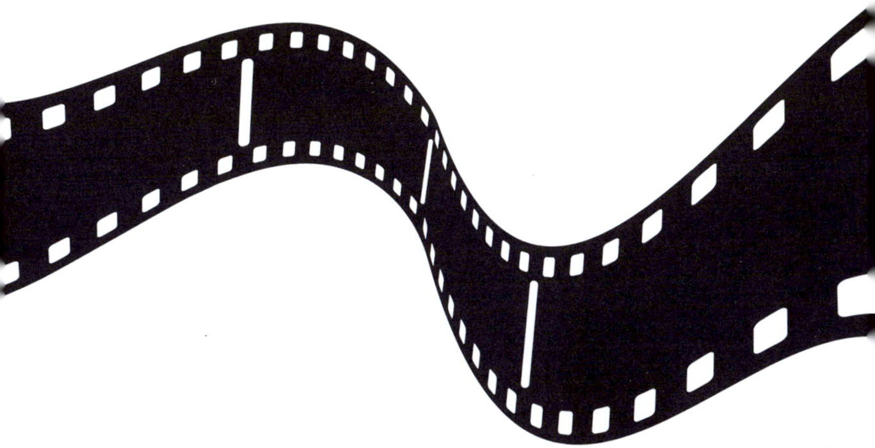

ROUND 4

1. BRAINSTORM

Complete the lists and spot the links – a point for each correct answer.

a) Which historical figure has been portrayed by Mick Jagger, Heath Ledger and George MacKay?

b) Which series of films has these subtitles: *Apocalypse* (2004), *Extinction* (2007), *Afterlife* (2010), *Retribution* (2012), *The Final Chapter* (2016)?

c) The novel *I Am Legend* by Richard Matheson has been adapted for the cinema three times, once in 2007 as *I Am Legend* starring Will Smith, once in 1964 as *The Last Man on Earth* starring Vincent Price and between those, a version in 1971 starring Charlton Heston – what was the title of that version?

d) Ann was born 1961, her sister Joan was born in 1962, their brother John followed in 1966. What is these acting siblings' surname?

e) What was *Hooch* in 1989, *Hachi* in 2009, *Marley* in 2008 and *Old Yeller* in 1957?

2. IT FOLLOWS

The first letter of each answer follows the first letter of the last. So, if the answer to c) is "Apple", the answer to d) will begin with "B". If you get to Z, go to A. Each question is worth one point.

a) The films *Slap Shot* (1977), *The Mighty Ducks* (1992), *Tooth Fairy* (2010) and *Goon* (2011) all feature which sport?

b) What is the name of the film from 1978 directed and co-written by Derek Jarman that sees Queen Elizabeth I transported forwards in time to 1977 by the occultist John Dee? The film featured various members of the punk scene, including Toyah Wilcox, Jordan (Pamela Rooke), Jayne County (then Wayne County) and Siouxsie Sioux.

c) Which character from the *Star Trek* films has been played by Ricardo Montalban (in 1982) and Benedict Cumberbatch (in 2009)?

d) In 1968, the first film to feature Herbie, the sentient Volkswagen Beetle car, was *The* ________ *Bug*?

e) What 2014 Disney film, starring Angelina Jolie, is a retelling of *Sleeping Beauty*?

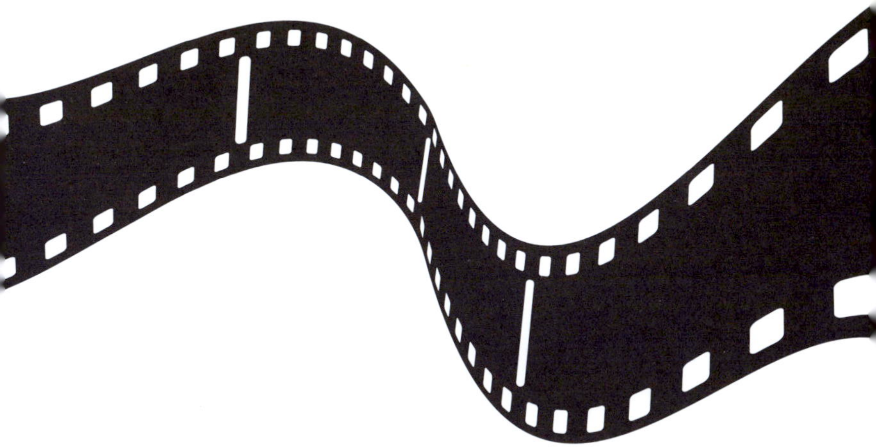

ROUND 5

THE LAST PICTURE SHOW

Say what you see! Can you identify the films from these picture clues? Each picture is worth a point.

1

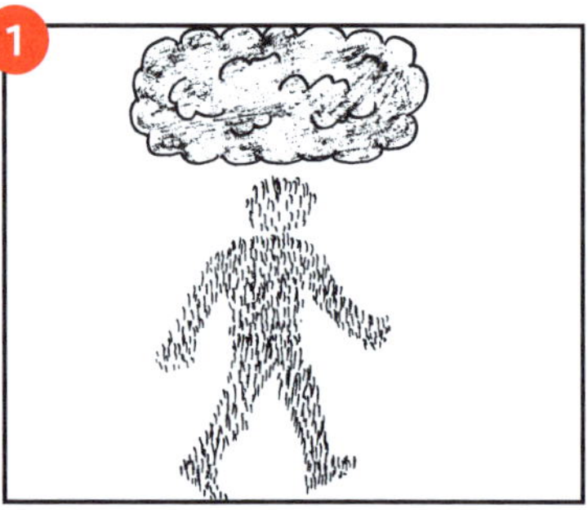

2

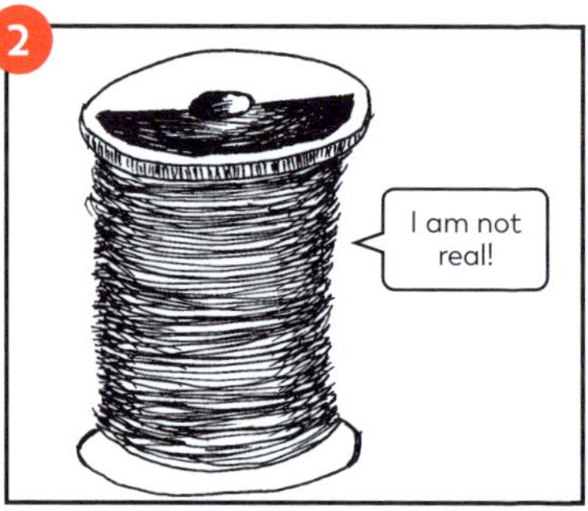

3

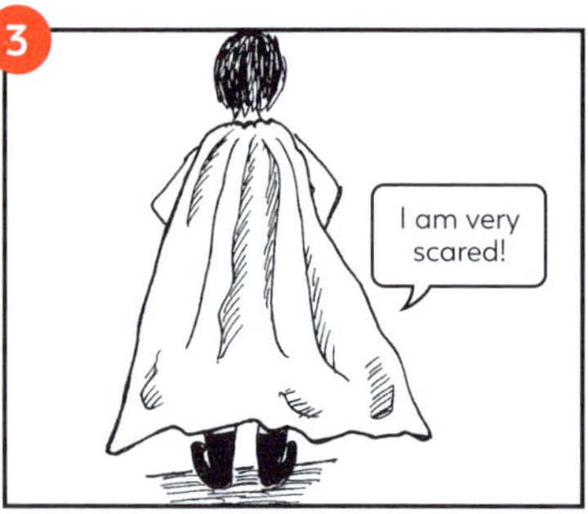

4

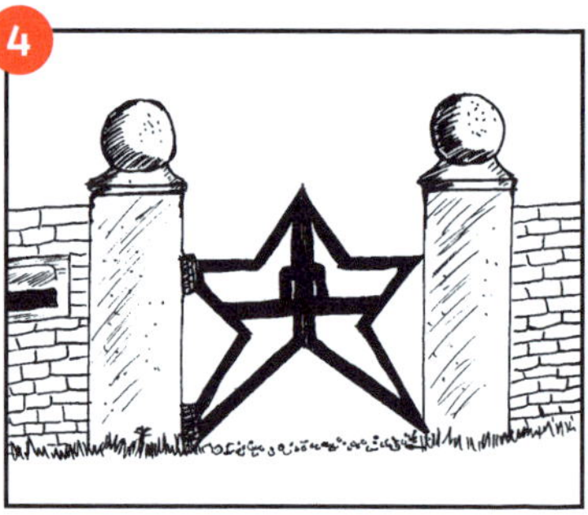

5

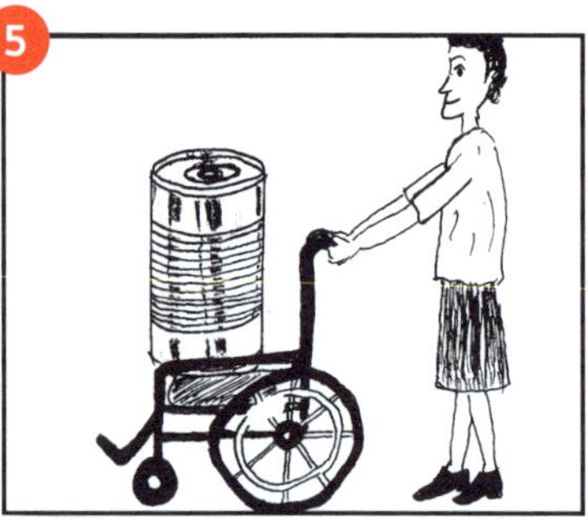

6

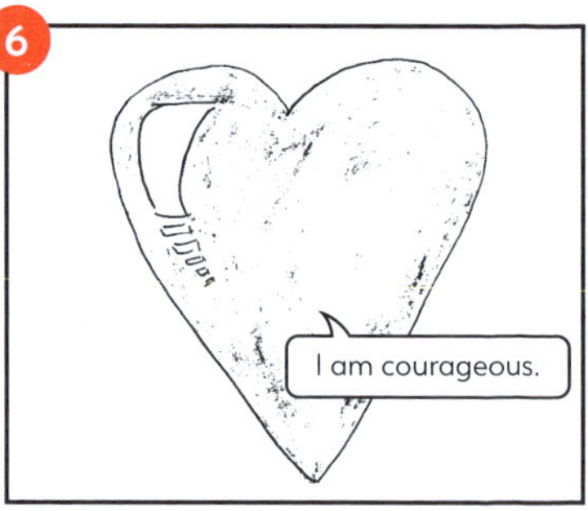

ANSWERS

ROUND 1

1. c) Paul Giamatti (1967). Paul Rudd was born in 1969 and Paul Bettany in 1971.

2. Sidney Poitier

3. b) *Dead Poets Society*

4. c) *Star Wars: Episode I – The Phantom Menace*

5. b) *Lincoln* by Steven Spielberg.

6. *Once Upon a Time in the West* and *One Flew Over the Cuckoo's Nest*.

7. a) Christopher Nolan doesn't use a smartphone. He says the internet is too much of a distraction.

8. b) Han Solo (*Star Wars*)

9. 1973

Steve McQueen and James Coburn were pallbearers at Bruce Lee's funeral.

10. *Footsteps* (1974), *Bugsy Malone* (1976), *Midnight Express* (1978), *Fame* (1980), *Shoot the Moon* (1982), *Pink Floyd – The Wall* (1982), *Birdy* (1984), *Angel Heart* (1987), *Mississippi Burning* (1988), *Come See the Paradise* (1990), *The Commitments* (1991), *The Road to Wellville* (1994), *Evita* (1996), *Angela's Ashes* (1999), *The Life of David Gale* (2003).

ROUND 2

1. a) Alan Rickman

1. a) i) *Die Hard*

1. a) ii) *Robin Hood: Prince of Thieves*

1. a) iii) *Harry Potter and the Deathly Hallows – Part 2*

1. b) Dennis Hopper

1. b) i) *Blue Velvet*

1. b) ii) *Speed*

1. b) iii) *True Romance*

1. c) Steve Buscemi

1. c) i) *Desperado*

1. c) ii) *Fargo*

1. c) iii) *The Big Lebowski*

1. d) Shelley Winters

1. d) i) *The Night of the Hunter*

1. d) ii) *The Great Gatsby*

1. d) iii) *The Poseidon Adventure*

> ***The Night of the Hunter*** **was the only film directed by Charles Laughton. A critical and box office failure at the time, it is now rightly seen as a classic.**

1. e) Sean Bean

1. e) i) *The Field*

1. e) ii) *Goldeneye*

1. e) iii) *The Lord of the Rings: The Fellowship of the Ring*

2. a) *Train*

2. b) *Bicycle*

2. c) *Cars*

2. d) *Motorcycle*

2. e) *Boat*

ROUND 3

1. a) *Dallas Buyers Club* and *The First Wives Club.*

1. b) *Crazy, Stupid, Love* and *In the Mood for Love.*

1. c) *The Girl on the Train* and *Money Train.*

1. d) *Manchester by the Sea* and *The Deep Blue Sea.*

1. e) *All the Money in the World* and *Ghost World.*

2. a) Ellen Ripley and Eli Roth.

2. b) Rose Sayer and Ridley Scott.

2. c) Alfred Pennyworth and Alexander Payne.

2. d) Erik Killmonger and Elia Kazan.

2. e) Apollo Creed and Alfonso Cuarón.

ROUND 4

1. a) Ned Kelly. Mick Jagger in *Ned Kelly* (1970), Heath Ledger in *Ned Kelly* (2003) and George MacKay in *True History of the Kelly Gang* (2019).

Mick Jagger was almost in a musical version of *Naked Lunch*. The book by William S. Burroughs was adapted by the author with Antony Balch to direct. After Jagger dropped out, Dennis Hopper was considered but the film was never made.

1. b) *Resident Evil*. There is also a reboot subtitled *Welcome to Raccoon City* (2021).

1. c) *The Omega Man*

1. d) Cusack

1. e) A dog. *Turner and Hooch*, *Hachi: A Dog's Tale*, *Marley and Me* and *Old Yeller*.

2. a) Ice hockey

2. b) *Jubilee*

2. c) Khan (Noonien Singh)

2. d) *Love*

2. e) *Maleficent*

ROUND 5

1. *Rain Man* (1988)
2. *Phantom Thread* (2017)
3. *Cape Fear* (1962/1991)
4. *Stargate* (1994)
5. *Pushing Tin* (1999)
6. *Braveheart* (1995)

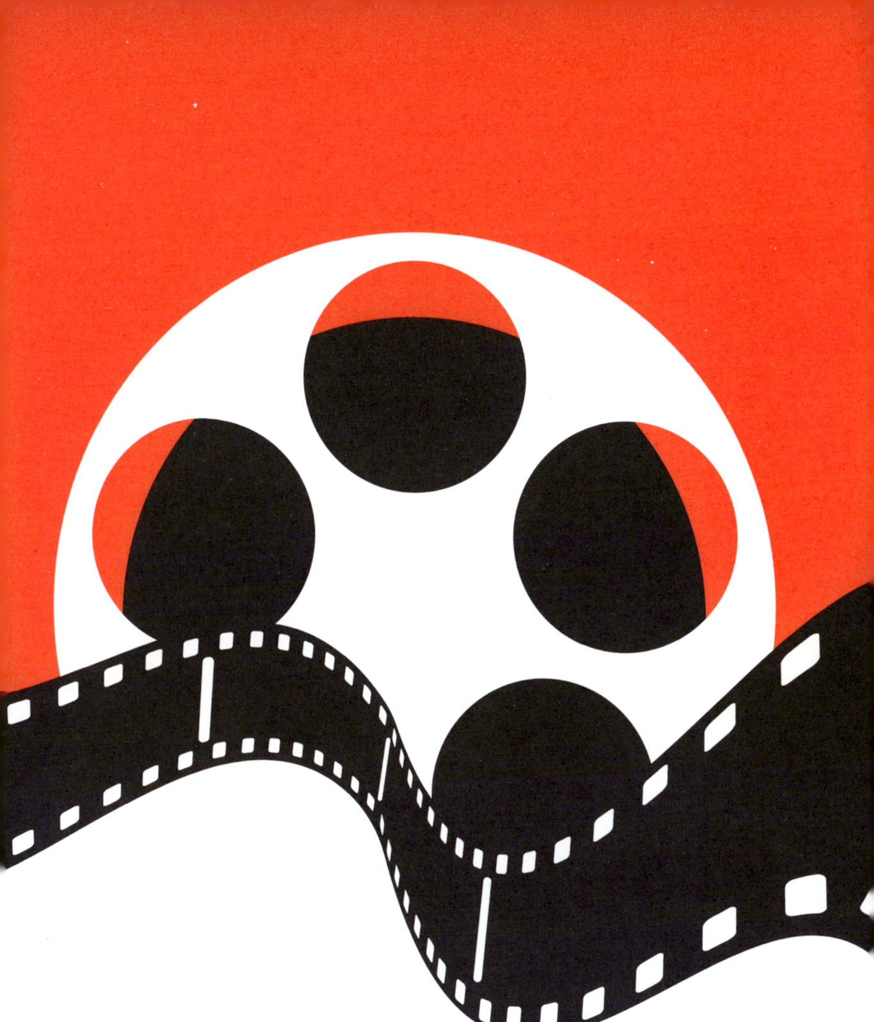

QUIZ 19

ROUND 1

STARTER FOR 10

Ten questions to begin!

1. THE FIRST QUESTION

Which of these classic musicals was released first?

a) *The Sound of Music*

b) *Gigi*

c) *Singin' in the Rain*

2. THE ANAGRAM

Unscramble the actor's name: COOPED IRON RADIAL

3. FILM QUOTE

What film is the following quote from?

"They're not gonna catch us. We're on a mission from God."

a) *Chariots of Fire* (1981)

b) *Bonnie and Clyde* (1967)

c) *The Blues Brothers* (1980)

d) *Kingdom of Heaven* (2005)

4. THUMBS DOWN

What film is this the one-star review of?

"Just because the characters are quirky and interesting doesn't mean the movie is funny or good. The character Jesus' potential was totally wasted. He could have been the funniest character but instead his lines fell flat and were boring."

a) *Kingpin* (1996)

b) *The Big Lebowski* (1998)

c) *Monty Python's Life of Brian* (1979)

5. ODD ONE OUT

Which of these films was not directed by Greta Gerwig? Bonus point if you know who it was directed by.

a) *Girl, Interrupted* (1999)

b) *Lady Bird* (2017)

c) *Little Women* (2019)

6. RHYMING FILMS

I'll give you the initials of two films whose titles rhyme with each other. I'll also give you one of the stars and the years they were released, just name the films for a point each.

BN, Mark Wahlberg (1997) and PH, Melanie Griffith (1990).

7. CELLULOID OR CELLULIED?

Which of the following is true about the film *Psycho* (1960)?

a) *Psycho* was the first film to feature paid-for product placement (Hitchcock was paid to use "D. Griffith" shower-curtain rings).

b) *Psycho* was the first film to be advertised at half-time during the Super Bowl.

c) *Psycho* was the first film to feature a toilet flushing.

8. WHAT MIGHT HAVE BEEN

Which of these roles did Frank Sinatra turn down?

a) Vito Corleone (*The Godfather* – 1972)

b) James Bond (*Dr. No* – 1962)

c) John McClane (*Die Hard* – 1988)

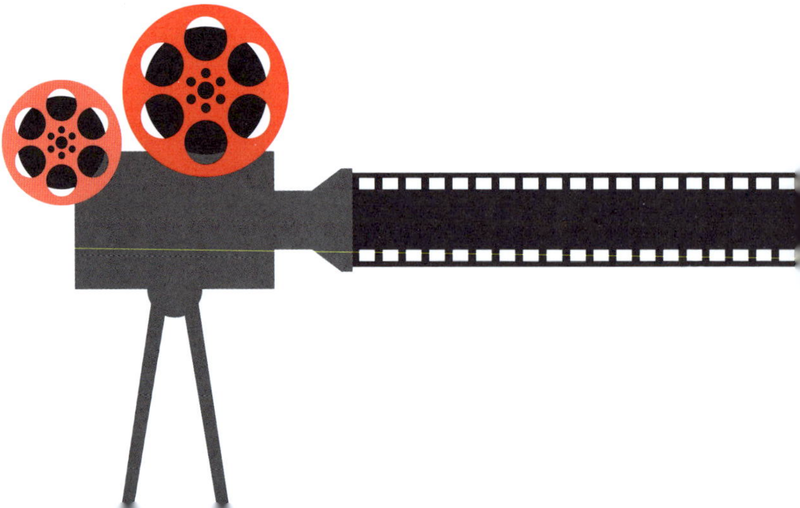

9. WHAT YEAR?

In what year did the following things happen?

Films released this year include: *Armageddon, Shakespeare in Love, You've Got Mail, There's Something About Mary, A Bug's Life, Saving Private Ryan, Velvet Goldmine* and *The Big Lebowski. Blade* starring Wesley Snipes is, at the time, the top-grossing film based on a Marvel character. *The Thin Red Line* releases in December, Terrence Malick's first film for 20 years. Elle Fanning, Daisy Edgar-Jones, Maya Hawke and Cailee Spaeny are born. Lew Grade, Lloyd Bridges and Frank Sinatra all pass away. *Lock, Stock and Two Smoking Barrels* sees the film debut of ex-footballer Vinnie Jones. But what was the year?

10. GIVE ME FIVE

A chance for five points! Name five films that Grace Kelly appeared in. There are 11 possible answers.

ROUND 2

1. THE HIDDEN

The titles of these classic horror films can be found in capital letters within the descriptions. Unscramble them to name the film for a point.

a) A priest, asked to cure a possessed child, must ensure he is all SET. HER TOXIC host may then be forced to leave. (1973)

b) Having avoided a plane crash, Alex and his friends hope to continue to cheat death but INSTEAD, FAIL IN NOT dying. (2000)

c) A young couple, the Woodhouses, move into an old New York apartment, and Mrs Woodhouse becomes pregnant. Everything seems fine until the EMBRYO BRAYS AS if it were a demon… (1968)

d) Christine Brown thinks nothing of getting rid of an old lady LODGER. "HA, MELT" thinks the evicted old woman as she casts a curse that will pursue the loan officer. (2009)

e) Beset by zombies while holed up in the Winchester pub, two friends wish they were back in their flat with video games, Cornettoes AND THE SOFA, HUED brown. (2004)

2. ONE OF OUR ______ IS MISSING!

Just fill in the missing word – there's always a theme, and this time it's... animals found in the Chinese zodiac.

a) *Jojo* ________ (2019)

b) *A Man Called* ________ (1970)

c) *Save the* ________ (1973)

d) ________ *Man* (2024)

e) ________ *Cogburn* (1975)

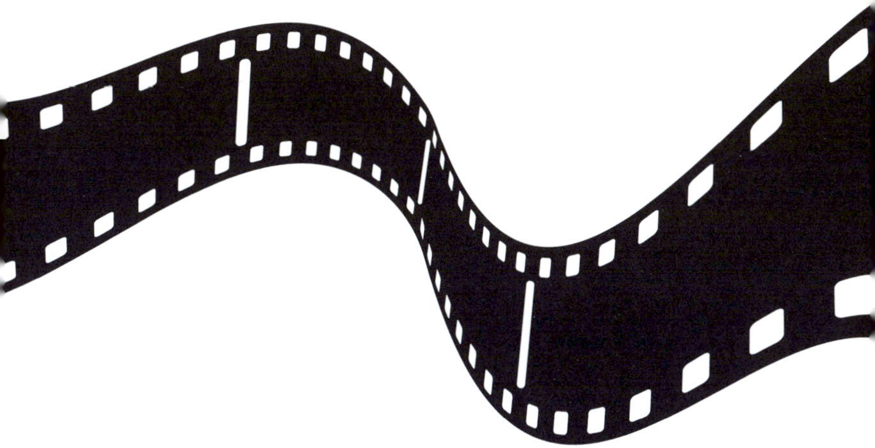

ROUND 3

1. LINK

I will give you a word that ends one film title and begins another, plus the star and the year – name both for two points.

a) The link is "Jungle". Film one – Glenn Ford (1955). Film two – Wesley Snipes (1991).

b) The link is "Summer". Film one – Zooey Deschanel (2009). Film two – Cliff Richard (1963).

c) The link is "Dead". Film one – Philip Seymour Hoffman (2007). Film two – Paddy Considine (2004).

d) The link is "House". Film one – John Belushi (1978). Film two – Vincent Price (1953).

e) The link is "For". Film one – Nicole Kidman (1995). Film two – Clint Eastwood (1965).

2. THE ODD COUPLE

I'll describe an actor and a film character that share the same initials. A point for each you can name.

a) **Actor:** American born in 1987. After breaking through on TV in *Gossip Girl* (2007–2012), she has since starred in films such as *The Shallows* (2012), *Savages* (2016), *A Simple Favor* (2018) and *It Ends with Us* (2024). She married Ryan Reynolds in 2012. **Character:** The space-adventurer doll given to Andy for his birthday in the first *Toy Story* film (1995), he is voiced by Tim Allen.

b) **Actor:** American actor born in 1952. Best known for portraying Janine Melnitz, the secretary and occasional

Ghostbuster in the *Ghostbusters* series of films (1984–2024). She also provides the voice for Bo Peep in *Toy Story* (1995), *Toy Story 2* (1999) and *Toy Story 4* (2019). **Character:** The titular character portrayed by Audrey Tautou in the international French hit directed by Jean-Pierre Jeunet in 2001. The character is a shy waitress who decides to try to help the lives of the people around her. Yann Tiersen's soundtrack was also a huge success and won the César Award for best music.

c) **Actor:** American, born in 1915. Over a career that began in 1956, two western roles stand out: Calvera in *The Magnificent Seven* (1960) and Tuco Ramirez in *The Good, the Bad and the Ugly* (1966). His final major role was Julius Steinhardt in *Wall Street: Money Never Sleeps* (2010). **Character:** Portrayed by Reese Witherspoon, the main protagonist of *Legally Blonde* (2001) and *Legally Blonde 2: Red White and Blonde* (2003).

d) **Actor:** American actor born in 1957. Found fame as Mr Pink in *Reservoir Dogs* (1992). Other roles include key collaborations with the Coen Brothers: *Miller's Crossing* (1990), *Fargo* (1996) and Donny Kerabatsos in *The Big Lebowski* (1998). **Character:** A scientist, played by Jeff Goldblum, who mistakenly (and disastrously) fuses his DNA with a fly in *The Fly* (1986).

e) **Actor:** American, born in 1936. Hugely successful as an actor and director, some of his key roles include the Sundance Kid in *Butch Cassidy and the Sundance Kid* (1969), Johnny Hooker in *The Sting* (1973) and Bob Woodward in *All the President's Men* (1976). In 1981, he won the Oscar for Best Director for *Ordinary People* (1980) and in 1978 he established the Sundance Film Festival. **Character:** An animated animal in a film (1988) that mixes cartoon and live action. Eddie Valiant (Bob Hoskins) is hired by studio owner R. K. Maroon to investigate if his star's wife (Jessica) is having an affair – but soon the titular character is in danger. The character is voiced by Charles Fleischer.

ROUND 4

1. BRAINSTORM

Complete the lists and spot the links – a point for each correct answer.

a) What connects Wallace Beery and Fredric March in 1932, Barbra Streisand and Katharine Hepburn in 1969 and Paul N. J. Ottosson and Per Hallberg and Karen Baker Landers in 2013?

b) What film comes next in this list? *Planes, Trains and Automobiles* (1987), *Ferris Bueller's Day Off* (1986), *Weird Science* (1985), *The Breakfast Club* (1985) and...?

c) What is the connection between these Best Picture Oscar-winning films? *Driving Miss Daisy* (1989), *Argo* (2012), *Green Book* (2018) and *CODA* (2021).

d) Which film franchise subtitles include: *Dream Warriors* (1987), *The Dream Master* (1988) and *The Dream Child* (1989)?

e) Which actor's only three (credited) roles were Cal Trask, Jim Stark and Jett Rink?

2. IT FOLLOWS

The first letter of each answer follows the first letter of the last. So, if the answer to c) is "Apple", the answer to d) will begin with "B". If you get to Z, go to A. Each question is worth one point.

a) Which 2023 film features a naked Barry Keoghan dancing to "Murder on the Dancefloor" by Sophie Ellis-Bextor?

b) *A Room with a View* (1985), *The English Patient* (1996), *Stealing Beauty* (1996) and *Tea with Mussolini* (1999) are all films set predominantly in which region of Italy?

c) In *Avatar* (2009) what is the name of the rare, valuable mineral on the planet Pandora that Earth wishes to mine?

d) Michael Keaton has played three characters based on creatures that fly: *Batman* (1989), 1992), *Birdman* (2014) and which other?

e) What is the name of the volleyball that is Charles "Chuck" Noland's (Tom Hanks) only friend on his island in *Cast Away* (2000)?

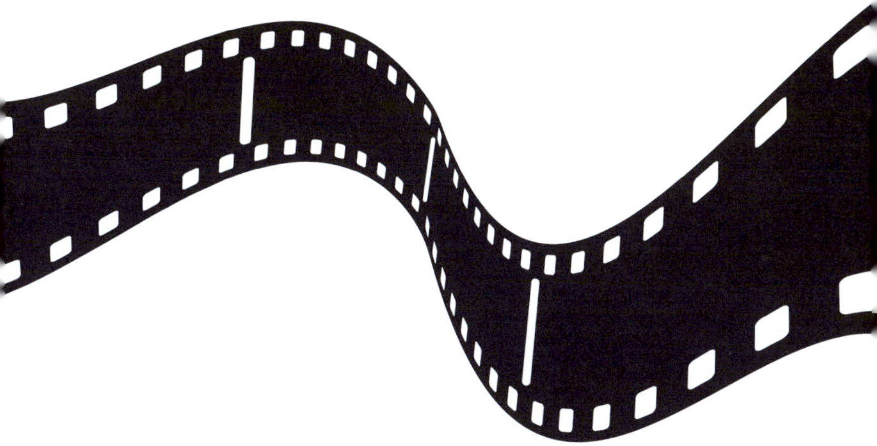

ROUND 5

THE LAST PICTURE SHOW

Say what you see! Can you identify the films from these picture clues? Each picture is worth a point.

1

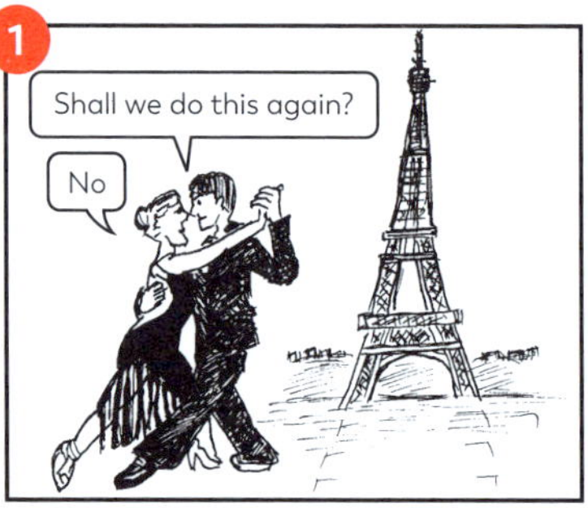

2

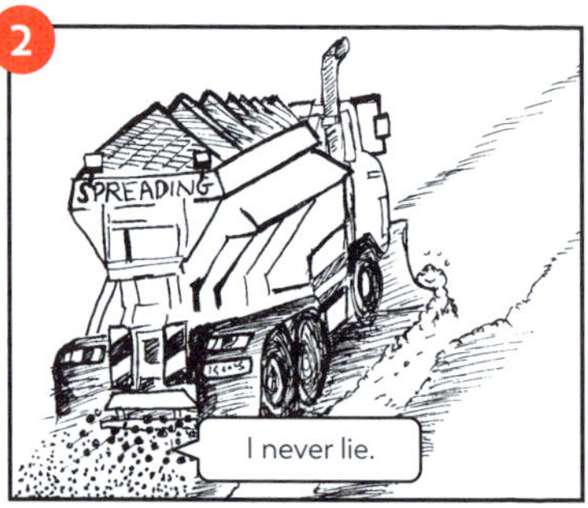

3

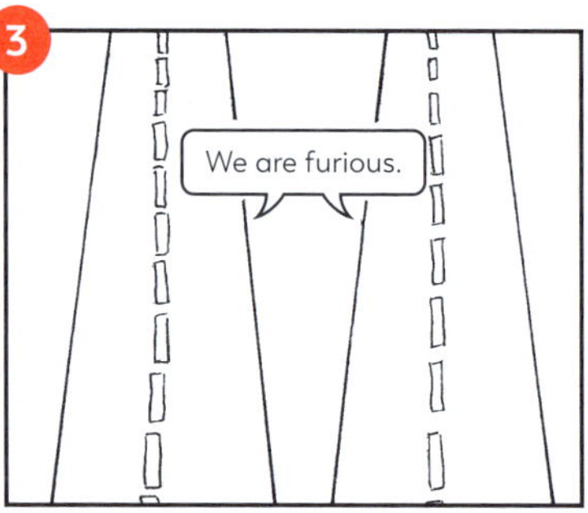

4

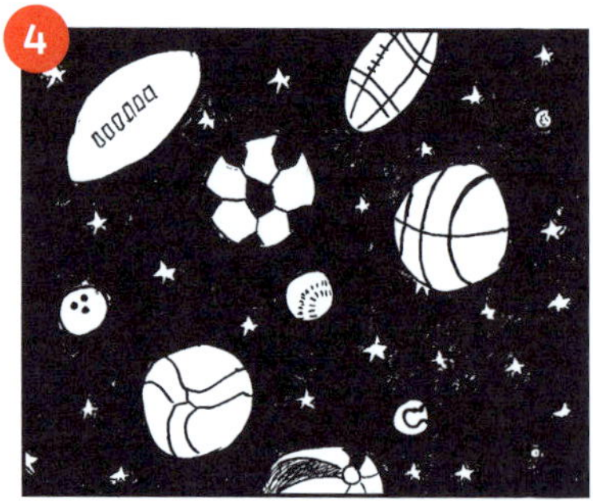

5

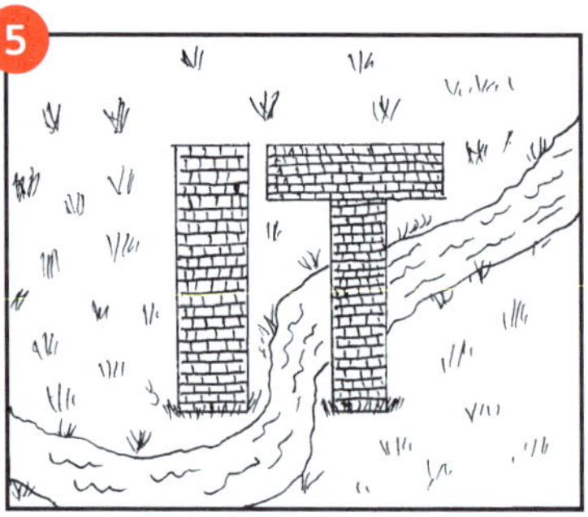

6

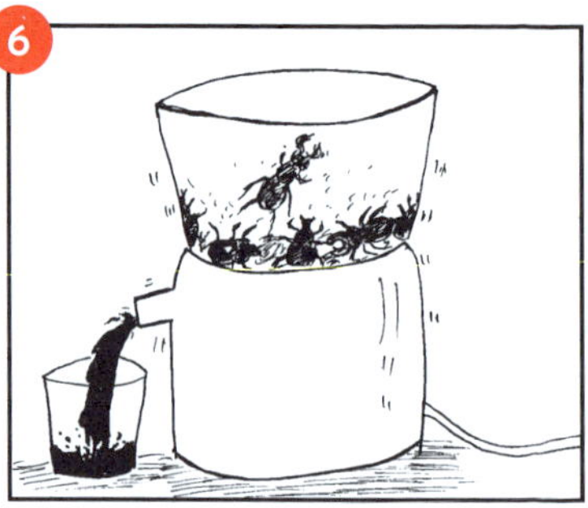

ANSWERS

ROUND 1

1. c) *Singin' in the Rain* (1952). *Gigi* was 1958 and *The Sound of Music* was 1965.

To get the famous swooping scene of Julie Andrews singing on the hill, a camera was mounted on a helicopter – unfortunately, every time it passed it blew Andrews down into the mud, until the tenth take when she was able to stay standing!

2. Leonardo DiCaprio

3. c) *The Blues Brothers*

4. b) *The Big Lebowski*

5. a) *Girl, Interrupted* by James Mangold.

6. *Boogie Nights* and *Pacific Heights.*

7. c) *Psycho* was the first film to feature a toilet flushing.

It wasn't the first film to show a toilet or play the sound of a flush, but it was the first to show a close-up of a toilet flushing. The Super Bowl didn't begin until 1966. Oh, and Del Griffith (John Candy) sells shower-curtain rings in *Planes, Trains and Automobiles* (1987), so that's just my little tribute to him.

8. c) John McClane (*Die Hard*)

Sorry. *Die Hard* is based on the novel *Nothing Lasts Forever* by Roderick Thorp. That book is a sequel to *The Detective*, which was filmed in 1966, starring Sinatra, so the film company were contractually obliged to offer him the role again. Sinatra, at 70 years old, turned it down. Other actors who were offered the role included Arnold Schwarzenegger, Al Pacino, James Caan, Richard Gere and Harrison Ford.

9. 1998

10. *Fourteen Hours* (1951), *High Noon* (1952), *Mogambo* (1953), *Dial M for Murder* (1954), *Rear Window* (1954), *The Bridges at Toko-Ri* (1954), *The Country Girl* (1954), *Green Fire* (1954), *To Catch a Thief* (1955), *The Swan* (1956), *High Society* (1956).

Grace Kelly retired from acting at the age of 26 to become Princess of Monaco.

ROUND 2

1. a) *The Exorcist*

1. b) *Final Destination*

1. c) *Rosemary's Baby*

1. d) *Drag Me to Hell*

1. e) *Shaun of the Dead*

2. a) *Rabbit*

2. b) *Horse*

2. c) *Tiger*

2. d) *Monkey*

2. e) *Rooster*

ROUND 3

1. a) *Blackboard* ***Jungle*** *Fever*

1. b) *500 Days of* ***Summer*** *Holiday*

1. c) *Before the Devil Knows You're* ***Dead*** *Man's Shoes*

1. d) *National Lampoon's Animal* ***House*** *of Wax*

1. e) *To Die* ***For*** *a Few Dollars More*

2. a) Blake Lively and Buzz Lightyear.

As well as being the first Pixar feature film, *Toy Story* was also the first film to be entirely computer-animated.

2. b) Annie Potts and Amélie Poulain.

2. c) Eli Wallach and Elle Woods.

2. d) Steve Buscemi and Seth Brundle.

2. e) Robert Redford and Roger Rabbit.

ROUND 4

1. a) They shared an Oscar. At time of writing, this has happened six times. Wallace Beery (*The Champ*) and Fredric March (*Dr. Jekyll and Mr. Hyde*) tied for Best Actor. Barbra Streisand (*Funny Girl*) and Katharine Hepburn (*The Lion in Winter*) tied for Best Actress. Paul N. J. Ottosson (*Zero Dark Thirty*) and Per Hallberg and Karen Baker Landers (*Skyfall*) tied for Best Sound Editing.

1. b) *Sixteen Candles* (1984) – these are films directed by John Hughes going back in reverse order to his first.

1. c) They won Best Picture without the director receiving a nomination for Best Director.

See also: *Wings* (1927) and *Grand Hotel* (1932).

1. d) *A Nightmare on Elm Street. A Nightmare on Elm Street 3: Dream Warriors, A Nightmare on Elm Street 4: The Dream Master, A Nightmare on Elm Street 5: The Dream Child.*

1. e) James Dean in *East of Eden* (1955), *Rebel Without a Cause* (1955) and *Giant* (1956).

2. a) *Saltburn*

2. b) Tuscany

2. c) Unobtanium

Yes, really.

2. d) Vulture. In *Spider-Man: Homecoming* (2017).

2. e) Wilson

ROUND 5

1. *Last Tango in Paris* (1972)
2. *True Grit* (1969/2010)
3. *Crossroads* (1986)
4. *Spaceballs* (1987)
5. *A River Runs Through It* (1992)
6. *Beetlejuice* (1988)

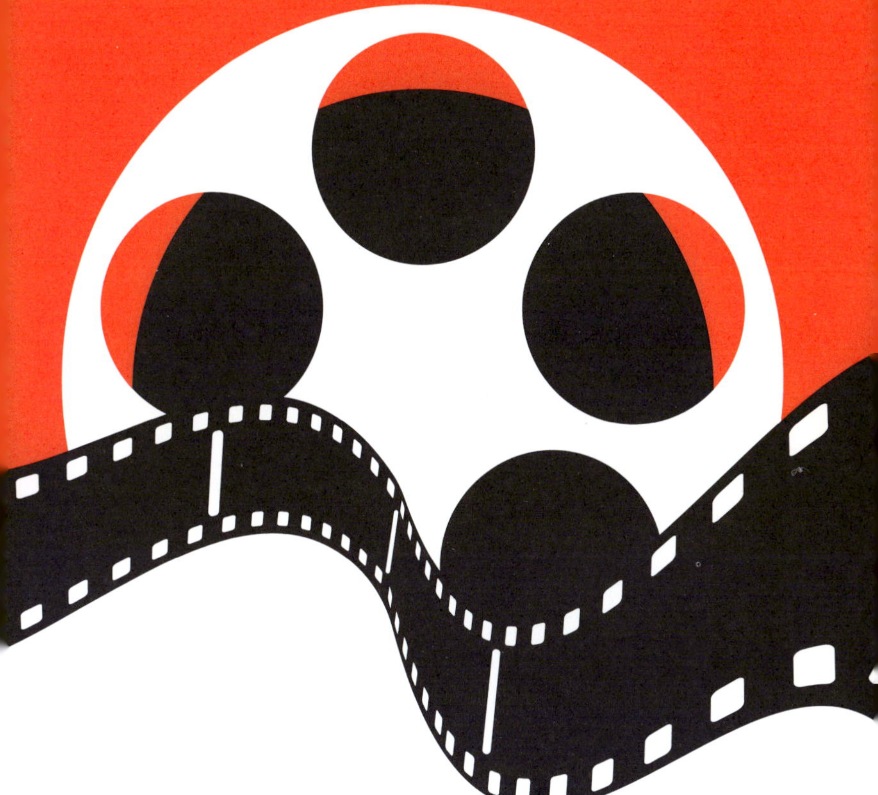

QUIZ 20:

THE CHRISTMAS QUIZ

ROUND 1

STARTER FOR 10

Ten questions to begin!

1. THE FIRST QUESTION

Which of these actors first appeared on screen as Father Christmas?

a) Richard Attenborough

b) Paul Giamatti

c) Kurt Russell

2. THE ANAGRAM

Unscramble the actor's name: TWEAK TINSEL

3. FILM QUOTE

What film is the following famous quote from?

"You say you hate Washington's Birthday or Thanksgiving and nobody cares, but you say you hate Christmas and people treat you like you're a leper."

a) *White Christmas* (1954)

b) *Gremlins* (1984)

c) *The Holdovers* (2023)

d) *Bad Santa* (2003)

4. THUMBS DOWN

What film is this the one-star review of?

"... actually terrifying, more of a horror movie than a Christmas movie."

a) *The Polar Express* (2004)

b) *How the Grinch Stole Christmas* (2000)

c) *Deck the Halls* (2006)

5. ODD ONE OUT

Which of these films was not directed by Chris Columbus? Bonus point if you know who it was directed by.

a) *Home Alone* (1990)

b) *Christmas with the Kranks* (2004)

c) *Scrooged* (1988)

6. RHYMING FILMS

I'll give you the initials of two films whose titles rhyme with each other. I'll also give you one of the stars and the years they were released, just name the films for a point each.

JATW, Arnold Schwarzenegger (1996) and TH, Cameron Diaz (2006).

7. CELLULOID OR CELLULIED?

Which of the following is a fact about the Grinch?

a) The Grinch was originally known as the Buggerlug.

b) Jim Carrey based his portrayal of the Grinch on his pet cat.

c) Dr Seuss drew the Grinch in black and white; animator Chuck Jones decided he should be green for the 1966 animation.

8. WHAT MIGHT HAVE BEEN

Which of these roles did Jim Carrey turn down?

a) Scott Calvin/Santa Claus (*The Santa Clause* – 1994)

b) Edward Scissorhands (1990)

c) Buddy (*Elf* – 2003)

9. WHAT YEAR?

In what year did the following things happen?

Christmas films released this year include: *Bad Santa* and *Love Actually*. Other big films of the year included *The Lord of the Rings: The Return of the King*, *School of Rock*, *Finding Nemo*, *Bruce Almighty* and *Lost in Translation*. Arnold Schwarzenegger becomes Governor of California, and we lose Hollywood legends Gregory Peck and Katharine Hepburn. But what was the year?

10. GIVE ME FIVE

A chance for five points! Name me five tracks from *The Nightmare Before Christmas* (1993) soundtrack. There are 19 possible answers.

ROUND 2

1. BAH, HUMBUG: FIVE QUESTIONS ON *A CHRISTMAS CAROL*

a) Who played Ebeneezer Scrooge in the following films?

- **i)** *Scrooge* (1951)
- **ii)** *Scrooge* (1970)
- **iii)** *A Christmas Carol* (2009)

b) In *The Muppet Christmas Carol* (1992), what does Mr Fozziwig's (Fozzie Bear) factory principally produce?

c) In *Scrooged* (1988), which American singer plays the Ghost of Christmas Past?

d) In the 2017 movie *The Man Who Invented Christmas* (a film about the writing of *A Christmas Carol*), who played Charles Dickens?

e) What is the name of the modern retelling of *A Christmas Carol* from 2022 starring Will Ferrell and Ryan Reynolds?

2. ONE OF OUR ______ IS MISSING!

Just fill in the missing word – there's always a theme, and this time it's… Christmas! (The words are Christmassy, the films are not.)

a) *Bell Book and* ________ (1958)

b) *Animal* ________ (1930)

c) *Mrs. Henderson* ________ (2005)

d) *Bob &* ________ *& Ted & Alice* (1969)

e) ________ *& Demons* (2009)

ROUND 3

1. HALLMARK OF QUALITY

These Hallmark Christmas films have punning titles, can you fill in the missing word? I'll give you the first letter.

a) *S_ _ _ _ _All the Way* (2021)

b) *The K_ _ _ _ _ Before Christmas* (2019)

c) *Sealed With a L_ _ _* (2023)

d) *L_ _ _ Hard* (2021)

e) *Check I_ _ to Christmas* (2019)

2. THE ODD COUPLE

I'll describe an actor and a film character that share the same initials. A point for each you can name.

a) **Character:** One of the most beloved characters in all Christmas movies. Portrayed by James Stewart in *It's a Wonderful Life* (1946). It's Christmas Eve in Bedford Falls and Stewart's character is contemplating suicide, but an angel is en route to save him and earn his wings. **Actor:** Scottish actor born in 1969. He rose to prominence playing King Leonidas in *300* (2006) and has since moved into rom-coms and action roles, including *Olympus Has Fallen* (2013) *London Has Fallen* (2016) and *Angel Has Fallen* (2019). He made his Christmas film debut in 2024 in *The Night Before Christmas in Wonderland* as St Nick (voice performance).

b) **Character:** The "real" name of the central protagonist from *Miracle on 34th Street* (1947 and 1994). Is he or isn't he the genuine Santa Claus? **Actor:** English actor born in 1985.

Rose to prominence in *Bend It Like Beckham* (2002) before starring in the huge hit *Pirates of the Caribbean: The Curse of the Black Pearl* (2003). She has starred in two Christmas films: *Love Actually* (2003) and the black comedy *Silent Night* (2021).

c) **Character:** The titular character from the 2011 animated comedy about the clumsy grandson of Santa Claus (Grandsanta) who attempts to deliver a bicycle that has been forgotten. **Actor:** American actor born in 1918. Possibly best known for a TV role (Ed Norton in *The Honeymooners*), though he did win the Best Actor Academy Award for the film *Harry and Tonto* (1974) and starred in *Going in Style* (1979) with George Burns and Lee Strasberg. In 1984 he played Santa Claus in *The Night They Saved Christmas*.

d) **Character:** The protagonist of the 1993 animated film *The Nightmare Before Christmas*, the Pumpkin King – the patron spirit of Halloween who is looking for something new, until he stumbles upon Christmas Town. He is voiced by Chris Sarandon (songs sung by Danny Elfman). **Actor:** English actor born in 1951. Probably best known for two roles: Solitaire in *Live and Let Die* (1973) and the TV role of *Dr. Quinn, Medicine Woman* (1993–1998). She has starred in a number of Christmas films: *Buttons: A Christmas Tale* (2018), *A Christmas Spark* (2022) and *A Royal Christmas* (2014).

e) **Character:** East German criminal mastermind portrayed by Alan Rickman in Christmas classic *Die Hard* (1988). His plan to steal $640 million in bonds is scuppered when a certain New York cop crashes his party. The character's brother Simon appeared in the later film *Die Hard with a Vengeance* (1995) portrayed by Jeremy Irons. **Actor:** English actor born in 1960. Found fame starring in romantic comedies such as *Four Weddings and a Funeral* (1994), *Notting Hill* (1999) and *Bridget Jones's Diary* (2001). Made his Christmas film debut playing the prime minister in *Love Actually* (2003).

ROUND 4

1. BRAINSTORM

a) Which character connects Jim Carrey, Benedict Cumberbatch and Boris Karloff?

b) Which actor connects *Fred Claus* (2007) and *Four Christmases* (2008)?

c) Which series of Christmas films has sequels subtitled: *Danger in the Manger!* (2012), *Dude, Where's My Donkey?!* (2014) and *Rocks!* (2018)?

d) Place these Christmas films in release order from earliest to latest for a point.

   i) *Your Christmas or Mine?*

   ii) *A Christmas Story*

   iii) *The Night Before*

e) What are Gimbels in *Elf* (2003), Duncan's Toy Chest in *Home Alone* (1990) and Kringles in *Candy Cane Lane* (2023)?

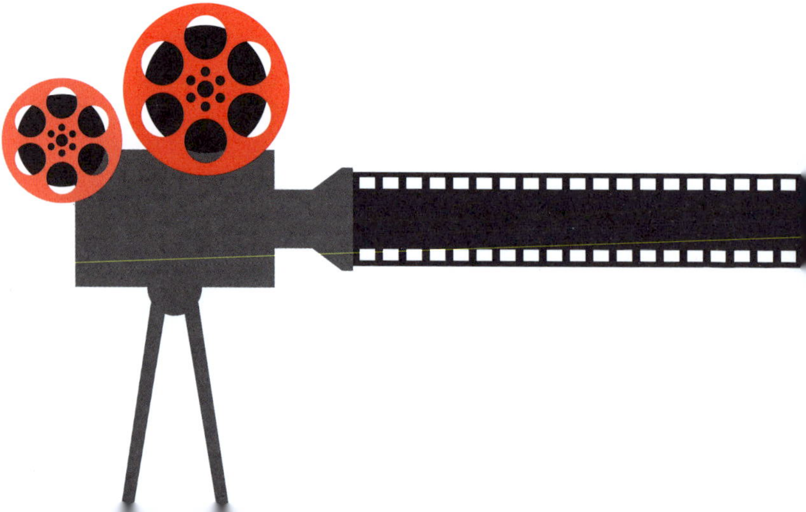

2. IT FOLLOWS

The first letter of each answer follows the first letter of the last. So, if the answer to c) is "Apple", the answer to d) will begin with "B". If you get to Z, go to A. Each question is worth one point.

a) What is the surname of the family lead by Clark (Chevy Chase) and Ellen (Beverley D'Angelo) in *National Lampoon's Christmas Vacation* (1989)?

b) In *Meet Me in St Louis* (1944), Judy Garland sings which beloved festive song?

c) Which Christmas classic is based on the short story *The Greatest Gift* by Philip Van Doren Stern?

d) What is the name of the rather dark Christmas movie from 1997 starring Michael Keaton as a neglectful father who is killed in a car crash and reincarnated 12 months later as a snowman?

e) In *The Muppet Christmas Carol* (1992), which Muppet plays Bob Cratchit?

ROUND 5

THE LAST PICTURE SHOW

Say what you see! Can you identify the films from these picture clues? (The clues are Christmassy but the films are not.) Each picture is worth a point.

1

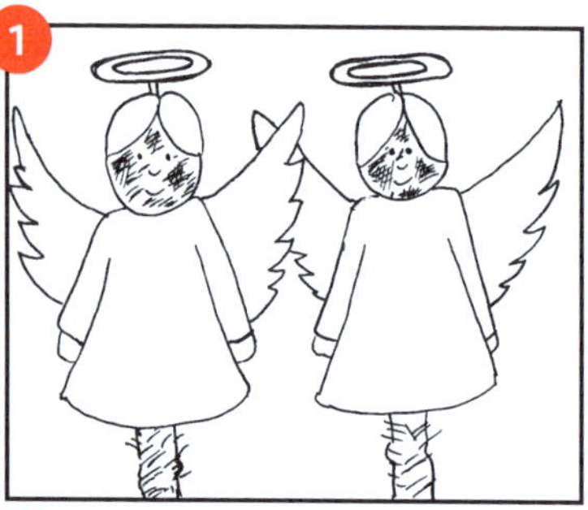

2

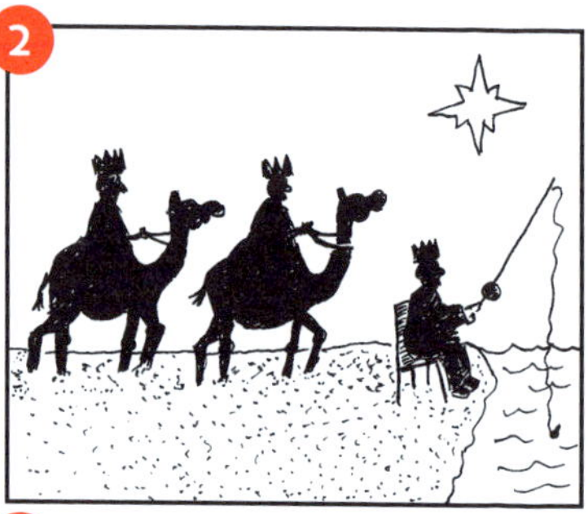

3

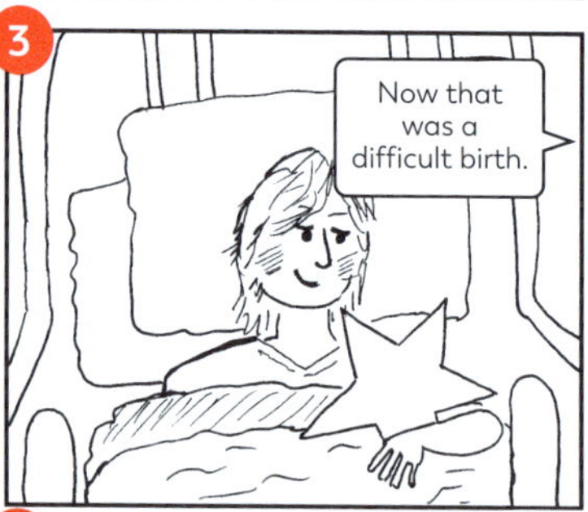

4

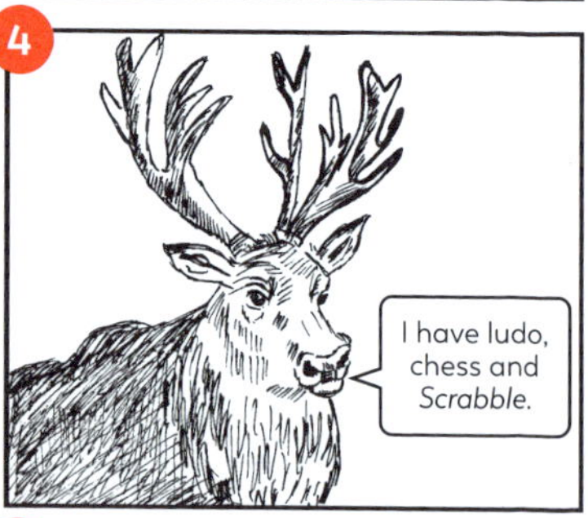

5

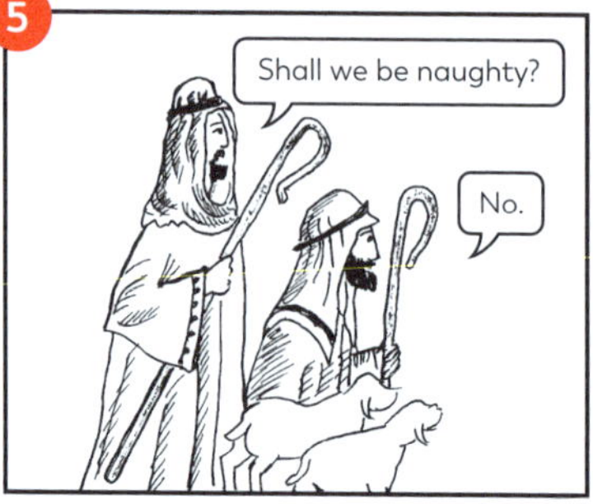

6

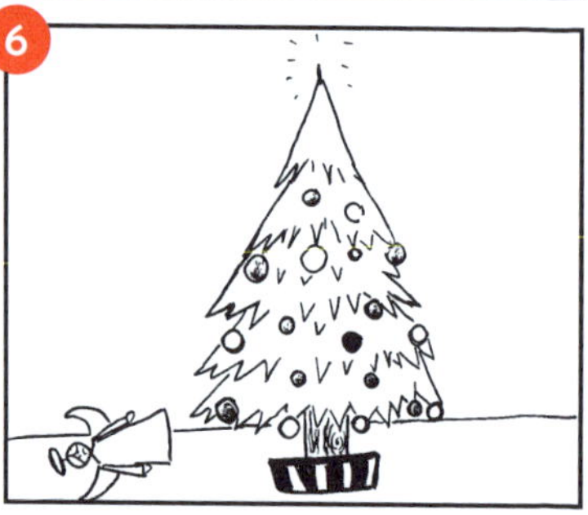

ANSWERS

ROUND 1

1. a) Richard Attenborough (1994) in *Miracle on 34th Street*. Paul Giamatti was 2007 (*Fred Claus*) and Kurt Russell was 2018 (*The Christmas Chronicles*).

2. Kate Winslet

3. b) *Gremlins*

> ***The Holdovers*** **is the first Christmas film to be nominated for Best Picture since the original** ***Miracle on 34th Street*****, in 1948.** ***It's a Wonderful Life*** **(1946) was nominated a year earlier.**

4. b) *How the Grinch Stole Christmas*

> **My other favourite one-star review was "He didn't steal Christmas, he borrowed it at best. Doesn't teach children to commit and see things through to the end."**

5. c) *Scrooged* by Richard Donner.

6. *Jingle All the Way* and *The Holiday*.

7. c) Dr Seuss drew the Grinch in black and white; Chuck Jones decided he should be green for the 1966 animation.

8. c) Buddy (*Elf*)

9. 2003

10. "This Is Halloween", "Jack's Lament", "Doctor Finkelstein/In the Forest (score)", "What's This?", "Town Meeting Song", "Jack and Sally Montage (score)", "Jack's Obsession", "Kidnap the Sandy

Claws", "Making Christmas", "Nabbed (score)", "Oogie Boogie's Song", "Sally's Song", "Christmas Eve Montage (score)", "Poor Jack", "To the Rescue (score)", also "Overture", "Open", "Closing" and "End Title (score)".

ROUND 2

1. a) i) Alastair Sim

1. a) ii) Albert Finney

1. a) iii) Jim Carrey (motion capture performance).

1. b) Rubber chickens.

1. c) David Johansen (of The New York Dolls).

1. d) Dan Stevens

1. e) *Spirited*

2. a) *Candle*

2. b) *Crackers*

2. c) *Presents*

2. d) *Carol*

2. e) *Angels*

ROUND 3

1. a) *Single*

1. b) *Knight*

1. c) *List*

1. d) *Love*

1. e) *Inn*

2. a) George Bailey and Gerard Butler.

2. b) Kris Kringle and Keira Knightley.

2. c) Arthur Christmas and Art Carney.

2. d) Jack Skellington and Jane Seymour.

2. e) Hans Gruber and Hugh Grant.

ROUND 4

1. a) The Grinch. Jim Carrey in *How the Grinch Stole Christmas* (2000), Benedict Cumberbatch (voice performance) in *The Grinch* (2018) and Boris Karloff voiced the Grinch in the animated *How the Grinch Stole Christmas* (1966).

1. b) Vince Vaughn

1. c) *Nativity. Nativity 2: Danger in the Manger!, Nativity 3: Dude, Where's My Donkey?!, Nativity Rocks!*

1. d) Correct order: ii) *A Christmas Story* (1983) iii) *The Night Before* (2015) i) *Your Christmas or Mine* (2022).

1. e) They are all shops.

2. a) Griswold

2. b) "Have Yourself a Merry Little Christmas"

2. c) *It's a Wonderful Life* (1946)

2. d) *Jack Frost*

2. e) Kermit the Frog

ROUND 5

1. *Angels with Dirty Faces* (1949)
2. *The Fisher King* (1991)
3. *A Star Is Born* (1937/1976/2018)
4. *Reindeer Games* (2000)
5. *The Good Shepherd* (2006)
6. *Angel Has Fallen* (2019)

ACKNOWLEDGEMENTS

Thanks to: my agent Stevie Finegan at Zeno Literary Agency and the excellent team at Summersdale, especially Sophie Martin, Imogen Palmer, Siobhan Coleman and Claire Berrisford.

I'd also like to thank the following people: Barnsey and Kev for all the late-night VHS (and Betamax!) watching in Wakefield. Robb (who will do very well at these quizzes), Gordy (who appreciates a good short film and a good long quiz) and Birdy, David and Wes (the Bookends!). I'd also like to thank Tony and Pip for the many enjoyable film conversations over dinner. And my brother, Neil, for introducing me (at probably far too young an age) to the films of Monty Python, John Belushi, Mel Brooks and many more.

Finally, thank you to my wife, Caroline, for all her help, advice and support. And, of course, for being the best person to watch a film with.